THE
50-PLUS
MARKET

MORE PRAISE FOR *THE 50-PLUS MARKET*

"Too often the 50-plus market is overlooked as an unattractive and unprofitable one. Dick Stroud clearly points out that this is very much far from being the truth. This book gives some insight as to the impact and attitude differences that marketers need to consider. There are also some excellent examples of how some organizations have got it right including those operating in the area of new media."

Christine Cryne, Chief Executive, the Chartered Institute of Marketing

"A wake-up call for marketers serious about growing their business, essential reading for anyone trying to understand the 50-plus market."

Richard Reed, Co-founder and Marketing Director, Innocent

"Marketers have been slow in recognizing the value of the 50-plus market. This book provides an excellent guide to understanding and marketing to the older consumer."

Chris Zanetti, Managing Director, Seven Seas

"Dick Stroud has provided the most thorough and comprehensive analysis of this market published to date. If this book does not generate a changed attitude by marketers towards this age group, then I fear that nothing will."

Peter Mouncey, Director of Research, Institute of Direct Marketing

"I am astonished that ad agencies and marketing folk still chase the younger age groups in blatant contradiction to the relative amounts of disposable income. Marketers must change their perception and approach to the 50-plus market. This book is a good starting point."

Dr Michael Chamberlain, Former Head of IBM's Business Consulting Services for Media and Entertainment in EMA

"Dick Stroud's book is a wake-up call to companies that are focused on mining ever-thinner seams of younger consumers, to see the opportunity that the 50+ market presents."

Andrew Walmsley, Founder, i-level

THE
50-PLUS
MARKET

Why the future is *AGE NEUTRAL* when it comes to marketing & branding strategies

Dick Stroud

IN ASSOCIATION WITH

OMD
INSIGHTS • IDEAS • RESULTS

**KOGAN
PAGE**

London and Philadelphia

To Stella

Publisher's note
Every possible effort has been made to ensure that the information contained in this book is accurate at the time of going to press, and the publishers and authors cannot accept responsibility for any errors or omissions, however caused. No responsibility for loss or damage occasioned to any person acting, or refraining from action, as a result of the material in this publication can be accepted by the editor, the publisher or any of the authors.

First published in Great Britain and the United States in 2005 by Kogan Page Limited
Reprinted in 2006 (twice)

120 Pentonville Road
London N1 9JN
United Kingdom
www.kogan-page.co.uk

525 South 4th Street, #241
Philadelphia PA 19147
USA

© Dick Stroud, 2005

The right of Dick Stroud to be identified as the author of this work has been asserted by him in accordance with the Copyright, Designs and Patents Act 1988.

ISBN 0 7494 4258 1

British Library Cataloguing-in-Publication Data

A CIP record for this book is available from the British Library.

Library of Congress Cataloging-in-Publication Data

Stroud, Dick.
  The fifty-plus market : why the future is age-neutral when it comes to marketing and branding / Dick Stroud.
     p. cm.
  Includes index.
  ISBN 0-7494-4258-1
  1. Marketing. 2. Middle aged consumers--Attitudes. 3. Older consumers--Attitudes. I. Title.
  HF5415.S874 2005
  658.8′0084′4--dc22

                                                                          2005019164

Typeset by Saxon Graphics Ltd, Derby
Printed and bound in the United States by Thomson-Shore, Inc.

Contents

Foreword

During the Age of Mass Marketing, which dominated the last half of the 20th Century, there was one group of consumers who were largely ignored – those who were 50 years of age or older. Marketers had several reasons for not including these people in their target audiences: 50-plus consumers were generally less mobile and consumed fewer products than their younger counterparts; life expectancies were much shorter than they are today and the belief existed that these consumers had already established their brand preferences. In addition to this, marketers assumed that the 50-plus market was already being reached due to the older generation's preference for newspapers and television – the media channels most used by marketers to deliver their *mass* messages. Today however, things have changed. Life expectancies are now longer; and the 50-plus consumers are more mobile and in many cases economically advantaged in comparison with the younger generation. Moreover, marketers no longer rely on *mass* messaging, but have evolved to address specific segments of their target audiences with tailored communication; and media fragmentation now requires new media strategies to effectively reach the best prospects.

As a result of this evolution, there is a need for a deeper understanding of this rapidly expanding and vibrant 50-plus market. To effectively capture the economic value of these consumers, marketers must acknowledge their differences as well as their similarities to the under-50s market. Messages and offers need to be relevant to and resonate with these individuals. Advertising and media strategies should reflect the new marketplace realities and marketers must consider that 50-plus consumers may interact with new media channels differently to the younger generation.

In *The 50-Plus Market,* Dick Stroud explores why this market is both important and valuable, and provides a foundation for the premise that 'the future is age neutral when it comes to marketing and branding strategies.' It is an important book which will help shape the way marketers unlock the potential of this previously untapped community of increasing economic power.

At OMD (one of the largest and most influential media communications specialists in the world), we began studying the 50-plus market in 2003, when we recognized how rapidly the market was expanding and how its importance as a rich pool of consumers was increasing. Our UFO (Understanding Fifties and Over) study has provided us and many of our clients with a deep insight into this group, which has allowed us to develop powerful ideas to deliver compelling business results. All of us at OMD are delighted to have had the opportunity to collaborate with Dick on this venture. We hope you will find value in this book and come away as excited as we are about the vitality and business opportunities inherent in the 50-plus market.

Joe Uva
President & CEO
OMD Worldwide, Inc.
Insights, Ideas, Results

Acknowledgements

There is a long list of people who helped in creating this book. The global media network of OMD, lead by Jo Rigby, Head of OMD Insight, was the key to providing the quantitative research for many of the book's conclusions. Janet Kiddle, the MD of Steelmagnolia organized the qualitative research programme to understand how the UK's leading marketers approach the older market. Richard Webber, the originator of Mosaic and Acorn, wrote the chapter explaining the importance of geodemographics in understanding and targeting the 50-plus market.

It would have been impossible to have given the book a global perspective without the contributions of Chris Evers (Scandinavia) – Founder of INSPIRUM, the Danish marketing consultancy and publisher that targets the 50 plus; Allein Moore (Asia) – Founder and Editor of *AdAsia*, a leading magazine about the advertising industry in Asia; Chuck Nyren (US) – a writer and consultant about advertising to the Baby Boomer generation; Frederic Serriere (France) – Chief Executive of Senior Strategic Network and publisher of TheMatureMarket.com; Reg Starkey (UK) – a veteran of the advertising industry, writer and broadcaster who focuses on the challenge of responding to the rising power of the older consumer; and, Gill Walker (Australia) – Director of Evergreen, an advertising agency specializing in marketing communication programmes for mature audiences.

I am indebted to all of the following people for finding time to be interviewed and giving their opinions and ideas about marketing to the older market: Sylvie Barr, Head of Marketing, Cafédirect; Alex Batchelor, Global Brand Director, Orange; Hugh Burkitt, Chief Executive, the Marketing Society; Charlie Crowe, Managing Director, C Squared; Winston Fletcher, Chairman, Advertising Standards Board of Finance;

Michael Harvey, Global Consumer Planning and Research Director, Diageo; Malcolm Macdonald, Emeritus Professor, Cranfield School of Management; Wally Olins, Chairman, Saffron Brand Consultants; Richard Reed, founder and Marketing Director, Innocent; Martin Smith, Sales Director, SAGA Publishing; Simon Thompson, UK Marketing Director, HONDA; Andrew Walmsley, founder and MD of i-level; Robin Wight, Chairman, WCRS; and, Chris Zanetti, Managing Director, Seven Seas.

My thanks also to the following people for their contributions: Mike Bingham, Managing Director, Senior Response, for his input about managing a call centre company catering for the 50-plus market. Ruth Simmons, MD of Songseekers, for her insight into the importance of music in the creative mix for older consumers; and Leslie Harris and Howard Willens, authors of *After Fifty* for their views on the US market.

Finally, my heartfelt thanks to the Kogan Page's editorial team for all of their help and encouragement.

The following chapters were contributed by other authors:

Chapter 1, Marketers on marketing to the over-50s

Janet Kiddle is the Founder of Steel Magnolia, the strategic research consultancy that specializes in understanding the 50-plus market. She combines specialist understanding of the target group with an understanding of brand marketers, brand planners and consumer insight teams. She has held senior positions with Saatchi & Saatchi/Team Saatchi and The Research Business International.

Chapter 7, The value of geodemographics

Richard Webber is the originator of Britain's two most widely used geodemographic classification systems, Mosaic and Acorn, and has experience of building neighbourhood classifications in 18 countries around the world. He is currently a Visiting Professor at the Centre for Advanced Spatial Analysis, University College London.

Chapter 12, Communicating with the over-50s

Jo Rigby is Head of OMD Insight, the OMD Group resource which serves both OMD UK and Manning Gottlieb OMD. She has worked at OMD since 2000 and prior to this she worked at Proximity London. Jo established UFO (Understanding Fifties and Over) in 2003, with the objective of gaining unique insight into the 21st century over-50s audience. This research study won the Marketing Research Award for Best Use of Customer Insight, the Media Week Award for Best Research Project, the Campaign Media Award for Best Use of Research. A second wave of UFO will be launched in September 2005.

Introduction

MARKETING BONANZA

Back in 1996 I wrote a book about a little-known technology called the internet and how it was going to change the world of business. I just couldn't understand why so many marketers didn't share my excitement about the internet's potential to create new markets and business channels. Those who didn't think it was important were subsequently proved wrong.

Today I feel exactly the same about the 50-plus market. It is obvious, at least to me, that we are on the precipice of a marketing bonanza. Up to now the over 50s have been largely ignored, yet even the most statistically allergic marketer can understand the data showing their economic power. There is a relentless shift in the economic centre of gravity towards older people. While our culture faces 'young', the economic reality is pointed to 'old'.

Having researched the topic of 50-plus marketing, I have come to realize that, in general, an adult consumer's age is of little use in determining their marketing behaviour. The evidence from my studies and interviews, confirmed by the research of media agency OMD, indicates that marketers would be wise to adopt the concept of 'age neutrality'. In very simple terms, this means that marketers should make no assumptions or decisions about adult consumers on the basis of their age, unless there is substantiating evidence. The principles of marketing to a 30-year-old are the same as marketing to somebody aged 75. Marketing theory is intrinsically age neutral.

A puzzle

Why then, don't companies grasp this business opportunity and do something about it? How can marketing directors ignore this group of affluent consumers? Why aren't the senior management of US and European companies demanding their advertising agencies target the older market?

For the last couple of decades, people like me have been shouting about the 50-plus market and its increasing importance as a key group of consumers, to little or no effect. It seems that business is impervious to these arguments. Marketing attention is showered onto the 18–35-year-olds while their parents and grandparents are pretty much ignored.

The solution

But just telling marketers about the importance of the 50-plus market is not enough. It is necessary to address the real reasons that companies are so reluctant to change and provide them with the tools and guidance to venture into the world of the older consumer. This is what this book seeks to do.

The book is not a social policy or a polemic document. Neither is it a set of predictions for the future or a collection of facts and figures. It is a very practical 'how-to' book designed for business people and marketers wanting to succeed in an environment geared towards the 50-plus market.

EXPERT HELP

In writing this book I sought and received a lot of help. I needed the input from other experts who could give a global view of the 50-plus market, as well as quantitative research that would tell me what's different about the attitudes of 30-, 50- and 70-year-olds and how these differ according to country and culture.

It was essential that I understood how leading marketers, both young and 'mature', view and respond to the 50-plus market. In the technical areas of media planning and geodemographics I needed the input from the leading industry practitioners. I was fortunate in receiving assistance from a great team of experts to research and write the book.

HOW TO USE THIS BOOK

The 50-plus Market is written as a story with a beginning and an end. Chapter 1 sets out the scope of the story by relating the views of leading marketers about the 50-plus market. Chapter 14 concludes by looking at the broader issues of the aging population and its effect on business. The intervening chapters separate the facts from the myths, looking at how the 50-plus market can be segmented and the implications for media planning, creative and interactive channels. Alternatively, the book can be used as a textbook that provides self-contained chapters explaining the facts and implications of the aging population, on each aspect of marketing.

Chapters 1 to 4 look at the facts, myths, prejudices and uncertainties about the 50-plus market and marketing. This analysis uncovers a group of older people (the Charmed Generation) that has a level of spending power that is unlikely to be matched by future generations. The analysis also reveals why the spending power of 18 to 35 year olds (Generation Broke) is in decline.

Chapters 5 to 7 uses OMD's research from Australia, the Czech Republic, France, the UK and the US to show how age affects peoples' attitudes and behaviours and what this means for segmenting markets.

Chapters 8 and 9 show why marketers need to change their approach to the 50-plus market and adopt the principles of age-neutral marketing and how this can be accomplished.

Chapters 10 and 11 discuss the impact of ageing on the way people use interactive channels, especially the Web, and how to make these channels '50-plus friendly'.

Chapters 12 and 13 review how the selection of media and the choice of advertising creative are affected by the need to target older people.

Chapter 14 considers a range of subjects, starting with the application of the Tipping Point theory to the 50-plus market and ending with a description of a world that is rapidly dividing into regions of old and young people and what this means to the marketer.

WEBSITE

The website accompanying this book can be found at www.the50plusmarket.com. There you will find the latest information about the 50-plus market and the blog I write about the subject. The site gives you a chance to tell me what you think about the 50-plus market and to ask questions.

STYLE

I find that some business books can be complex, difficult to understand and lacking in excitement. I have endeavoured to make this book light-hearted, engaging in tone and amusing. Where I have encountered ill-thought-out arguments, I have said so, and to all those that I have offended, my apologies. I hope that I have provided you with some new and interesting insights into the 50-plus market and that the 'age-neutral' approach to marketing is one that you will follow.

1

Marketers on marketing to the over-50s

How do leading marketing practitioners react to the 'ageing' of consumers? Do they perceive the steady rise in the numbers of those over 50 to be a problem, an opportunity or an irrelevance? Is it something that keeps them awake at night or never crosses their minds?

To answer these questions, I worked with Janet Kiddle – a leading expert in researching the over-50s – interviewing old, young, client and agency marketers. This chapter documents their opinions.

As all of these people are marketers, it is not surprising that we encountered a wide range of views – some of them diametrically opposed to each other. It was fascinating to hear the opinions of leading young marketers along with older gurus of the industry.

We asked a range of questions. How does ageing affect consumer behaviour, attitudes to new brands and responsiveness to advertising? We also sought their views about how marketers will cope with the business changes resulting from the ageing population.

Our aim was not to seek a consensus or derive the definitive answer to these questions, but to understand how the best minds in the industry perceive the effect of an ageing population on marketing.

Where possible, we have used the marketer's own words to express their opinions. We could not use all of the interviewee's quotes, but their collective views contributed to the opinions expressed in the chapter.

IS THERE AN ISSUE?

When I first conceived the idea of writing this book, an old friend and long-time marketer, Mike Detsiny, asked one of those very short but horribly revealing questions: 'Why?' He then expanded it to 'Is there really an issue with marketing to older consumers. Isn't it one of those perennial things the media talks about when they are short on other topics?' This question seemed like a good place to start in our interviews.

Research from Help the Aged shows that just 5 per cent of advertising targets the over 50s, even though this age group represents nearly half of peak-time TV audiences and dominates radio-listening figures. Other research shows the figure to be somewhere between 10 and 15 per cent. Whatever statistic is correct, the figure for advertising is low.

Mike Waterson, Chairman of the World Advertising Research Centre (WARC), is uncompromising in his view that 'Advertisers and marketers are astonishingly neglectful of older audiences, even for products primarily sold to older people.'

Research carried out among the over-50s in the US by the AARP and in the UK by Help the Aged reveals that the majority feel advertising portrays them negatively. A great many simply don't relate to advertising at all, feeling that it is not intended for them, but for the young.

The marketers we interviewed believed that if there was an issue, it didn't apply to the way that they behave. Perhaps that is not surprising.

We encountered strong support for the view that positioning a brand to appeal to people with a similar set of values, beliefs and needs was far better than defining a market simply by age. Many felt that brand values will be shared, in varying degrees, across all age groups.

Sylvie Barr, Marketing Director of Cafédirect, voted the UK's 'Marketer of the Year' in 2004, said 'The age of our customer is not the primary factor in our approach to marketing. What matters most is Cafédirect's ethos and our brand values and this drives everything we do.' This was supported by Alex Batchelor, Orange's Global Brand Director, who said, 'With our market segmentation we try to ignore age as much as possible. You can have 70-year-olds who buy all the latest gadgets alongside 30-year-olds.'

When Richard Reed, founder and Marketing Director of Innocent Drinks, was asked about the importance of age in his choice of advertising media, he said 'I don't ever look at the age of viewers or readers.'

These views are an acknowledgement that the importance of a brand to an older age group has to be evaluated on a case-by-case basis. There are no general marketing 'rules' that apply.

Several people believed that the way in which society perceives older people determines how marketers behave. Robin Wight, Chairman of WCRS, observed, 'There is a big difference between youth and youthfulness. The first is defined by chronological age, the second is a state of mind.' He went on to talk about the importance of the age one feels, rather than age of the face reflected in the mirror in the morning. As a society, our values and aspirations are to be youthful. This creates a tension between the business realities of an ageing population that is economically powerful and an inspirational centre of gravity that is young.

Wally Olins, Chairman of Saffron and a leading expert on branding, said, 'Age is not something valued by Western society. There are signs that this attitude is spreading to the East. This is the culture in which marketers work and it influences their decisions.' He continued, saying 'Our society portrays the old as boring, lacking excitement and not sexy. Why should anybody be concerned with the old! Why should marketers be any different?'

It was surprising that the most vocal proponents of an age-neutral approach to marketing were the youngest marketers we interviewed.

The mismatch between the economic value of older people and the marketing attention they receive seems to be part of a larger cultural issue – namely, society is institutionally ageist. It is not surprising that, living in a culture where young is good and old is boring, marketers behave as they do.

Having established their opinions as to whether or not the ageing population is an issue for marketers, we then sought their views about how ageing affects consumer behaviour.

DOES THE WILLINGNESS TO TRY NEW BRANDS DECLINE WITH AGE?

We had a full range of responses to this question. Some thought that the assumption that older people are less willing to try new brands was wrong, others believed that it was too simplistic as an explanation of brand behaviour and a minority thought it correct.

Michael Harvey, Diageo's Global Consumer Planning and Research Director said 'I doubt if a person's willingness to try new brands declines with age.' In reference to older people he believes that 'Their brand repertoire will change but for different reasons to a younger person.' He quoted the example of the beer market and said 'As people get older their preferences change as they cannot consume the volume of product that they could when younger.' Older men often move to a higher alcoholic strength beer in order to get the same effect from drinking but in lower volumes. He then went on to say, 'We have found that drinks preferences, formed during a person's 20s, are retained in latter years. The one exception is wine, which has been adopted by all age groups and people have come to it later in life.'

Robin Wight agreed with the statement, but felt that the relationship between age and brand promiscuity has changed over the past 20 years in the way illustrated in Figure 1.1. This shows brand promiscuity still declining with age, but at a later stage in a consumer's life. The really difficult thing is putting dimensions on the two axes!

He believed it was a natural response that, as people age and have the opportunity to experience more brands, they will naturally decide their preferences, so it is not surprising that brand promiscuity declines. It is a function of experience rather than attitude. Simon Thompson, Honda's UK Marketing Director, supported this view: 'Our research clearly shows that it is increasingly difficult to change car brand preferences as people get older.'

Charlie Crowe, MD of C Squared, takes a different view. He believes that 'Many of the assumptions marketers make about the role of age in conditioning consumer behaviour are outdated and irrelevant. The marketing profession is talking about the issue, but is only just starting to do anything about it.'

Sylvie Barr has had the interesting experience of seeing her products being purchased initially by older people and then adopted by the young. She explained, 'In Cafédirect's early days, customers of Fairtrade

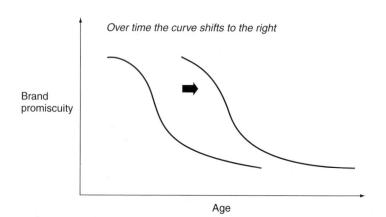

Figure 1.1 *How the relationship between brand promiscuity and age changes with time*

products were mainly the 45+. Now, with Fairtrade and world issues a part of the school curriculum, I see schoolchildren motivated by exactly the same issues as our long-standing customers. Our brands appeal to people from all ages, be they teenagers or their grandparents.'

The views of our marketers suggest that the willingness to try new brands can decline, but for a collection of reasons, not some universal trait in human behaviour. We also heard many examples of brand behaviour and age being totally independent. The conclusion from this diverse set of views is that there is no simple or generalized rule about ageing and brand behaviour.

OLDER PEOPLE ARE LESS RESPONSIVE TO ADVERTISING THAN THEIR JUNIORS

There was little support for this view. As Wally Olins succinctly said, 'It is a simplistic argument which hasn't much value.' All agreed, though, that older people responded in a different way because of their age. Michael Harvey summarized his view as follows: 'They [the over-50s] are more responsive to communications of a different sort that recognizes them as individuals and accepts their stand in life.' Alex Batchelor thought that 'They are not less responsive but they are less interested in style over substance.'

Chris Zanetti, MD of Seven Seas and Director, Merck Consumer Healthcare, said, 'Seven Seas has a range of products that targets the over-50s that we support through advertising and our tracking shows that we have very high indices for advertising responsiveness for both TV and direct marketing.' He went on to say that 'Younger consumers want to know what is in a product but they are more interested in lifestyle and image, whereas older consumers want the facts.'

Martin Smith, Sales Director at SAGA Publishing, related that many advertisers believe they need to have a different approach when advertising to older age groups: 'When I talk with clients and agencies they often think it is necessary to customize their advertising for the over-50s.' His response to this idea is 'I tell them that our readers are mainstream consumers and to use their existing campaigns, but getting marketers to understand this message can pose a challenge.' The message does seem to be getting through to the marketing departments of some major companies, however. Mainstream brand advertising from companies such as Bose, Suzuki, Mitsubishi and L'Oréal is the fastest-growing area of SAGA's advertising revenue.

It was evident from these discussions that little research is carried out when developing advertising to assess whether or not it appeals to the older consumer unless the brand is overtly targeting this audience.

APPEALING TO OLDER CONSUMERS ALIENATES THE YOUNG

Most thought that this is often true and reflects the society in which we live – one where appealing to youth is more important than alienating the old. A good creative – marketing-speak for advertisement – can engage a wide range of ages, but it is the exception, not the rule.

Michael Harvey believes that a great example of an ad that worked across all age groups was Guinness's 'Swimmer' advertising campaign. The premise of the ad – shown in Figure 1.2 – is that, as a young man, Marco won a medal in the Olympic Games and now each year the villagers gather to watch him race 'against the pint'. It takes 119.5 seconds

Figure 1.2 *Guinness's 'Swimmer' advertisement*

to pour the perfect pint of draught Guinness, so that's how long he's got to swim from a buoy in the bay back to shore and sprint to the bar before the barman finishes pouring the pint. The celebrations begin as Marco drinks his well-earned pint. As Michael Harvey says:

> For younger adults, it was just so cool to see this old guy still performing and clearly still up for the swim even though his brother gave him a little bit of help so that each year he won the race against the pint. For older consumers it was an ad that had a product message in it, which was 'good things come to those who wait'.

In other words, it was an enjoyable product with good taste values and coincidentally there is someone who is a good role model for people in their 50s as he shows that he is young at heart.

It is interesting that the brewer Anheuser-Busch has also adopted the image of an older, male swimmer. It had a full-page ad in an issue of *AARP The Magazine* showing an athletic 50-ish man climbing out of a swimming pool with goggles on his forehead. A glass of beer sits next to a bottle of Michelob Ultra in the upper right-hand corner. The tag line says, 'If this is your fountain of youth, this is your beer.' It seems that imitation really is the sincerest form of flattery.

Honda's UK advertising has produced campaigns that are perfect examples of age-neutrality. Simon Thompson's approach is that 'Honda's advertising creative is age-neutral. When we focus on specific age groups it is achieved by our media planning.'

Figure 1.3 shows a series of stills from Honda's advertising campaign called 'Cog'. The ad showed an intricate chain-reaction involving 85 car parts from the Honda Accord. Like a set of dominos, each one hits the next and ends with the final part releasing a fully built car that slowly rolls down a ramp.

Simon Thompson says about it, 'We want to show it is a superbly engineered quality car. It shows the passion and obsession that the engineers have put into each part.' In 2003, this ad swept the board of advertising awards.

Stills from the 'Grr' campaign are shown in Figure 1.4. This advertisement was an enchanting way of showing how the dirty and noisy diesel engine can become clean and quiet. The animated sequence narrates the story of Honda's better diesel engine, all set in a colourful world of talking rabbits, flowers and rainbows. The first still shows a rabbit, with ear mufflers, being passed by a flight of old noisy, smoky diesel engines. By the end of the sequence, shown in the last still, the new Honda diesel has been born.

Figure 1.3 *A series of stills from Honda's 'Cog' advertising campaign*

Jim Thornton, Creative Director of Leo Burnett, an advertising agency, said of the ad, 'It unashamedly appeals to women and children as well as petrol heads without ever patronizing them.' The appeal of the ad to children is not surprising as, Simon Thompson believes, 'It has always been the case, and always will be the case that children have a strong influence over the car purchase decision.'

The Honda and Guinness examples show that age-neutral advertising can be outstanding and world class, judged against any criteria.

Those disagreeing with the assertion that appealing to older consumers alienates the young did so because they held the view that if you are communicating values and a need that spans different age groups, then age is irrelevant. Alex Batchelor's explanation for this view is that 'The

Figure 1.4 *Two stills from Honda's 'Grr' advertising campaign*

reality is older people are more eclectic than they used to be. Most people are quite good at recognizing when things are aimed at them.'

Andrew Walmsley, founder of the interactive agency i-level, was clear in his view that 'Some advertising should alienate older viewers. For example, if you are targeting youth products and attempting to engage consumers by characterizing them as rejecting traditional values.' He then went on to say, 'What's dumb is when advertising fails to engage a signif-icant section of a brand's user base because marketers and agencies aren't interested or don't know how to engage them.'

The role of advertising and how it relates to older people seem to be something of a paradox. Older people are perceived as being more advertising 'savvy' and capable of filtering out messages not intended for their consumption. The possession of this ability means advertising can be biased towards young people, even though their media consumption, especially of TV, is lower than that of older generations.

We concluded each interview by seeking interviewees' opinions about the cultural and organizational challenges that marketing faces in coping with demographic change.

HOW WILL MARKETING ADAPT TO THE POWER OF THE OLDER CONSUMER?

Each of our marketers speculated on how the practice of marketing will adapt to the rising power of older consumers and the challenges this creates. It is easy to blame junior brand managers who are in their mid-20s for being remote from the older target audience and not understanding or valuing its importance. However, it is not the brand managers who are responsible for setting a company's marketing agenda and, as Michael Harvey succinctly says, 'To adapt to the power of the older consumer, marketing will need to understand how to target these people, which I don't think older marketers have got to grips with yet, so what chance do younger marketers have?' Maybe, then, the myth that it is all the fault of youthful marketers is not correct.

Charlie Crowe believes that many of the problems reside with agencies: 'The age, social and ethnic profile of society is rapidly changing. Clients are kicking their agencies to become aligned with this new reality.' In their defence he did go on to say that, 'To be fair, in some cases it's the other way around.'

Wally Olins thinks that marketing's reticence to change is a significant problem: 'In my experience, marketers are lazy and will take the easy option. It is much easier to keep doing what you know rather than moving out of your comfort zone.'

Some markets have always had older consumers because the product is only of relevance to them when they reach a certain age. The 'age ghetto' sectors include exciting things such as equity release mortgages, free flu jabs, discounted car insurance and remedies for various medical ills. Perhaps these are not the products likely to excite the young marketer?

It is in the multi-age markets, though, where companies have not confronted the implications of the ageing population and the obsession with targeting the young. Almost everyone acknowledges that the issue of the 'age thing' is on their radar, but most are reticent about addressing it with any seriousness. For this to change, our interviews highlighted a couple of attitudinal barriers that marketers must overcome.

The first is the 'dying brand' syndrome that is characterized by the view that it is bad, if not fatal, to have a customer base biased to the over-50s. Marketers need to reframe their attitudes and think of their brand as having significant growth potential for customers aged 50 and above.

The second mental leap required is to question the assumption that a marketing campaign 'will get them anyway'. To adopt the language of modern warfare, if advertising's primary target of attack is the young, then, it is assumed, their parents and grandparents will automatically sustain collateral damage.

TV advertising's bias towards the under-35s, it is argued, is to balance the fact that this age cohort spends less time viewing television than other age groups. It would also be argued that this doesn't matter, as older people, as a secondary audience, are also exposed to the same advertising. Andrew Walmsley, however, highlighted the flaw in this theory: 'This argument is sound as long as the nature of the advertising is not so youth-orientated that it alienates the older viewer.'   .

Chris Zanetti believes that marketers must take the ageing population seriously. In his view, the biggest challenge will be in adapting their channel marketing.

The final word about the challenges that marketers face goes to Michael Harvey: 'I think the demographic shift to older consumers does demand a fundamental change in thinking. You do need to go from mass communications to the masses to individual communications to the masses. Older people expect (and want) to be valued and respected as individuals.'

WHAT'S THE RELATIVE IMPORTANCE OF THE AGEING POPULATION?

How important is the issue of the ageing population compared with other changes in the social, regulatory and economic environment?

Most of our interviewees felt that the implications of the ageing population was not as big an issue, in their markets, as other changes going on in society and the regulatory environment. For example, in the alcoholic drinks business, having socially responsible marketing is more important than this question because if companies don't react appropriately to the social and regulatory environment they won't have a business. Similarly, the fast-food industry needs to respond to government guidelines on food education, advertising the healthiness of its products. Thus, staying in business is a more pressing need than addressing the marketing opportunities of the over-50s.

The network mobile phone market is heavily regulated and trying to reduce the bills of all is seen as more important than working with handset manufacturers to develop phones that are easier for older consumers to use. In fairness, this is beginning to change, but very late in the day.

The food industry is confronted with regulatory and consumer pressures to overhaul the nutritional balance of its products and improve labelling. Reappraising the age profile and targeting its customers is of secondary importance to these issues.

Chris Zanetti, however, rates the issue of the ageing population as one of his 'core marketing pillars'. Like those working in the food and drinks businesses, he also ranks the impact of EU regulations – in particular relating to what claims can be made about his products – as a major issue.

Clearly, there is competition for management's time and resources between coping with tactical priorities and managing strategic change. At the moment it would seem that the former is winning. The following apocryphal tale of boiling frogs has important lessons when balancing the importance of tactical marketing imperatives against strategic change.

If you put frogs into a container of cold water that is slowly heated, the frogs die. You might wonder, 'Why don't they jump out of the water?' The answer is that, as the water heats very slowly, they fail to notice their changing (and dangerous) environment before it is too late to act. No doubt the frogs were more concerned about the short-term opportunity of finding a mate!

Marketers have a big advantage over frogs: they are at least aware of the ageing population issue. However, they are tempted to perceive it as being important but something that they will deal with when they have the time. The hectic world of marketing means that issues demanding immediate attention push potentially more important but less time-critical items down the 'to do' list. Adopting a marketing strategy compatible with an ageing population is an easy task to delay while solving the problem of the day. This, though, is a dangerous way to go on.

Several of our interviewees believed that the short time horizons of brand managers made it difficult for companies to grapple with the bigger strategic issues. We were forbidden from attributing the following quote, but it sums up this predicament: 'Most brand managers are rarely in their job for more than 18 to 24 months and are primarily motivated by gaining status with their peers in the industry.' So, for them, the 'age thing' will come way down their priority list. Even if this is only partially true, it is a frightening thought.

WHAT KEY MESSAGES CAME FROM OUR INTERVIEWS?

Trying to distil 15 interviews into a few paragraphs is difficult. Janet and I each selected our primary conclusions and were, much to our surprise, in total agreement.

The usual rules of marketing still apply

There is not a special subset of marketing that applies to older people. All the basics about understanding the customer's motivations, needs and purchasing behaviour are equally valid. The fatal mistake is to assume that the older consumer shares the same mindset as the young or, even worse, to use an identikit model of an older person, pieced together from simplistic stereotypes.

Don't confuse youth and youthfulness

Understand that a youthful attitude can exist among people in their 20s through to their 80s. Remember Robin Wight's view that 'Everybody in their head is 25.' Understand that our self-image is very different to the reality we confront in the mirror each morning. The classic mistake is to try to appeal to the youthful instinct of older people with the imagery, language and humour of the young.

Marketers are only human

We live in a world that places an irrational value on the new, the young and all things modern. Equally, things that are old, the old and the past are devalued. It hasn't always been this way and may change in the future, but today that's the way it is. Marketers live in and are part of this culture, so it not surprising that they are instinctively youthcentric.

The same but different

Just because the English and Americans share a common language doesn't mean that we think the same, share the same humour or react to advertising in the same way. Of course there is a large area of common understanding, but there are still differences, too. A similar relationship exists between different age cohorts. Most of the time, older people are able to understand the language, culture and motivations of the young. They have a great deal in common – not least being their parents and grandparents!

Marketers would do well to realize that even though older people understand the zeitgeist of the young, there are times when engaging with them on their own terms would produce the best results.

Age-neutral advertising is difficult but not impossible

It is possible to produce advertising that is age-neutral. It is not easy, but when it works well, it creates outstanding ads – judged by any criteria. The Guinness and Honda ads are brilliant examples of what can be done.

There's always something more important

Every industry has its own set of problems to which it can apply the saying, 'If we don't get today right then tomorrow will never come.'

The results of demographic and economic change may be gradual, but they are relentless and predictable. The challenge for marketers – and it is a huge challenge – is to balance the continual stream of short-term events while also confronting the implications of the longer-cycle changes to their markets.

The final words in this chapter come from Robin Wight, who perfectly summed up the challenge facing marketers in understanding older people. The reality of today's older consumer is a 'Non-ageing mind, in an ageing body, with a maturing wallet.' We just wish we could have thought of this definition!

PEOPLE WE INTERVIEWED

Tim Ambler	Senior Fellow	London Business School
Sylvie Barr	Head of Marketing	Cafédirect
Alex Batchelor	Global Brand Director	Orange
Hugh Burkitt	Chief Executive	The Marketing Society
Charlie Crowe	Managing Director	C Squared
Winston Fletcher	Chairman	Advertising Standards Board of Finance
Michael Harvey	Global Consumer Planning and Research Director	Diageo
Malcolm McDonald	Emeritus Professor	Cranfield School of Management
Wally Olins	Chairman	Saffron Brand Consultants
Richard Reed	A founder and Marketing Director	Innocent
Martin Smith	Sales Director	SAGA Publishing
Simon Thompson	UK Marketing Director	Honda
Andrew Walmsley	A founder and MD	i-level
Robin Wight	Chairman	WCRS
Chris Zanetti	Managing Director	Seven Seas, Director, Merck Consumer Healthcare

2

The future is getting old(er)

Researching the facts and figures to write this chapter was easy. Any article or book about older consumers contains a section, littered with data, proving their marketing importance. Paradoxically, the more charts and tables that are used to prove the point, the less effect they seem to have.

Health warnings on cigarette packets is another example of where confronting people with abstract facts results in the opposite reaction from that intended. Cigarette packets, in the UK, contain warnings covering 30 per cent of the front and 40 per cent of the back with gory statements such as 'smoking kills' or 'smokers die younger' or, more clinically, 'smoking clogs the arteries and causes heart attacks and stroke'. What result have these dire warnings had on young people? In 2002, more 20–24-year-olds smoked than did in 1988. If you can't change a 24-year-old's behaviour by telling them that they are killing themselves, what chance do you stand of convincing them to take notice of the over-50s with a litany of facts and figures?

Marketing's equivalent to the health warnings on cigarettes is the 'boiler plate' sentences that appear in most commentaries about marketing and the over-50s. Here are examples from the US, Canada and the UK (see tinted text on page 18).

I sense that when younger marketers see these statistics, they filter them out and pigeonhole whatever follows as something that will be banging on about old people. The numbers blur into each other, lose their meaning and are ignored. Marketers continue as before, aware, but ignorant of the facts.

It is a sad indictment of marketing, but when I come to evaluating and using statistics about demographics and consumer spending, the prevailing attitude is, 'Don't confuse me with the facts, I am happy with my prejudices.'

The 78 million Americans who were 50 or older as of 2001 controlled 67 per cent of the country's wealth, equivalent to $28 trillion. Households headed by someone in the 55–64 age group had a median net worth of $112,048 in 2000 – 15 times the $7,240 reported for the under-35 age group. And within five years, about a third of the population is going to be at least 50 years old.

The over-50s increased from 5.4 million in 1991 to nearly 7.3 million in 2001. By 2013 it will reach 9.5 million, one-third of all Canadians. People over 50 are responsible for more expenditure than any other group in Canada – some $35 billion a year.

The over-50s hold 80 per cent of the nation's wealth (£280 billion), 40 per cent of its disposable income and spend £240 million on consumer goods each year. They represent 42 per cent of the UK adult population and by 2011 this will have increased to 22 million people.

MARKETING 101

The following two questions have been taken from the first lesson of a course about marketing fundamentals.

▌ Question 1   What is the most attractive segment of a matrix that represents the growth of consumer numbers and amount of consumer wealth? Do you choose a fast- or slow-growing group of consumers? Do you choose consumers with low or high wealth?

▌ Question 2   What is the most attractive segment of a matrix that represents the level of consumers' disposable income and the degree of competition for their business? Do you choose consumers with low or high disposable income? Do you choose sectors where the competition is low or high?

The collected responses to these questions from the world's marketers are shown in Figures 2.1 and 2.2.

Of course there are numerous other factors that affect the answers to these simplistic questions, but, in the absence of any other information, you would have expected the answers to be:

▌ Answer to question 1 High growth in consumer numbers and high consumer wealth (the top right-hand corner).

▌ Answer to question 2 Low level of competition and high disposable income (bottom right-hand corner).

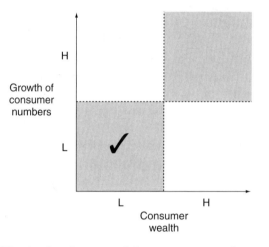

Figure 2.1 *Matrix showing growth in consumer numbers and level of consumer wealth (H = high, L = low)*
Source: 20plus30, 2004

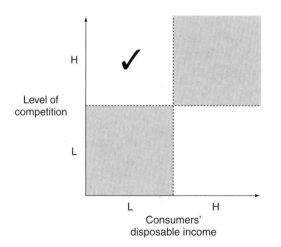

Figure 2.2 *Matrix showing level of competition and degree of consumers' disposable income (H = high, L = low)*
Source: 20plus30, 2004

No, there is not a misprint in the figures – the ticks are in the right places as marketers actually prefer to concentrate their resources on market sectors where the:

- growth in consumer numbers is *low*;
- consumer wealth is *low*;
- disposable income is *low*;
- level of competition is *high*.

Time and time again, companies ignore a group of consumers that is rapidly growing in number, has a high level of wealth and income and attracts little competition. If you haven't already guessed, this paradox occurs due to the obsession with younger rather than older people.

Surely there must be some extremely powerful arguments to justify this bizarre situation? Well, not really powerful arguments, more a collection of hunches, anecdotes and undisguised prejudices, which are the subject of the next chapter. What follows next here is the evidence that proves, categorically, that the future is getting older.

THE OLDIES ARE COMING

Marketing's prized group of consumers is the 15–34-year-olds. Their parents and grandparents – the 50–69-year-olds – are invariably of secondary interest. Figure 2.3 shows how the numbers of people in these groups will change over the next decade and a half. I don't think the conclusion from this graph needs too much explaining. There are going to be a lot more oldies and only a few more youngsters. For those wanting the actual predicted figures, 3,000,000 more 50–69-year-olds and 160,000 more 15–34-year-olds.

An alternative way of expressing these numbers is to see the age groups that increase in size and those that decline during the next 15 years. Again, the chart (Figure 2.4) doesn't need a great deal of explanation. There are a lot of tall black bars among the older age groups and as many negative white (declining) ones in the age groups from 0 to 49 years.

A similar, but less pronounced, trend is occurring in the US. Figures 2.5 and 2.6 show the US's equivalents of Figures 2.3 and 2.4. In the US, the 50–69 age group grows three times faster than the 15–34, but not at the same rate as in the UK. All age categories, with the exception of the 40–49-year-olds, grow during this period, but none so fast as the 50 plus.

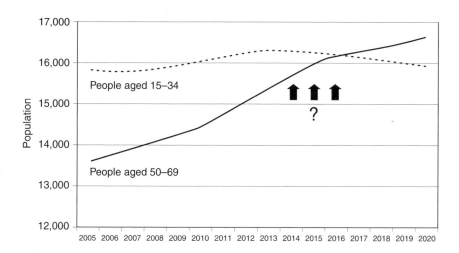

Figure 2.3 *Graphs showing the predicted numbers of the UK population aged 15–34 and 50–69*
Source: Government Actuary's Department, 2000

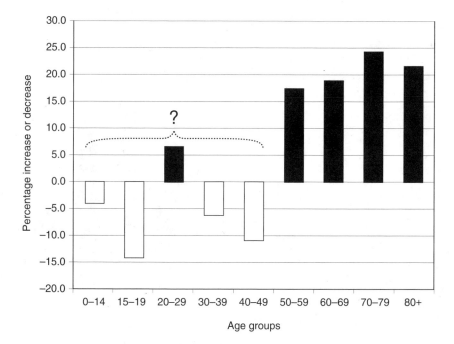

Figure 2.4 *Changes in the numbers of people in different age groups between 2005 and 2015 in the UK*
Source: Government Actuary's Department, 2000

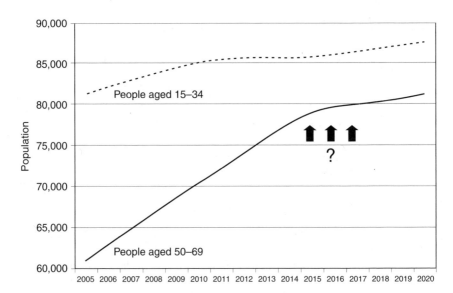

Figure 2.5 *Graphs showing the predicted numbers of the US population aged 15–34 and 50–69*
Source: Census Bureau, Department of Commerce, US, 2004

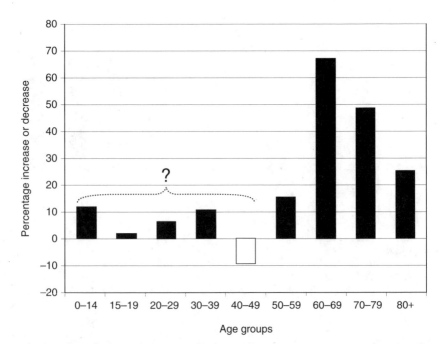

Figure 2.6 *Changes in the numbers of people in different age groups between 2005 and 2015 in the US*
Source: Census Bureau, Department of Commerce, US, 2004

NICE GRAPHS BUT SO WHAT?

The numbers used for this analysis are infinitely more accurate than any piece of consumer attitude research you have ever read. Nothing short of severe climate change, plague or pestilence, war or an asteroid strike can possibly change them.

There is one overriding conclusion to be drawn from this analysis: the numbers of older consumers are growing faster than those of the younger variety. This means that if you focus on the 15–34 market sector:

you will see virtually no increase in your market growth resulting from the change in customer numbers. If your customers are in the 50–69 category, you will increase your business by over 20 per cent without having to increase your market share.

You are consciously choosing a group of consumers whose numbers are at best stagnant and in some cases declining *and* consciously ignoring a group that is rapidly increasing.

Your advertising product development and sales channels will ignore (and probably alienate) the fastest-growing group of consumers.

If the pattern of ageing in the UK and US were an aberration, then there might be the germs of an excuse for marketers being obsessed with the under-35s. However, compared to many countries, the UK and US are distinctly youthful in their age profile. Italy and Japan are 'geriatric' when compared to the US. Figure 2.7 shows how the percentages of the population over 50 changes by country and year.

In 2005, Australia, like the US, had a 50-plus population in the 40 per cent band. The UK appears in the 50 per cent band, Italy in the 60 per cent and Japan in the staggeringly high 80 per cent band. As the years pass, the percentages increase further and the countries move into higher bands. The populations get a little older day by day.

Companies trading with Japan and Italy are already encountering the effects of their populations ageing. Soon, the under-50s will become the minority in Japan. China's massive population – 450 per cent the size that of the US – is fast approaching the point where it will age more quickly than any other country in history.

% of the 50+ compared with those under-50s				
90%+		Japan (90%)	Japan (96%)	Italy (91%) Japan (105%)
80%	Japan (85%)			
70%			Italy (79%)	
60%	Italy (63%)	Italy (69%)		UK (63%)
50%	UK (51%)	UK (54%)	Australia (54%) UK (59%) US (51%)	Australia (58%) US (54%)
40%	US (42%) Australia (43%)	US (47%) Australia (48%)		China (47%)
	2005	2010	2015	2020
Year				

Figure 2.7 *Percentages of population over 50 in different years for Australia, China, Italy, Japan, the UK and the US*
Source: United Nations' population forecasts, 2004

Not all of the world is experiencing hyper-ageing. For example, parts of the planet are very young and will remain that way for the foreseeable future. The marketing implication of a world that is fragmenting into old and young is discussed in Chapter 14.

FOLLOW THE MONEY

People in the UK aged between 50 and 54 have, on average, 30 per cent more income than those in the 25–29 age group. Those aged between 55 and 59 have an income that is about 20 per cent more than those who are younger.

Figure 2.8 shows how income varies by age for UK adults. Around the age of 50, income peaks, then falls, reaching a plateau from the age of 60 onwards. Interestingly, this plateau level is the same as the average income earned by those aged between 20 and 24.

This analysis comes as no great surprise – older people tend to earn more than younger people. What is baffling, though, is why, nevertheless, at least 80 per cent of marketing effort in the consumer goods industry is focused on the relatively poor group of younger consumers.   .

Individuals' net wealth is even more skewed towards older people than income. 'Net wealth' is what a person owns when their debts have been subtracted from their savings and investments.

Until the age of 35, the average level of UK citizens' net wealth doesn't rise above £5,000. From that age onwards, it steadily climbs and peaks somewhere around the age of 65. This analysis is shown in Figure 2.9.

In the US, the pattern of income and age is similar to that in the UK. Instead of showing the income of individuals, the graph in Figure 2.10 plots the income of households in the US by the age of the head of the household. Notice anything a little strange? The income in households where the head is aged less than 35 years is lower than for all other ages, other than those in their mid-70s.

Perhaps it is not surprising that the 2001 Consumer Expenditure Survey in the US showed older consumers being the primary purchasers of transportation, healthcare, housing, food, pensions and personal insurance.

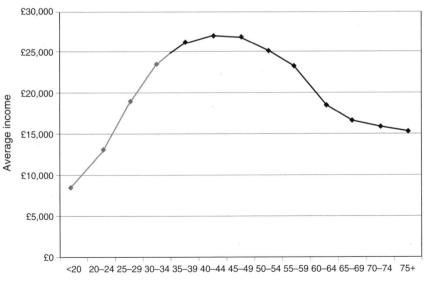

Figure 2.8 *Analysis of incomes in the UK for the period 2002–2003*
Source: Inland Revenue, 2004

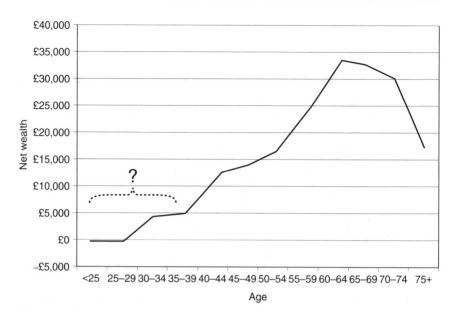

Figure 2.9 *The distribution of net financial wealth in the UK*
Source: Institute for Fiscal Studies, 2002

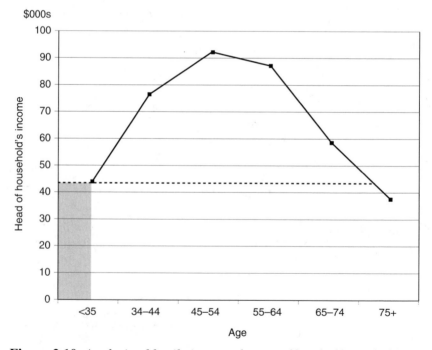

Figure 2.10 *Analysis of family incomes by age of head of household in the US*
Source: Federal Reserve Bulletin, January 2003

NICE GRAPHS BUT SO WHAT, PART 2?

On average, older people have more money to spend than younger ones. However you want to analyse, dissect, chart and present the ways in which income and wealth vary by age, you will always come back to the same conclusion: people under the age of 35, on average, are poor compared with their parents and grandparents. This means that if you focus on the 15–34 market sector, you have intentionally chosen a group with:

low levels of disposable income

the highest marketing/consumer spend ratio – that is, the amount of marketing spend divided by the level of consumer expenditure.

These are obvious statements, but ones that need to be made. The macro-economic analysis of age, income and number of consumers we have undertaken here will not apply to every single marketplace, as the dynamics and attractiveness of markets are affected by many things other than the number of consumers and their income. However – and this is a major factor – you cannot ignore the irrefutable evidence that proves the economic centre of gravity is moving from young to older people.

This chapter can be summarized in the following simple, logical statement:

older people have higher incomes than younger ones – in some cases a great deal higher
AND
numbers of older consumers are growing a great deal faster than the younger variety, which
IMPLIES
that marketers must have *exceptional* reasons for ignore ignoring older age groups.

FUNDING PENSIONS AFFECTS CONSUMER SPENDING

The concurrence of a population that is ageing with one in which its older members are disproportionally wealthy raises some interesting issues. The point where the rubber firmly hits the road is the implications this creates for funding pensions.

Governments have no easy choices to make for their citizens. They can ask them to retire on a pittance, pay more tax, save more or work for longer. Whatever happens, one thing is certain: consumer spending patterns are going to change for the worse.

Pensions and how to pay for them are complicated subjects, but the basic facts are simple and obvious. Fact number one: we are living longer. Fact number two: we are having fewer children. It doesn't take a genius to deduce that there will be fewer people working who will have to support an increasing number of older people, which we demonstrated earlier. The term 'support' doesn't just mean paying pensions; it also includes providing health and residential care, both of which are expensive.

This situation is not good, but it is only the start of the bad news. Today's pension position is pretty grim, with 50 per cent of people in the UK having such low levels of savings and private pensions that they are entitled to additional handouts from the State. If we look forward, in 10 years' time today's pensioners will appear wealthy. The picture in 30 to 40 years' time is too horrible to consider.

All the solutions to the pensions crisis are nasty. To recap, it either means working longer, saving more money, starting to save money at an earlier age, paying more tax or, most likely, a combination of all four remedies. The UK's *Financial Times*, not known for hyperbole, has said, 'The traditional British penchant for muddling through has bequeathed a system that is incomprehensible, inequitable and inadequate.'

What is the exact magnitude of the problem? If pensioners in the UK are to remain as well off as they are today and retire at the same age, then an additional 8 per cent of the country's gross domestic product (GDP) – £48 billion – will have to be spent on pensions by 2050.

In differing degrees, this problem affects all countries with an ageing population. In President Bush's 2005 State of the Union address, he launched his campaign for 'private accounts' as a way of privatizing the US's social security. In the proposed US model, individuals will pay into their own 'private' pension accounts, which are then invested in a mix of investments. The attraction of this for government is it caps its financial commitment to paying pensions.

Whatever the solutions, they have a common theme: money that would have been spent on consumption must be transferred by the individual, employer or government to paying for people's old age. This affects the amount of money in consumers' pockets, especially those of the young.

What might seem like a theoretical economic argument thus has some significant implications for marketers. The way in which, historically, pensions have been funded is a central factor in the creation of the generation of people we have now who enjoy a secure and prosperous financial future. How pensions will be funded in the future is key to creating the next older generation, who will be relatively poor by comparison.

THE 'CHARMED GENERATION'

Some of the circumstances surrounding the 'charmed generation' are special to the UK, but, in differing degrees, they are also present in Europe, Australia, Canada, Japan and the US.

In the UK, part of the group of people who are retired and who will retire in the next five to ten years have a level of wealth and income that is unlikely to be repeated in future generations. They are thus the 'charmed generation' and represent a business opportunity that, once gone, is unlikely to be repeated.

The reason for their good fortune is explained by the four Ps: pensions, property, parents and prudence – not to be confused with marketing's 4Ps!

Pensions

Many people of this generation receive, or will receive, a defined benefit pension. This scheme pays the highest level of guaranteed income, relative to the person's salary, of any type of pension. It is unaffected by the stock, bond, currency or any other market. Its recipients receive a guaranteed level of income for the rest of their lives.

In the UK's commercial sector, the number of active members of these schemes today has fallen by 60 per cent since 1995, 50 per cent since 2000 and could fall by a further 10–20 per cent in the future. This generous form of pension provision is fast disappearing. So, unless there is a drastic change in pension law, the era of receiving a guaranteed level of pension from an employer is over. Like the parrot in *Monty Python* (the renowned TV comedy show), the defined benefit pension scheme is dead, it is no more, it has ceased to be. Defined pensions have expired and gone to meet their maker!

Government employees are the only group who are guaranteed a defined benefit pension. The cost of meeting pension commitments for civil servants, teachers, National Health Service employees and the emergency services has risen so quickly that it now dwarfs the level of public-sector debt. The estimated, unfunded public-sector pension liabilities had reached £690 billion by March 2005. The size of this figure is staggering, as is the problem it presents to government. Public-sector pensions will be forced to undergo radical change.

The unpalatable alternative is for people to spend a sizeable amount of their income – maybe as much as 25 per cent – on funding a private pension. Money that is funding a pension is not being used for consumer spending.

Property

In the UK, the proportion of people under 45 years old owning their own property has declined since 2001. If you are 30 or younger, you are less likely to own a property now than 20 years ago.

The barrier to becoming a homeowner is the relatively high cost of property. If you were buying a house between 1960 and 1970, it would have cost you three times your annual earnings. Today it is exactly six times.

In 1994, three in every five first-time buyers came from the 18–30 age group. In the last 10 years, property prices have trebled and now only two in every five first-time buyers are of this age.

The conclusion to be drawn from this analysis is that much of the UK's property assets are owned by the 45+ and that the financial barriers for future generations to join the ranks of property owners will keep rising. Saving for a deposit and paying the mortgage consumes a disproportionally large chunk of income and, like paying for pensions, money spent on housing debt is not spent on consumption.

Parents

Another repercussion of the rapid rise in property prices is inherited wealth that the over-50s are receiving at the death of their parents. Few older people have used the equity in their property to fund their retirement, which means that most of the property value is being passed on to their children as an inheritance. Today's 50-year-olds need to fund, on average, 20 to 30 years of post-retirement life, however, so releasing equity (wealth) from the value of their homes will become an increasingly important way in which to achieve this.

Already, a fifth of people moving between owned properties on which there is no mortgage say that the reason for them doing so is that they want a smaller and cheaper house. From this you can infer that they are seeking to transfer some of their property value into cash.

Nearly 40 per cent of people in the UK aged between 51 and 60 who have a pension believe that the equity in their home will be part of their retirement assets. For some, in fact, property wealth will be an integral component of their retirement income. Currently, £2,250 billion of value resides in housing equity (that is, the property value less the outstanding mortgage). This is nearly double other forms of wealth, with the exception of pensions. Unlike savings and investments, housing equity is more evenly distributed throughout the population and so can be used by more people.

The outcome of the over-50s' dependence on property wealth has a worrying implication for their sons and daughters: property wealth spent on funding mum and dad's retirement will not be inherited. We have witnessed the birth of the SKI phenomenon – spending the kids' inheritance.

In truth, nobody knows how much of retired peoples' housing equity will find its way back to their children or be consumed funding their own retirement, what effect the reduction in the number of young people will have on housing prices and what will happen when interest rates rise. Further, if housing prices are at an artificially high level and plummet, so will one component of the 'charmed generation's income.

Where there is little doubt is that converting the equity held in property into income will be a central issue in the pension-funding process.

Prudence

The UK's level of debts on credit cards, mortgages and loans has reached the gigantic figure of £1,004,290,000,000.

Very little of this vast mountain of debt resides with today's retired generation. They come from the pre-credit card era, when debt was something to avoid at all costs. Things are different for younger people, however, and those close to retirement. As the Director General of Age Concern said, 'Older people have historically been reluctant to get into debt, but some of the next generation of pensioners appear to have quite different attitudes.' It appears that many 50-year-olds are spending rather than saving and this is setting the trend for 40- and 30-year-olds. There is a cohort of people entering retirement with considerable levels of debt that has to be serviced by retirement, rather than earned, income. This change in behaviour is likely to affect intergenerational transfers of wealth as older people have to use their property value to repay debt rather than pass it on as inheritance.

The terrifying prospect is that interest rates increase. At the beginning of 2005, the UK's base rate of interest was 4.75 per cent. For much of the 1970s and 1980s, the interest rate was twice and sometimes three times this level. If the rate were ever to increase to these historic levels again, then it would divert a massive amount of expenditure from consumption to debt repayment. It is a thought best not considered.

For the debt-free retired generation, though, the higher the interest rate the better, as it increases the income they receive from their savings.

The 'charmed generation' grew up during a period when the State paid for higher education and all but the very wealthy went to State-funded schools and used the free health service. Now, the burden of paying for education and health is increasingly transferring from the State to the individual. This generation has benefited from good pensions, rocketing property assets and low debt.

It is not surprising, when you look at the wealth profile of the UK, that so much of it is concentrated with the 50-plus. Sadly, the children and grandchildren of this group are very unlikely to accumulate the same levels of wealth. In a decade's time, the 50-plus cohort might have (almost certainly will have) a very different wealth profile. It will still contain the very rich and very poor, but the group of people who benefited from the unique combinations of the 4Ps will be missing.

Not all members of the 'charmed generation' are wealthy

The report produced by the Pensions Commission in 2004 as a policy document for the UK government concluded that 'The present level of pension rights accrual is both deficient in total *and increasingly unequal.*'

This inequality is demonstrated in Figure 2.11, which shows how the mean and median levels of net wealth vary by age. It is impossible to deduce from the mean (average) value how the wealth is distributed (that is, there may be a few very wealthy people and lots of poorer ones or, alternatively, everybody could have approximately the same level of wealth). The median value is a more useful measure. It represents the middle value of net wealth in each age range. So, for the age range 60–64, the average net wealth is nearly £35,000, but the median is close to £5000, implying that half of the people's net wealth is below this value.

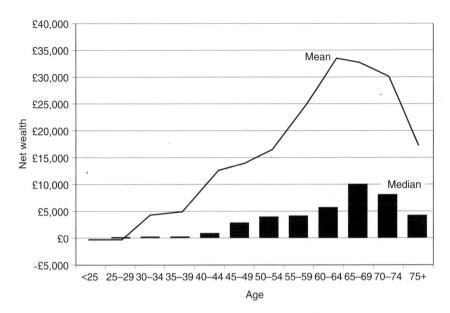

Figure 2.11 *The mean and median values of net wealth by age*
Source: Institute for Fiscal Studies, 2002

Even the most statistics-averse marketer can see that the median value is far less than the average value for the whole age range. There are a few people in each age group with a lot of financial wealth and far more with little or none. Indeed, of the £165 billion financial assets owned by 50–59-year-olds, over 84 per cent are owned by a quarter of the group.

Another measure of inequality – or, perhaps, it is the cause – is the unequal distribution of older people who have not retired but just 'stopped working'. Figure 2.12 shows, for the age group 50–59, the unequal distribution, by levels of wealth, for those who are retired or semi-retired and those who have stopped working for such reasons as being unemployed, sick or needing to care for a dependant. The poorest 20 per cent of this age group have nearly all disappeared from the work market, while the richest 20 per cent have retired or are semi-retired.

The more you look, the more evidence you will find of the disparity in wealth. Savings and home ownership are higher among those with pensions than those without.

Income and wealth inequality is very much part of society in the US as well. The AARP published a study in 2004 showing that there is an increasing level of wealth and income inequality for Americans aged 41 to 59 (baby boomers). The top 1 per cent of this group owns more wealth than the whole of the bottom 80 per cent. In each year of the survey – from 1989 to 2001 – the inequality gap widened.

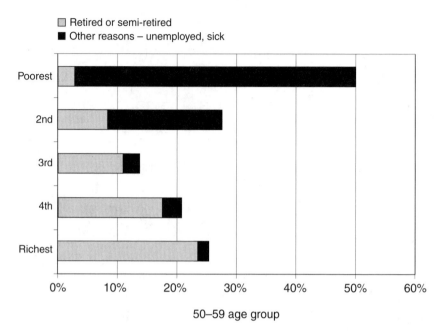

□ Retired or semi-retired
■ Other reasons – unemployed, sick

50–59 age group

Figure 2.12 *Reasons for men aged 55–59 not working in relation to wealth*
Source: Pensions Commission, 2004

The message for marketers is blindingly simple: some retired people, and those near to retiring, are going to have a lot of spending power. A lot more in this age group, however, will have very little – a trend that will become more pronounced in the future. This puts a premium on establishing marketing relationships with the post-retirement affluent. The question every marketer must answer is: does their customer base contain the rich or the poor over-50s? This is not such a simple question to answer because it depends whether or not their customer's income is predominantly dependent on paid employment.

At the point when people stop working because of retirement or exiting from the workforce, their financial position can radically change. For instance, the income of a self-employed person may have been high compared to that of a government employee. At the point when work income stops and retirement income starts, however, their respective financial positions may be reversed. The government employee has a guaranteed pension for the rest of his or her life, while the self-employed person may not have made pension provisions and is then dependent on State support.

The groups of people listed in Table 2.1 are a first approximation of the 'winners and losers' in terms of having adequate pensions.

Table 2.1 *Groups of people most likely to have adequate and inadequate pensions*

Those with adequate pensions	Types of people likely to have inadequate pensions
▌ Members of private-sector direct benefit schemes that are still accepting payments. ▌ Most public-sector employees. ▌ Senior executives with high-paying pension schemes. ▌ People on low incomes who will receive equivalent levels of State benefits.	▌ People not paying into a pension scheme and those making insufficient payments. These people are most likely to be found among the: – lower middle-income groups – smaller and mid-size firms – service sectors – self-employed.

Source: Pensions Commission, 2004

NICE GRAPHS BUT SO WHAT, PART 3?

The popular media's depiction of the over-50s swings between portraying them as a sad bunch of people, destined to pensioner poverty, and a fun-seeking and healthy group, determined to spend their wealth rather than leave it to their children. Even such a broad description has to contain some elements of the truth!

Among the retired and the soon to be retired is a group of fortunate people with little debt, receiving income from investments, pensions and property. Future generations will have such people but never so many as there are today. The concurrence of the 4Ps that created the 'charmed generation' is not likely to be repeated for the foreseeable future. So, this group represents a one-time opportunity for marketers. Once this cohort has aged and lost its ability and enthusiasm to spend, it will not be replaced by another of equal wealth. If you miss this opportunity it is gone for good.

Life for many of the other over-50s will not be so good, even now. At least 50 per cent of the over-50s stop working and have little in the way of savings and no private pension. Worse still, many more are retiring who have substantial levels of debt. The types of products and services purchased by this group will be totally different from those chosen by their wealthy counterparts. Marketers must understand the radical differences between these two groups

The importance of translating property wealth into income is central to how many people will fund their retirement. During the next decade, there will be a bonanza in the financial and support services associated with property equity release.

Finally, the ways in which companies collect customer information must reflect the differences between the pre-retirement affluent (those with wealth derived from work income) and the post-retirement affluent (those with income from pensions and property). In many cases, the two groups will be the same, but this will not always be the case. Some customers' income will plunge when their income stops and inadequate pensions start.

'GENERATION BROKE'

The 'charmed generation' has a mirror image. It is called 'generation broke'.

The name for this generation was coined in a briefing paper published in 2004 by Demos, the US think tank. In the press release accompanying the report's launch, there was the following profound statement: 'younger Americans (18–34) face a "perfect storm" of debt, massive student loans, slow wage growth, underemployment and rising costs.' The press release went on to say, 'ironically, this coveted demographic for advertisers and marketers are slipping into a downward debt spiral that is unmatched in modern history.'

'Generation broke' is not just an American phenomenon. It is estimated that the average student in England and Wales now leaves higher education owing around £12,000 and this figure keeps increasing. According to the Demos report, young adults (25–34) in the US are experiencing record levels of debt. The statistics are frightening. These young adults' average credit card debt increased by 55 per cent between 1992 and 2001. Households in this age group, with credit card debt, spend nearly 24 per cent of their income on debt repayments. In households with incomes below $50,000 (approximately two-thirds of the total), debt servicing can rise to 40 per cent of income. Adults aged 18–24 are experiencing even higher rises in credit card debt – up 104 per cent between 1992 and 2001.

The 18–34 age group has suffered from a combination of factors that have resulted in this precarious financial position. Many of the costs associated with young adulthood have increased dramatically during the past 10 years. Housing costs have risen by a significant amount when compared to salaries. Education costs – something that was once free – are now an expensive entry into adulthood. Salary levels have been suppressed and many permanent jobs have been replaced with short-term contract employment. To make matters worse, this generation has experienced the full might of credit card and retail store companies' marketing machines. There has never before been an era when buying on credit has been so simple.

With all of these financial commitments and temptations, it is not surprising that the one thing this age group is not doing is contributing enough to securing its pensions. In the UK, between 2002 and 2003, the number of under-35-year-olds saving for pensions declined. This wasn't a tiny little drop, but a huge fall – 13 per cent of men and 12 per cent of women in this age group dropped out of saving for a pension in a single year! During the same period, the percentage of 45–64-year-olds paying into pensions increased by around 7 per cent.

Since 1997, an additional 1.7 million people have entered the UK workforce. During that same period, however, the number of people both working and contributing to a pension has not increased by one person.

It is plain that this situation cannot continue. Either through higher tax or enforced saving, the 18–35s are going to have to pay a large chunk of their incomes into pensions. This is bad news for marketing's favourite age segment as every penny paid into a pension scheme is one penny less spent on consumption.

Financial life is going to get bleaker for these 18–35-year-olds. They are going to have to fund their own retirement plus that of their mums, dads and grandparents. Marketers had better get used to the idea that this age group is going to become relatively poor as they are forced to stop spending and start saving. The marked differences in the financial outlooks for these two generations are shown in Table 2.2.

There are some negative factors affecting the 'charmed generation's ability to spend. Needing to fund up to 30 years of post-retirement living affects the rate of spending, as does the demand to help with their children's finances, especially with housing and relieving their debt burden. However, compared to the catalogue of issues confronting 'generation broke', these are minor irritants.

The conclusion from analysing the 18–35 age group is that their future is littered with financial commitments that will constrain their ability to consume. These woes will not affect all members of this generation and there will remain an attractive subgroup worthy of marketing attention. At an aggregate level, however, you have to conclude that this age group's marketing attractiveness is declining.

Table 2.2 *The factors affecting the spending power of the 'charmed generation' and 'generation broke'*

'Charmed generation'		'Generation broke'	
Pension income	✓	Paying to fund pension	✗
Property equity	✓	Low growth in pay	✗
Low debt (beginning to change)	✓	Debt from funding education	✗
Accumulated savings/investments	✓	High housing debt repayments	✗
Need to fund long period of retirement	✗	Saving to acquire property	✗
Intergenerational wealth transfer	✗	Likely tax increases to fund ageing population	✗

Source: 20plus30, 2004

THE MARKETER'S TESTIMONY

Marketers made a range of responses when confronted with the arguments contained in this chapter. Table 2.3 lists these responses, accompanied by a slightly cynical interpretation of what is really meant by their reactions and the actions that they are likely to take as a result.

A simple technique to encourage senior marketing and business managers to really think about the implications of this analysis is the 'marketer's testimony' (see Figure 2.13). This is a short document that should be signed by the marketing and senior business managers in companies that primarily target the 18–35 age group.

Table 2.3 *The responses from marketers to this chapter's demographics and economic analysis*

Reaction to the analysis	Real meaning and resulting actions
'I know all of this and it's reflected in how we market.'	It is a tiny number of marketers who have genuinely and thoroughly investigated the relevance of this analysis. Rarely has a recent and comprehensive audit been conducted to evaluate the significance of these demographic changes.
'I don't think it will affect us.'	When translated this means, 'I have no idea if it will affect us and I don't intend to find out.'
'It's something we should look at.'	This, almost certainly, means nothing will happen. The genuine interest and concern is soon replaced by a more pressing issue.
'Perhaps it will affect us, but not in the short term.'	Same answer as above.
'This could have a serious impact on our business.'	This might result in some action being taken, but, more likely, it will become an item on a lengthy 'to do' list.
'This really makes me think.'	Another item that will be added to the 'to do' list. Unlike the previous response, though, it will be placed in the 'very important' category.
'We must evaluate the implications.'	This response has a 50:50 chance of resulting in action being taken.
'I will personally make sure we understand the implications.'	This response has a good chance of resulting in significant activity to understand the implications of these trends on the business.

Source: 20plus30, 2004

THE MARKETER'S TESTIMONY

I understand the implications of the demographic and economic changes affecting the number and relative wealth of consumers. Please tick to confirm that you understand the facts and implications of each point.

The numbers of people aged over 50 will increase significantly during the coming decade.	☐
The numbers of people aged 18–35 will remain static and in places decrease.	☐
On average, a person aged over 50 has a higher level of wealth and income compared with the average 18–35-year-old.	☐
A significant number of members of the age group who are retired and those retiring in the next five to ten years have a level of wealth and income that is unlikely to be repeated in future generations. They represent a business opportunity that, once gone, is unlikely to be repeated. They are called the 'charmed generation'.	☐
The generation aged 18–35 are experiencing financial pressures caused by high levels of debt, the need to fund a pension and the change in employment conditions and this is a situation that is likely to continue. On average, their relative financial importance as consumers will decline. They are called 'generation broke'.	☐

Even though the demographics and economic trends indicate the reducing economic importance of 18–35 consumers, I recommend retaining our current focus on this group for the reasons detailed below. These are listed in priority order.

Reason 1

Reason 2

Reason 3

Reason 4

Reason 5

I, being of sound mind and body, do acknowledge that I have thoroughly read and understood the meaning and implications of this document.

Name	....	Date	....

Figure 2.13 *The marketer's testimony form. Proof that the implications of the changing demographic and economic value of different-aged consumers is understood*

IMPLICATIONS FOR THE MARKETER

Many, if not the majority of marketers, focus on the 18–35 age group, even though, compared to other age cohorts, their numbers are hardly growing and they are relatively poor.

! Where companies have a youthcentric strategy, it is the duty of senior management to explain why it is appropriate for them.

There is an ample supply of data about population patterns and the associated distribution of income and wealth.

! Understanding macroeconomic consumer data and then using it to guide future strategy is part of the marketer's role.

A subsegment of those who are retired and who will retire in the next five to ten years has a level of wealth and income that is unlikely to be repeated in future generations. This is the 'charmed generation'.

! Companies should understand whether or not this group of wealthy consumers is relevant to their business. If it is, then there needs to be some urgency in targeting them.

Many of those who are about to retire will suffer a significant reduction in their standard of living. This is the start of a trend that will become more prominent in the future.

! Companies should understand the impact on its customers' expenditure levels as they move from pre- to post-retirement incomes.

For many young people, their future is littered with financial commitments that will constrain their ability to consume.

! Marketers should not assume that the spending power of 18–35-year-olds will continue at its current rate. Their levels of expenditure should be closely monitored.

SUMMARY

▮ Whichever way you analyse the data, the conclusions are the same: compared to the over-50s, the 18–35 cohort is growing at a slower rate and is relatively poor. In the next 15 years, the number of 50–69-year-olds in the UK will increase by 3,000,000. The number of 15–34-year-olds will struggle to grow by 160,000.

▮ Despite these statistics, marketers retain their fascination with the young.

▮ The same patterns of ageing, wealth distribution and marketing indifference exist throughout Europe, Japan, Australia and the US.

▮ In the UK, some of those who are retired and who will retire in the next five to ten years have a level of wealth and income that is unlikely to be repeated in future generations. They are property owners, have little debt and receive income from investments, pensions and inheritances. They are the 'charmed generation' and represent a 'one-time' opportunity for marketers. Once this cohort has aged and lost its ability and enthusiasm to spend, it will not be replaced by another of equal wealth. If you miss this opportunity it is gone for good.

▮ Another and larger part of this age group is financially ill-prepared for retirement and will suffer a significant reduction in its standard of living.

▮ The message for marketers is astoundingly simple. Some retired people, and those near to retiring, are going to have a lot of spending power. A lot more in this age group will have very little – a trend that will become more pronounced in the future. This puts a premium on establishing marketing relationships with the post-retirement affluent.

▮ The mirror image of the 'charmed generation' is the many 18–35-year-olds suffering from the financial problems of credit card debt, repaying student loans, slow pay growth, under-employment and rising property costs. For many younger people, their future is littered with financial commitments that will constrain their ability to consume.

▮ Marketers must understand how the different generations' consumption levels are being affected by economic factors, even if they then wish to ignore the conclusions.

3

Myths and marketing myopia

The previous chapter detailed the reasons for the growth in importance of the over-50s – namely, their increasing numbers and spending power. Such compelling evidence, you would expect, would have the marketing world frantically devising new strategies to target older consumers. Nothing could be further from the truth.

Ranged against the data that proves the need to question marketing's fixation with the 18–35 age group is an array of arguments, hunches and myths to justify maintaining the status quo. Some of the arguments are plain silly, but others are rooted in a homely, commonsense logic that makes them sound believable, at least on first hearing. A few of the arguments are valid for specific combinations of countries, products and markets. Unfortunately, many of them have assumed the mantle of universal truths even though they possess little supporting evidence. This chapter discusses these arguments and assesses their value in justifying the pro-youth, anti-oldies bias.

THE TOP FIVE ALL-TIME FAVOURITES

You can guarantee that at least two – and sometimes all five – of these reasons will appear in any debate on the subject of age and marketing. They are, without doubt, the top five favourites. The scores allocated to them are totally subjective, like most of the arguments. Here is what the scores mean:

■ 0/10 = the argument is without value and worthless;
■ 5/10 = there might be specific situations where it is true but it cannot be generally applied;
■ 10/10 = it is an argument that marketers should always consider.

Appealing to the old alienates the young

There always have been and always will be good reasons to target younger people. Long may it continue! There is probably no faster way to destroy a fashion campaign targeted at twentysomethings than to use their grandparents as role models.

Where this argument becomes unstable is when products are sold to people of all ages. Marketers create an artificial problem that they are forced to resolve. Do we appeal to the 18–35s or the 'others'? Why is it necessary to choose between them?

Chapter 6 shows the problems of using age to segment markets and explores why it is dangerous to make assumptions about the motivations of people in different age groups.

As the examples given so far (Honda and Diageo) have proven, it is possible to appeal to multiple age groups at the same time.

From an advertising agency's perspective, it is much easier to focus on a narrow age demographic and use 'alienating the young' as the justification than broaden the appeal. Beware the motivations of people using this argument!

This argument does have value in youth markets. When applied to multi-age markets, though, it should be phrased 'appealing to the old *can* alienate the young.' Remember, the word 'old' can be substituted for 'young' in this phrase to produce the reverse of this argument.	5/10

Older people are unwilling to try new brands

Of all the anti-age arguments, this is probably the one that is most frequently used. What better way of retaining a youth focus than by pushing the over-50s into a marketing wasteland labelled 'brand dead'?

Analysing this argument is an important theme of Chapter 5. In some countries (such as the Czech Republic), the argument appears to have some substance, but, in most others (such as Australia), it is shown to be worthless. There might be specific combinations of market and product where this behaviour exists, at least for the current age cohort of over-50s. For instance, persuading an over-50-year-old to change to a new car manufacturer might have been difficult five years ago, but today's 50-year-old could be very different. Overall, there is little to no evidence to substantiate the 'rule' that older people are unwilling to try new brands.

The factors affecting consumers' brand loyalty are many and varied – fashion, habit, value in changing, quality, price competitiveness, to name a few. The idea that you can use the blunt instrument of age as a predictor of brand behaviour should be self-evident fantasy.

For the existing age cohort, this 'rule' might be true in certain countries and for combinations of product and market. Under no circumstances, however, should the argument be applied unless there is thorough and recent research to justify this conclusion.	5/10

It is important to get them when they are young

This is marketing's equivalent of the Jesuit maxim 'Give me a child for the first seven years, and you may do what you like with him afterwards.' It pushes the bounds of credibility to think that marketers can generate the same level of commitment from people to their chocolate bars as priests can from them to God.

The previous argument assumes that ageing is accompanied by a sclerosis of brand preferences, whereas this assumes certain preferences can only be established when people are young.

Special cases might exist where this argument is correct. For instance, historically, once a person has made the decision about the supplier of their banking services they have stuck with them for life. This probably has more to do with the effort–reward equation of changing rather than any affinity with the bank.

The drinks industry believes that categories of drinks consumption, not necessarily the brand, become established in early life. This applies as much to coffee and tea as to types of alcoholic beverage. There might be some physiological reason for taste being connected to age.

Persuading people to try some types of meat, fish and dairy foods is much harder if they didn't experience them as a child. However, there is no reason to think that the mechanism that determines these early life preferences can also be applied to washing powder and mobile phones.

For certain products, especially food and drink, this argument may have some validity, but it has no universal value to marketers.	5/10

We get them anyway

A marketing campaign targeted at the 18–35 age group is assumed to 'pick up the older consumer anyway.'

To adopt the language of modern warfare, if advertising's primary target of attack is the young, then, it is assumed, their parents and grandparents will automatically sustain collateral damage. In media-buying language, the over-50s are the 'spillover' generation.

This argument may be correct in terms of media exposure, but where it descends into absurdity is when it is linked to the type of creative that is supposedly 'spilling over'. If a creative is designed to influence a young audience, it doesn't matter how visible it is to older age groups, it is unlikely to have much affect.

A study in the UK by the agency Millennium found that, of the 350,000 respondents, all aged over 50, 86 per cent said that they found most current advertising irrelevant to them. Studies in other countries have reached similar conclusions.

A totally flawed argument.	3/10

Older people are stuck in their ways

Articles about marketing to the over-50s are often accompanied by bizarre photos of old people straddling a Yamaha superbike, perched on the latest Stewart surfboard or bungee jumping from a bridge. It is as if the media feel impelled to refute this argument by showing that the terms 'adventure' and 'old' are not mutually exclusive.

Many marketers instinctively believe that the spirit of change, adventure and experimentation wane with the passing years.

The evidence from OMD's research (discussed in Chapter 5) shows this to be true in some countries, but in others – including Australia, the US and the UK – it is a fallacy. You can be a 'stuck in their ways' just as easily at 30 as you can at 70. Many parents complain that their older children don't have the spirit of adventure that they associate with their own youth.

Of course, age-related illnesses and the natural deterioration of the body affect the scope of physical challenges an older person can undertake, but this does not appear to have stopped a large number of retired people from seeking new experiences and adventure from travel. Indeed, the prime audience for overseas adventure holidays is the over-50s and this is the fastest-growing sector of the international youth hostel market.

In some countries it applies, but in others it is a fatally flawed argument.	3/10

There is something suspicious about books that use lists of historical quotations to substantiate their arguments. The author appears unable to rely on the power of his or her own arguments and so needs the support of other people's wisdom. Thus, I include only the following quotation from Herbert Spencer, a British social philosopher, and I do so because I could not find a better collection of words to describe the basis of these arguments and the results they have on marketing:

> There is a principle which is a bar against all information, which is proof against all arguments and which cannot fail to keep a man in everlasting ignorance – that principle is contempt prior to investigation.

Certainly all of these, and the following, arguments cry out for detailed investigation before being used to make profound marketing judgements. Some marketers cling to them like a drowning man does to driftwood in defence of their entrenched position.

STRONG CONTENDERS FOR BEING ALL-TIME FAVOURITES

The next group of arguments are regularly used to justify the marketing status quo and so are contenders for joining the all-time favourites list. They each have phases of being particularly popular. In the main there is very little substance to any of them, as is shown by their scores. The arguments are set out in Table 3.1.

Table 3.1 *Arguments that are strong contenders for joining the all-time favourites list*

Argument	Description	Score
The young are the future of our brand	This is a valid statement of marketing strategy, but does not qualify as a universal rule. It has as much general credibility as saying 'The over-50s are the future of our brand'.	5/10
	It is difficult to argue against the image of a fresh-faced, energetic youth, credit card in hand, when it is held up against a decrepit adult, credit card replaced by a walking stick, waiting to collect a pension payment. It rings all of the same emotional bells as 'children are the future'.	
	Even so, you cannot base a brand strategy on a single statement of faith unless all of the other determining factors have been thoroughly researched.	
We don't want an ageing and dying customer base	Taken to its extreme this argument implies that you would never have any customers. From the instant anyone is born they become members of a 'dying customer base'.	0/10
	The argument relies on a simplistic zero-sum game notion that if you have an older customer base you have to forfeit one that is younger. Some of the big corporate successes of the coming decade will owe their success to exactly the reverse of this argument.	
It costs more to reach the young	The foundation of this argument is that, because the numbers of 18–35s are declining and they are hard for marketers to reach, they demand a disproportionate level of advertising spend.	3/10

	It treats young people like diamonds. They are intrinsically attractive, scarce and getting scarcer and more expensive to obtain, hence their value is high. This logic dictates that advertisers should also pay a premium to reach nomads in the Gobi Desert. It may be a statement of fact, but it is of no marketing value, unless you are committed to targeting the young for some other reason.	
Older people are technophobic	Daily, the evidence mounts showing this to be a grossly oversimplified argument. This argument is invariably supported by two examples: texting via mobile phones and DVD/video remote controls. The first is used to illustrate that young people are fast at adopting new technology and the latter to prove that the old are incapable of mastering complicated electronic devices. Chapter 10 shows the danger of basing a view of a generation on a couple of exceptional examples. It might be true that groups of the over-65s are averse to using PC and Internet products, but that does not mean the opposite applies en masse to their juniors.	3/10
Older people are not interested in fashion and 'showing off'	One of the most quoted documents propounding the need to concentrate on the 18–35 age group is 'You're Getting Old', from the planning director at the advertising agency Young & Rubicam. This is how it substantiates the fashion argument: 'when you were 18 and the music, the clothes and the expressions that were in varied from month to month. Well they still do. And if yours don't any more, you're likely to be over 35.' It goes on to say, 'Older people aren't bothered about standing out in a crowd. Their need for social display goes.' For certain groups of the over-50s, these statements are absolutely correct. For others, it could not be further from the truth. The receptivity to fashion doesn't just apply to clothes. It also includes holidays, places to live, luxury items, leisure activities and health treatments. The 'showing off' gene doesn't decay at 35, it just craves a higher price tag! For certain products this argument maybe valid, but it should not be generally applied.	5/10

The comments made at the end of the all-time favourites list earlier apply at least as much to these arguments. They range from the simplistic to those that apply only in particular combinations of products and markets. They all make the classic mistake of perceiving both the over-50s and the 18–35-year-olds as amorphous undifferentiated masses. Nothing could be further from the truth.

OTHER ASSORTED ARGUMENTS

The final group is a collection of the arguments that appear from time to time. They are of even more dubious worth than those covered so far.

'We know all about marketing to boomers'

The culprits for creating this argument are the age gurus who have promoted the idea that there are a few basic rules to master for appealing to the over-50s.

Chapter 6 discusses the options for segmenting the older market and the flaws in attributing sets of universal values and behaviours to age groups. The 'baby boomer' generation is the one that has suffered the most from being dissected and simplified into checklists of dos and don'ts. It is equivalent to horoscopes that propose you can split the world into 12 groups of people whose behaviour and future can be summarized in a daily newspaper column.

Such simplifications have resulted in massive generalities being made about baby boomers and older generations. Marketers have been encouraged to see a significant part of the adult population as a homogeneous mass that can be described by snappy statements of the kind 'Baby boomers are self-centred and demanding' and 'Baby boomers will always push the boundaries of society.' As somebody who has made an extensive study of this subject, I can assure you that we are a very long way away from knowing all of this stuff.

'To be cool you have to be young'

For the past few years, Research International (a global market research agency) has been studying the issues that make a brand 'cool'. In 2004, it published a list of the factors contributing to brand 'coolness'. Of the 10 factors that we perceive as important, 'young' was the least important, following behind 'unique', 'innovative', 'authentic', 'witty', 'daring', 'unconventional', 'timeless', 'effortless' and 'self-assured'.

So much for that argument.

'All of the over-50s are rich' or 'All the over-50s are poor'

For those defending their youthcentric approach, in a market dominated by low-income consumers, then the 'they are all rich' is a convenient argument. Strangely, the diametrically opposite conclusion is used to substantiate the reason for not targeting older people in a luxury market.

As the previous chapter demonstrated, the income and wealth profiles of the different generations are complicated and cannot be summarized by these simplistic arguments.

'They might have wealth, but they will not spend it'

The over-50s are avid shoppers. For instance, they purchase 35–50 per cent of all travel, 65 per cent of new cars and 50 per cent of face care products.

As with all such arguments there will be a lifestyle group of the over-50s who save rather than spend and who gain their thrills from seeking out the lowest prices. Equally, a group of their peers will annually pay £40,000 for a round-the-world cruise, renew their luxury car annually and get their thrills from sampling the best Michelin three-starred restaurants. Thus, there is not a shred of evidence to support this all-encompassing argument.

'Their lifetime value is too short'

Marketing is normally criticized for having short-term objectives, fuelled by one of the highest staff turnover rates of any profession. This makes it doubly odd to hear the argument that, as the shelf life of older people is relatively short, it is not worth bothering to capture their business.

In 2005, women in the UK aged 50 can expect to live, on average, for another 32 years. A 65-year-old man should live for 16 more years. Japanese life expectancy is over 81 years and in the US it is 77 years.

Not only is the length of post-50 spending increasing, it is growing disproportionately for the wealthy compared to the poor. Even if you were to assume that a 50-year-old's active purchasing life is shorter than their life expectancy, it is not unreasonable to expect them to be active consumers for least another 25 years. Further, as the vast majority of new products and services don't make it to their third birthday and the best guess is that the average life of a brand is somewhere between 10 and 15 years, then to be concerned that you 'only' have another 25 years of a customer's purchasing potential is sheer idiocy.

IS IT ALL MYTH AND MARKETING MYOPIA?

OMD's research shows distinct differences by country in the way older people react to everything from trying new brands to using technology (see Chapter 5). Older Australians, for example, show an appetite for adopting new ideas and being open to change, whereas their peers in France are more reluctant. The idea that you can generalize about behaviour, therefore, is manifestly wrong.

As we have seen, for some types of products, in selected markets, for specific types of older consumer, some of the 15 arguments we have looked at will be correct. However, none of the arguments has universal value.

They are most misleading when considered as a group. If you aggregate together the small grains of truth that they each contain, it can appear to result in a half-convincing argument. In general, though, these supposedly 'self-evident' truths are myths that result in a nasty variety of marketing myopia. If this was the worst outcome, then the problems would be resolved over time as the weight of research and the realities of demo-graphic and economic change exposed their flaws. However, a much worse problem is that, for a many people, it doesn't matter if the argu-ments are right or wrong. Their value is an excuse for maintaining the status quo. No amount of research or evidence will convince these people to change. Their minds have been made up and the 15 statements are invaluable ammunition in defending their obsession with the 18–35 age group.

HOW AGE-NEUTRAL ARE YOU?

The questionnaire shown in Table 3.2 is a very simple way to estimate how age-neutral is your attitude to marketing to the over-50s. Simply note

Table 3.2 *Questionnaire to estimate level of age-neutrality*

Factors that influence marketing to the over-50s		
To what extent do you agree with these statements? **(On a scale of 1–10)** (10 = totally agree, 1 = totally disagree)		
Each question requires two answers. One scores your level of agreement, when applied to your own marketplace. The other scores your response for all market sectors.		
The all-time favourites	My market sector	All market sectors
1. Appealing to the old alienates the young		
2. Older people are unwilling to try new brands		
3. It is important to get them when they are young		
4. We get them (the over-50s) anyway		
5. Older people are stuck in their ways		
Total score		
Multiply total by 3	= **A**	= **D**
The strong contenders		
1. The young are the future of our brand		
2. We don't want an ageing and dying customer base		
3. It costs more to reach the young		
4. Older people are technophobic		
5. Older people are not interested in fashion and 'showing off'		
Total score		
Multiply total by 2	= **B**	= **E**
Other assorted arguments		
1. We know all about marketing to boomers		
2. To be cool you have to be young		
3. All of the over-50s are rich. All the over-50s are poor		
4. They might have wealth, but they will not spend it		
5. Their lifetime value is too short		
Total score	= **C**	= **F**
Grand total (A+B+C)		
Grand total (D+E+F)		

how much you agree or if you disagree with the series of statements listed in the table. First, score them for how the statements apply to your own market sector and, second, your agreement or disagreement with them as general rules of marketing. When answering these questions, it is important to think how well you could justify your responses or if they are an instinctive gut feeling.

How to interpret the scores

The scores give an approximate guide as to how influenced you have been by the arguments discussed in this chapter. It is possible to have a high score for your own market sector, especially if is a well-researched area. It is much more concerning if there is also a high score for the general applicability of the statements.

My market sector	
Score	**Implications**
300–250	Unless you have reached these opinions as a result of detailed research, they represent extremely biased views that will damage the effectiveness of your marketing.
249–200	You are convinced that most of the statements are true. Unless you can substantiate these opinions with research, you should consider if prejudice rather than logic is driving your decisions.
199–150	You are more certain than not about the value of these statements. It may mean that you operate in a market sector that is atypical or are allowing unproven statements to cloud your judgement.
149 – 100	In the main you are undecided by the value of the statements. There is an element of uncertainty about their validity that could be affecting your marketing decisions.
99–50	You appear to discount most of the statements and are unusually age-neutral in your approach.
<50	Either you are fee from bias or you have reached these opinions from a detailed analysis of your market. Whatever the reason, your marketing will be unhampered by artificial constraints.

All marketing sectors	
Score	**Implications**
300–250	You are suffering from a severe case of age-bias. You should reread this and the previous chapter.
249–200	A dangerously high score, indicating that you are making huge assumptions about the behaviour of older people. Beware.
199–150	This is a high score and you should be concerned. You think that most of the statements might be true when applied to any market or product.
149 – 100	You believe that there is some truth in these statements. You need to be careful that these doubts are not adversely influencing your decisions.
99–50	A balanced approach to the influence of ageing on people's behaviour.
<50	Excellent – your views about the over-50s are unencumbered by marketing myths.

IMPLICATIONS FOR THE MARKETER

This chapter contains a single, but incredibly important, implication for marketers:

! *There are no universal truths about marketing to older people.*

SUMMARY

▌ There is an array of arguments, hunches and myths that are regularly used to justify not focusing more resources on the over-50s. Some of the arguments are plain silly, but some are rooted in a homely, commonsense logic that makes them sound believable, at least on first hearing.

▌ A few of the arguments are valid for specific combinations of countries, products and markets. Unfortunately, many of them have assumed the mantle of universal truths, even though there is little or no supporting evidence.

▌ In any discussion or article about marketing and the over-50s, you can rely on seeing all, or a good number, of these arguments:

– appealing to the old alienates the young
– older people are unwilling to try new brands
– it is important to get them when they are young
– we get them (the over-50s) anyway
– older people are stuck in their ways.

Each statement contains some grains of truth, but none has the certainty to influence a marketing campaign, let alone a marketing strategy.

▌ In addition to these arguments, there are 10 more that range from being half-believable to plain daft.

▌ The results of the market research conducted by OMD (discussed in Chapter 5) show graphically the silliness of many of the arguments. For instance, older Australians show an appetite for adopting new brands, ideas and change that is not shared in some other countries.

▌ Some of the 15 statements discussed in this chapter will be correct for some types of products, in particular markets, for specific types of older consumers. None of the arguments has universal value, however.

▌ This chapter concludes with a simple set of questions that allow the reader to measure the extent to which their marketing judgement is influenced by these arguments.

4

A global snapshot

The previous chapters discussed the subject of marketing to older people from various directions. Insights from leading marketers, demographic and economic data, and a discussion of marketing stereotypes and myths all contribute to forming a picture of how marketers perceive this group.

This chapter rounds out the picture we have so far by giving you a global snapshot of how the situation differs around the world. Rather than using data and charts to do this, it uses the views of marketers working in different countries and geographical regions. They provide, in their own words, an insight into how companies and marketers are reacting to their populations growing older. The ways in which they tell their stories are very different from each other, but there is a single consistent message: companies and marketers are failing to react to the reality of the changing age demographic.

A YOUNG AND OLD WORLD

To provide a context for these comments, Table 4.1 shows the percentage of the population in a selection of countries or regions over the age of 60.

The world is ageing at different rates. France, the UK and Scandinavia are 'old' and getting older. The US and Australia are in a phase of 'middle age' and Asia is 'young'. How these age profiles will change in the future is discussed in Chapter 14.

Table 4.1 *Percentage of the population in each country or region aged over 60*

Region	% of population over 60
Asia	9.9
USA	16.2
Australia	16.7
France	20.5
UK	20.8
Scandinavia	21.2

Asia

Allein Moore – founder and Editor of *AdAsia*, a leading magazine about the advertising industry in Asia.

The retiree sits on the concrete bench below the block of apartments, watching the world go by with tired, old eyes. He is dressed in a singlet and pyjama bottoms. He is waiting for his daughter-in law to come home and prepare him a meal. This Asian man retired three years ago and this is a typical day.

Across the city is another old man. This 'towkay' is the patriarch of a family enjoying the wealth created by the shipping line founded by the elderly and now frail gentleman. He came from China before World War II and slept on sacks by the dockside before beginning to climb out of poverty. Despite his advanced years and their Western education, the sons not only defer to the father but also even fear him.

Such contrasts remain common across Asia. Devotion to and honouring parents is a Confucian ethic that is still strong in Chinese societies. Respect and care for elders also runs strongly in Muslim, Hindu and Buddhist religions, which are common in many parts of Asia. Encouraging families to take care of their parents suits the governments in Asia well. It relieves them of the necessity of providing State pensions or other financial help to impoverished older citizens. Few countries in Asia have much in the way of national pensions or other guaranteed financial or medical assistance for the greying population. Incidentally, do not be fooled by the lack of grey-haired old folks in Asia. Dying the hair as the silver threads appear is almost universal and as Asian hair is jet black it is an easy thing to do.

Asian couples used to have many children, not only due to a lack of knowledge about contraception, but because numerous offspring guaranteed that the parents would have sons and daughters ready to take care of them in their old age. They believe that it is their right to have this support after bringing up their children. Most Asian parents expect financial help from their children and for one of the family to provide a roof over their heads once they retire. A Chinese son or daughter who does not give money regularly will get a scolding, either from the parents or from other siblings.

As mentioned, there few pensions provided either by companies or by the State and in the past most Asians struggled all of their working lives and reached their 50s and 60s with no savings. Only 8 per cent of Singaporean retirees have a personal income.

Most Asians have been worn out by years of hard work and see retirement and dependence on their families as a relief. They have been happy to abdicate responsibility for their lives to a son or daughter. Large MPV vehicles are popular in Asia because the new middle-class families can take out their children, the maid and their elderly parents.

The downside of this close relationship is that many elderly people in Asia soon rely completely on their offspring for support. They become frightened to take the bus or go to the doctor without being accompanied by their son or daughter. When I was heading the creative department of an ad agency in Singapore, one of my staff asked for the day off to accompany her mother to the hospital for a check-up. 'Of course', I replied. Then I asked, imagining an ancient old lady, 'How old is your mother?' 'Oh, she is 53', came the reply. As I was 57 at the time, I found this quite surprising. However, this employee was not being unduly protective of her mother as, after looking younger than their years, many Asians embrace old age and senility with amazing alacrity. Retirement age in Singapore used to be 55 and only now are there moves to make it 60.

The expectation of early retirement is causing the same concerns as it is in the West. Life expectancy in many Asian countries is rising, especially in Singapore, Malaysia and Thailand. Unfortunately, the respect for elders and their role in society that has glued village life together for hundreds of years has been eroded by the rapid development of modern societies, industrialization and major cities. The exciting developments that are bringing wealth and new opportunities right across Asia result in a focus on the new. Singapore, for example, has lost many of its historic buildings and local places of interest in the drive to build new shopping centres and modern office blocks. This loss of historic buildings and traditional culture is happening right across Asia.

The focus on modernization and adoption of Western values also means that youth is now highly prized. For decades, the majority of the population in Asia was young. Disease killed off many and years of toil ensured that few survived long into their senior years. It is only now that senior citizens are becoming a sizeable minority and the first generation of 'old folks' have retired with money in banks, property and shares. However, now that youth has become a highly valued commodity, difficulty in finding another job as a redundant 40-year-old is as common in Asia, as it is in the West. With the rapidly changing technology, it is perhaps inevitable that younger people are seen as being more in tune. Experience may mean little in industries that are themselves less than 10 years old.

Sadly, in my opinion, senior citizens in Asia – by virtue of their education and inclination – are less adventurous than someone of a similar age in Europe or the US. They will not readily try new foods, let alone skydiving and riding motorcycles – activities the UK's media always associates with the new generation of older people. This cautious mindset makes it harder for them to adopt new lifestyles and try new products. However, the speed with which Asia has welcomed changes and adopted new technology, such as mobile phones, suggests that this will not be a handicap in the future.

As mentioned, there is a growing group of affluent Asians. In the rapid expansion that has taken place along the Pacific rim, many people have acquired considerable wealth. Singapore has more Mercedes-Benz cars on the road than any European country, excluding Germany. Hong Kong, I believe, has more Rolls-Royces than the UK. In Hong Kong and Singapore more cognac is consumed than in either London or New York. BMW has discovered a lucrative market in the status-conscious Asians. China, too, is rapidly increasing the number of multimillionaires in the world. One has only to look at the phenomenal growth in the number of golf clubs to observe how readily the affluent adopt and even surpass the West in certain social activities. Naturally, the people with the most time for golf are in the twilight of their careers or retired.

Currently, there are few companies of which I am aware that are aiming their products specifically at the older consumers in the Pacific region. The pharmaceutical industry is probably one of the few that deliberately targets this group, as it recognizes that ill health often accompanies old age. Unfortunately, the adoption of Western-style eating habits – especially the consumption of snack foods – is having a detrimental effect on the health of many Asians. Already diabetes and heart disease among the over-50s in the more developed countries in Asia is causing major concern. The demand for private healthcare has grown and cities such as Singapore and Bangkok are establishing themselves as medical centres in the region. Incidentally, plastic surgery is also becoming an important industry in this part of the world and Korea has seen a rash of new surgeries being set up to serve its own citizens who spend fortunes on eyelid and nose surgery.

Looking young is important in markets where so much emphasis is placed on youth. Market research company Synovate found that Asian men are high spenders on everything from facial cleanser foam to moisturizer. The fear of losing virility weighs heavily on the minds of ageing men in Asia. The sales of Chinese herbs, powders made up from the rhino's horn, tiger's penis, snake's blood and other remedies to restore sexual vigour are still brisk. Chinese businessmen are not slow to get second wives whom they keep in a different city as this is seen as sign of their virility as well as their wealth. Youth is admired for the memories of sexual vigour it offers, but older Asians are unlikely to bungee jump, try rollerblading or visit the movies.

While marketers in Asia currently seem to ignore the 'greys', it is obviously a market that will grow once locals lose this perception of themselves as a generation that sits back and watches life go past until death arrives. Culturally, there is a fatalism that tends to encourage acceptance of the illnesses and restrictions accompanying ageing. The new generation of 'greys', however, who have enjoyed the benefits of economic growth in Asia and seen their property investments boom as well as their shares portfolios expand, will offer a new market to advertisers and marketers. In other words, Asians are getting older and richer and will be seeking new ways to spend their Singapore and Hong Kong dollars, dangs, rupiah and rupees.

What of China and its population of 1.3 billion people? The country's rapid industrialization and the resultant social upheaval have been well documented. In its urban areas, China now has a vibrant, growing consumer class.

The changes to China's population profile are set to be equally dramatic. In the next decade, the proportion of its population aged over 65 will rapidly increase, accompanied by a decrease in the growth of its working-age population. China's rate of ageing will be faster than that of any other country in history. The statistics are incredible. From 1975 to 2000, China's dependency ratio – the number of working-age adults supporting each person over the age of 60 – was constant at approximately 8. Since then, it has been falling. By 2030, it will fall to less than 2. At about the same time, the proportion of China's population over the age of 60 will exceed that of the US.

China's one-child-per-couple rule is a major contributory factor to this distortion in its population profile, but it is not the only one. Even without this policy, the numbers of older people in the population would be increasing. The one-child policy has simply accentuated this pre-existing trend.

The distorted age profile is not the only result of China's interventionist policies. Its cultural bias in favour of males has also had an effect. In the 2000 census, the official figures showed a ratio at birth of 118 boys to 100 girls. The normal ratio is about 105 to 100.

It is impossible to predict how China's market for older consumers will develop. The country's rapid economic growth, its ageing population and a marketplace where the State still has the ability to exert a high level of intervention makes forecasting impossible. Whatever happens, with a population that is approximately four-and-a-half times that of the US, it is not a market that can be ignored.

Australia

Gill Walker – Director of Evergreen, a marketing communications consultancy specializing in working with mature audiences.

Australian companies are starting to understand the commercial impor-tance of older consumers, but the majority of marketers are standing on the edge of the diving board, too scared to jump! The media is continu-ously discussing the 'ageing population' and its impact on the economy, but the reporting is usually negative rather than stressing the positive implications.

In 2005, my company gave a series of seminars to 40 of Australia's top advertisers and their media agencies about the importance of older consumers to marketers. It was an excellent opportunity to understand how advertisers and agencies think about this group. Their comments and perceptions were surprising. The majority of advertisers didn't realize that people over 50 had more disposable income than people in their 30s – the contrasting financial positions of the two age groups has not been grasped. Many 30-year-olds are still repaying their university debt and only just able to buy a property. A large number of the over-50s own their property, are debt-free, benefited from a free university education and are without family commitments. Their contrasting financial positions – especially the levels of disposable income – were not fully appreciated.

Unfortunately, the myth that ageing is accompanied by increasing brand loyalty is alive and well. Many marketers still use this fallacy to justify their neglect of the over-50s audience. Maybe this concept was true 30 years ago, when the boomer generation were in their 20s and 30s and the dominant cohort, but times have changed and so has the attitude of the over-50s towards trying new brands.

The DDB Needham study has tracked brand loyalty over 20 years. It shows that all adults up to the age of 50 have the same propensity to stick to well-known brands. Another conclusion from the study is that brand loyalty among the over-50s has decreased. The proviso is that the new brands must be appropriate to their needs and presented in a relevant and accessible way.

These results are supported by Charlie Nelson – one of Australia's leading economic forecasters. His research measured what consumers think about the ways in which companies communicate with and understand their needs. He called this measurement the 'empathy index'. He found that this index declines with age, especially after the age of 55, and is lowest among the 55–59 age group. Associated with a low empathy index is a reduction in brand loyalty.

Some industries in Australia are adapting their marketing to reflect the changing profile of the population's age; others are not. You can get some measure of the 'leaders and laggers' by reviewing how companies use the media and innovate new products. Table 4.2 shows how industries compare. Interestingly, of the non-age-related industries, only banking and insurance are leaders in both categories. Note that when an industry is labelled a 'leader', it does not mean that all of the media and product innovation takes account of the older market but that they are making efforts in that direction.

There are two reasons for companies being so slow to embrace the over-50s as a lucrative group of consumers. Like all other parts of the world, the Australian advertising industry is staffed by young people – the average is 33 years old. The industry's youthfulness partly results from the waves of downsizing, starting in the early 1990s, that saw middle layers of staff removed.

There is another explanation for the rarity of older people in the industry. Younger people are attracted to advertising for totally understandable reasons. The high-volume, process end of advertising work is competitive and frenetic. For younger people, the frenzy and competition equals excitement and energy. After a few years, this style of work becomes repetitive, the emotional gain declines and people start thinking about things like the 'work/life balance'. That's the time when lots of people leave the industry.

Advertising agencies have a challenge communicating with older people when their employees are, on average, 20–30 years their juniors.

Table 4.2 *Industry 'leaders and laggers' in their approach to the over-50s market*

Use of Media		Product innovation	
Laggers	Leaders	Laggers	Leaders
Food	Banking	Food	Banking
Department stores	Insurance	Confectionery	Insurance
Computer	Telecoms	Retailers	Cosmetics
Fast food	Automotive	Clothing	Travel
Clothing	Retirement services		Retirement services
Travel			

Young people generally have few, if any, memories on which to base their understanding of older people. This cannot be supplemented by their peers as they are of a similar age with a matching lack of experience. An advantage of getting older is the range of real-life experiences you amass. If you lack your own experiences, then you have to borrow them from others. Acquired experiential knowledge is never as good as the real thing.

Since becoming involved in advertising to older consumers I have developed a few simple rules that guide me.

▎ Great advertising can be ageless. It is possible to create advertising that works across multiple generations.

▎ Good art direction is paramount. It doesn't matter how great the creative concept is if the audience has to work hard to read or hear it. They won't be bothered to stick around.

▎ Mature minds respond to advertising at their pace, not that of the advertiser. Older people respond to and appreciate advertising, but on their terms, when and how they want it.

▎ Advertisers should focus on the consumers' experiences with the brand, rather than representing their brand as the hero.

Some companies have successfully understood the older market and translated this into successful advertising campaigns. Here are some examples from the Australian market.

▎ L'Oréal used models that are appropriate to the consumer, such as Dayle Haddon. This uses mature women in a positive sense, celebrating age rather than focusing on the negatives of osteoporosis and incontinence!

▎ SmithKline Beecham's Panadol campaign employed a cross-section of talent, including a very active mature surfer who uses Panadol because it doesn't interact with his other medications. We don't need to know his age as viewers can work it out for themselves and understand the relevance of the message.

▌ Heinz created an excellent ad for canned soup aimed at older men. The ad says, 'The old fool thinks he can make curry out of soup.' It portrays older men in a positive and light way, with the language that they are likely to use about themselves. A picture of the Heinz ad is shown in Figure 4.1.

▌ Tourism Tasmania took the time to understand its audience, resulting in an awarding-winning campaign.

Figure 4.1 *Heinz soup advert targeted at older men*

■   Southern Cross Broadcasting realized the value of its 40-plus audience and invested heavily in educating marketers and advertisers about the opportunity this group presented to the company.

Australia is probably little different from other countries in the things stopping marketers from adopting a more balanced and positive approach to the older age cohorts. There is the unwillingness to understand, or accept, the data that show the spending power and growth of the over-50s market. It is too easy for marketers to rely on referencing people of their own age, interests and experiences and being reluctant to step out of their comfort zone and into a world that they don't understand. This results in too many companies devoting their energies, focusing on and fighting over, the decreasing, fragmented and poorer younger audience.

France

Frédéric Serrière – CEO of Senior Strategic, publisher of theMatureMarket.com and an expert on France's senior market.

Companies in France fall into two categories. There are those that are already targeting the mature market, some of which have been doing so for many years. Companies such as Vacances Bleues (tourism), Damart (clothing) and, more recently, Beiersdorf with its Nivea Vital range of anti-ageing products. These companies face the challenge of appealing to the new generation of older people, the baby boomers.

The other, much larger, group of companies still focuses on younger age groups. Many of these companies realize that the mature market presents a unique opportunity for growth, but very few have translated this knowledge into changing the way that they market. Companies in the banking and insurance industries show signs of change, but the car and retail industries continue as normal, focusing on young people.

Companies' reticence to changing their marketing approach is usually quoted as being due to the unwillingness of older customers to change brands. Also, younger people are thought to be easier to target than older ones. I believe, however, that the main reason for companies continuing to pursue their youthcentric approach is the commercial pressure to focus on short-term results. Middle managers are not permitted the time to pause, research and think about the mature market. Short-term performance stops companies planning for the longer term.

In France, when a company decides to target the mature market, it is because a 'high-level leader' is prepared to make the decision and personally take the risk. Middle-ranking managers can only influence the Day-to-Day marketing tactics, not the overall strategy.

During 2004 there was a definite change in companies' attitudes to the older market. I think most of them are now aware that 'something should be done', but perceive the changes as being limited to the way in which they communicate with the market. They don't realize that changes need to be made in all aspects of their business. Much of this preoccupation with communications is due to the way in which some 'experts' have focused exclusively on this aspect of mature marketing. To successfully address the older market you need to take a global view, encompassing all aspects of marketing and the sales channels. Communications are important, but they are only part of the equation.

Some companies in the cosmetics industry have understood this fact. Both L'Oréal, with its brand Age Perfect, and its competitor, Nivea's Vital, have achieved success in appealing to older women. The tourism company Vacances Bleues has been very successful with the over-50s, getting 90 per cent of its business from this age group without overtly targeting them by age. Trying to appeal to the over-50s by defining them as an age group is, of course, a cardinal sin!

Another reason stopping companies targeting older people is the uncertainty about how it should be done. This has not been made any easier by the quality of advice being given by some of the senior marketing gurus. For example, it is common to hear that generational marketing is a powerful technique. I agree that it might be useful, but it is not sufficient in itself to determine your marketing approach. Explaining a person's consumer behaviour on the basis of when they were born and what they experienced in their early life is not precise enough for marketing purposes. This is because saying that all people of the same age behave in the same way is plainly wrong. Other than for things such as awarding discount cards, as French railways are proposing to do for the over-60s, age has little use as a targeting mechanism.

In my view, psychographics is a powerful tool for segmenting the older market. When you study two people such as Richard Branson and Tony Blair, you can see that their profiles are totally different. Another factor that must be incorporated into marketing to the senior market is the importance of 'cognitive age'. This is the difference between perceived and actual age – that is, somebody who is 60 years old having a mental image of themselves as being 45–50.

Whatever approach you use to understand the older market, it is obvious that today's 50- to early-60-year-olds are very different from the same age cohort of a decade ago. Their attitudes, how they behave as consumers and their willingness to try new brands are different. Marketing managers need to understand and act on this, otherwise they will have some bad nights' sleep in the future!

Scandinavia

Chris Evers – Founder of Inspirum marketing consultancy, past MD of the Danish Marketing Association and Marketing Director of the Danish branch of Age Concern.

Scandinavian companies are slowly becoming aware of the commercial value of older people. Most of the focus has been on older people as members of the workforce rather than as consumers. Consequently, the debate and initiatives have been about ways in which to extend people's time at work. Like the UK and US, Scandinavian countries are looking for ways in which to manage the financial and social implications of the ageing population and combat ageism.

When I was Managing Director of the Danish Marketing Association, we held a conference called 'The Grey Gold'. We had 450 attendees from most of Denmark's biggest companies. The conference was well received and generated a lot of press coverage. What was the effect of this event on companies marketing strategies? Sadly, very little change happened. No companies adapted their advertising to take account of the older age group.

Ten years later, there is still a focus on youth in advertising and the development of products and services. Not that much has changed in all that time.

In 2000, I became the Marketing Director of the Danish branch of Age Concern. I formed an alliance with 10 companies in different areas of business, including insurance, banking, travel and white goods. The idea was for these companies to benefit from contact with the organization's 500,000 members, which represents 25 per cent of Denmark's over-50s population. We anticipated that the company's marketing departments would need assistance with marketing to the mature market, so we created a consulting team to help them to target older consumers.

After holding many meetings (at least 100), we had just three companies that became actively involved in the project – Codan, an insurance company, Shell and Thiele, an opticians. This is resounding proof that most Danish companies ignore the mature market. The situation is the same in Sweden and Norway.

In Denmark, there have been some attempts by companies in the financial services industry to adapt their marketing to the changing age demographics. The financial products they have created are fine, but how they are advertised is terrible. People over the age of 50 are either represented as balancing on a surfboard with a hula-hoop or as lonely figures, aimlessly feeding their pigeons. In all of the focus groups that I have conducted with people in this age group, nobody has recognized these stereotypes as applying to them.

The travel Industry is making some efforts to change its advertising, but when it succeeds it seems to be more by luck than judgement! I don't know of any of the travel companies that has a strategic approach to this older age cohort.

Denmark is no different from the UK and the US, with the vast majority of marketing budgets being targeted at the youth market. It is difficult to say exactly how much is spent on this group, but estimates put it as high as 95 per cent of the total.

Companies, like governments, concentrate on the short term and are reticent to move into unknown areas. Many Danish companies perceive there being a risk to their brand identity if they overtly target older people. These are the main reasons for so little progress having been made in changing marketing attitudes. Not working with older people means that marketers have little knowledge about them as consumers, which makes them more likely to stay with the age groups that they understand, so the downward spiral continues. We have the crazy position where the 20–30 singles are divided into numerous segments, while the 50-plus age group is left as one an amorphous lump.

Age is an imprecise and dangerous way to segment consumers. Life stages and life events are much better approaches. In Scandinavia, marketers don't spend anywhere near enough time trying to understand what motivates the different generations of over-50s to think and act as they do. Until we have this understanding, we will not be able to communicate in their language and in ways that they understand.

There are still so many preconceptions about how older people think and act. The idea that older people are brand loyal is a complete myth, if I am to believe the feedback from my focus groups. A few types of products are seen as dear old friends and are unlikely to be changed, but most other product categories attract the same level of brand loyalty as you would expect from the young.

The focus groups show some evidence that older men are less concerned about showing off than younger ones. They take the view that they might have the money to buy an expensive brand of sailing jacket, but if another does the job equally well, then why spend the money? It is dangerous to generalize from this response and say 'older men are less fashion conscious', as a sizeable number of them are very aware of the names on the labels of the clothes that they wear.

Unfortunately, in Denmark and the rest of Scandinavia, the phrase 'getting old' engenders a flood of negative emotions. Ageing should be associated with the positive things in life – free time, experience, wisdom, humour and, for many, a sizeable income. Marketers need to understand what it is like to be over 50 in Scandinavia today. I think that if they understood the reality, rather than relying on the myths, we would achieve a more balanced approach to marketing across the different ages.

UK

Reg Starkey – a veteran of the UK's advertising industry, writer and TV broadcaster, his focus is the advertising industry's challenge to respond to the rising power of the older consumer.

Popular psychologist M. Scott Peck's first line in his journeyman classic *The Road Less Travelled* (Hutchinson, 1983) is: 'Life is difficult.' In my experience, 'Advertising is difficult.'

As the legendary advertising man Robin Wight wrote in a house ad years ago, 'Nobody wants to read your ad', yet, in today's high-tech environment, virtually anyone can produce what passes for advertising, virtually anywhere. 'Desktop advertising', where technique is more highly valued than content, is the curse of the twenty-first century.

When I came into the advertising business, advertising was regarded as an art by some agencies and as a science by others. Of course, advertising was, is and always should be an imaginative mixture of the two. David Bernstein described it succinctly as 'applying imagination to facts.'

Our worlds were different then, of course – the real world and the world of advertising. Choice was so limited, on the streets and in the media. A centre break ad in the soap opera *Coronation Street* would regularly 'reach' up to 20 million people, while the centre break in flagship news programme the *News at Ten* would deliver a more upmarket ABC1-profiled audience, also measured in double-digit millions. The remote control had not been invented, so changing channels, seeing what was on 'the other side', usually demanded walking from the sofa or the armchair to the TV set and back. Also, few people had TV anywhere other than in the sitting room.

What was certainly true then was that viewers frequently agreed with the assertion that the commercial breaks were better than the programmes that surrounded them. I haven't heard that thought expressed recently. My alternative suggestion is that, in that era, the advertising idea was paramount and the production values were simply its servant. Today, it seems to me, too often the roles have been reversed and the technique does not so much support the idea as becomes the idea, more's the pity.

The most relevant point is made by Steve Harrison, Creative Director of HTW, when he reminds youthful clients and prospects that 'baby boomers' have been exposed to more advertising ideas – good or bad (indifferent = bad) – than any creative director working in the business today. You only have to sit in on a group discussion or listen when out socially to see how consumers have become advertising-literate and advertising-critical.

Of the 22,000 people aged over 50 who responded to a Millennium postal survey in 2001, 86 per cent claimed that they did not relate to most of the advertising they currently see. This unambiguous majority, even allowing for the self-selected nature of the sample, should disturb all advertisers from their current youth-obsessed complacency.

These quantitative findings are supported in qualitative research by anyone who has ever bothered to recruit respondents over 45 years of age and then risked inviting their opinions on current advertising.

The situation may be changing – I trust it is – but in the last decade, 45 was the upper end of most qualitative recruiting. The omnibus surveys sampled around 1,000 people in order to reflect the national profile, but generally in the 1990s you reached the age of 45 and advertisers assumed that your brand choices were set for life. You were beyond persuasion. At any rate, you would see the messages aimed at the young, so, they assumed, it was safe to ignore you.

This ill-informed, ageist attitude might have been commercially justifiable 40 years ago when the post-war baby boom was transforming the marketplace, when there were more young people earning good money and fewer older people still recovering from experiencing World War II, but things are different now. Figuratively speaking, it's as if a boa constrictor swallowed a camel after the war and can now be seen to be struggling and suffering as its two humps move through its long, distended body. There is no population bulge behind the current bulge.

Demographics is a relatively precise social science and the long-term driver of economic cycles. The opportunity is here and now. The paradox is that the youth market is now the market of the past and the mature consumer markets are now, and will continue to be, the markets of the future.

Denial of this reality represents 'contempt prior to investigation'. The trends are set and nothing short of severe climate change, plague or pestilence, war or an asteroid strike can possibly change them. Indeed, in 2005, for the first time in UK history, the over-60s outnumbered the under-16s. Consequently, today's 'mature market' is not a niche market – it is *the* market. It's the only growing demographic, so for advertisers to ignore this fact is to imitate King Canute or a frightened ostrich.

The legendary Bill Bernbach, leader of a creative revolution in New York in the 1960s, said that we should 'concentrate on the unchanging elements of human nature.' That we should 'tell it like it feels' rather than tell it like it is. According to Professor Peter Cochrane, there will be more technological changes in the next 20 years than in last couple of centuries. Will this modify Maslow's hierarchy of needs in any way whatsoever? Frankly, I doubt it.

In my interviews with 30 opinion-leaders aged between 50 and 80 years old, I was struck by the similarities rather than the differences between them when it came to choosing their all-time favourite ads. Hamlet cigars came up time and time again – simple ideas, well executed, continually entertaining, with practically zero wear-out factor. Not surprising, then, that it is considered to be one of the best UK TV ads of all time. The series was inexpensive to make, yet has stood the test of time, which few of today's trendy commercials can ever hope to do.

Another vintage campaign that was nominated time after time, even though it was made a quarter of a century ago, was the Leonard Rossiter and Joan Collins series for the drink Cinzano. The ad, set on board an aircraft, sees Leonard Rossiter accidentally spilling his drink over the debonair Joan Collins.

What can today's marketers learn from these two historical examples? That there is no simple formula – 'advertising is difficult', remember. If it were as easy as choosing a popular celebrity to feature, how come John Cleese's commercials for the supermarket chain Sainsbury's performed so badly, while Prunella Scales' umpteen commercials for its arch rival Tesco worked so well for so long?

One campaign was based on a good idea – 'Every little helps' – and the other on an unpopular one – 'Value to shout about'. One was produced with wit and style; the other was loud, in every sense, and in your face.

So much advertising today appears to be aimed exclusively at the young – no wonder at least four out of five older consumers currently feel excluded from it. An example is the advertising for the clothing company fcuk that is by the young for the young and will only work with the young.

Now, however, the centre of gravity has shifted – it makes so much less commercial sense than yesterday when the world was young. We older consumers know that advertising which ignores us, excludes us, patronizes us, offends us, insults our intelligence, treats us like stereotypes, provides inadequate information or rewards or fails to engage us for any reason whatsoever will fail.

We continue to consume products, services and media until the day we die. We make or influence purchasing decisions from the cradle to the grave. So, if the 'baby boom' generations are dead set on making the most of every remaining day, advertisers should be with them all the way.

US

Chuck Nyren – writer and consultant on advertising to the 'baby boom' generation.

I don't think advertising agencies in the US have caught up with their clients, most of whom are now convinced that targeting the 40–60 demographic is not only viable but a very smart idea – maybe even the key to their survival and growth.

Ad agencies are intransigent when it comes to targeting anybody older than 35 and it's the baby boomers themselves who are to blame. They were the people who brought about this youthcentric paradigm. From the late 1960s to the other side of the 1980s, boomers were fixated with advertising to their own age group.

Most ad agencies today give lip service to targeting boomers, saying that they reach them anyway because older people 'think' that they are still aged in their 20s and 30s and so they respond to ads aimed at that demographic. This is a huge miscalculation. Today's 50-year-olds are redefining what middle age is – they're *not* trying to be 20 or 30 years old again. They certainly don't respond well to advertising overtly targeted at the twenty- and thirtysomethings. In the US, only 10 per cent believe that advertising understands their needs – a number that hasn't changed in the past five years.

For ad agencies, there is a stigma when advertising to an older demographic. It's not very sexy. They just don't want to be known as an 'uncool agency'. It's bad for the image.

It is something of a cliché, but nearly all advertising creatives and most of their executives and media planners are aged between 20 and 35, with maybe some in their early 40s. They don't want to advertise to anybody but themselves. Again, these are lessons well taught by the boomer generation, so it's partly their fault.

Before the 1960s, advertising agencies had a good mix of young and old. Account executives would assign creatives based on their cultural strengths – young for young, old for old, women for women and so on. Later on, when racial and cultural demographics were brought into the mix, ad agencies hired African-Americans, Latinos and so on to fashion and create campaigns for these target markets. Now, with this huge, potent demographic – the 'baby boomers' – nothing has been done to bring boomer creatives back into the fold. So, advertisers ignore them.

Advertisers are the victims of myopia. If there is to be change, it will have to come from their clients. They must demand that advertisers target the older age demographic and creatives understand how they think and act. While I'm not thrilled about clients dictating the shots creatively, I think that it's fair for them to insist on suitable creatives for their target markets.

The advertising industry in the US – and, I suspect, many other countries, too – should understand that this is the first generation in which most women are feeling good about reaching their 40s and 50s. While they still want to look younger and stay healthy (who doesn't?), their overall self-image is improving as they age.

A good barometer of this is the success of *MORE* magazine – an American publication 'celebrating women 40-plus'. In September 2004, it forecasted hitting the million circulation level and has attracted advertising from General Motors, P&G and Revlon. This magazine is overtly targeting 'baby boomer' women and gives ageing a very positive spin – not an antiseptic one like some of the specialist old people's magazines. Instead, *MORE* has tapped into a new zeitgeist – 'baby boomer' women are more powerful, more in charge of their lives than women have ever been before. They also know that the odds are they'll be active for another 30 or 40 years and they're ready to rumble!

What changes have there been in the ways in which companies value the commercial importance of older consumers? It's sad to say, but change has been slow. There is a group of marketing pundits trying to change things, but it's not easy. I think Europe and Australia are probably ahead of the US in accepting older people as an attractive consumer market. In the US, there are a few advertising agencies specializing in the older age group and none of them has made a real mark in the advertising world. I'm guessing and hoping that things will change in the next five years.

You cannot discuss the relationship between advertising and older consumers without mentioning the issue of brand behaviour and brand loyalty. I am adamant that the 'boomer' generation is not wedded to brands, as some marketing firms and most advertising agencies claim. Actually, I don't think advertising agencies *really* believe it – they just use this as another excuse not to advertise to this age group.

Like most people I have a few brands that are 'comfort brands'. For me, it's ketchup and sweatpants. For people outside the US, sweatpants are cotton jersey trousers used for exercising. I am unlikely to change brands for these products, but everything else is up for grabs. I'll try new coffee, new tea, new shoes, new types of cars, new toothpaste, new anything. I think this is a commonly held viewpoint.

Today's 50-year-olds fuelled the computer boom and are now driving the home entertainment boom. These are new products and new brands. Brand loyalty is meaningless with most technology products. I don't see any of the home entertainment companies targeting older customers. Are plasma screens better or worse for older eyes? I don't know. Which speakers are balanced and mixed for mature ears? I don't know. Perhaps older ears have different needs and require more highs, more defined, compressed lows. It seems that it has escaped the marketers in these companies to even ask, let alone answer, these questions.

Finally, there is the question of perceived versus actual age. Everybody thinks that they are a bit younger than they are because they have no future perspective, only the past perspective. I'm 53, but I really don't know what that means or even what it feels like to be 53. However, I *can* remember what it was like and what it felt like to be 42. I have past and future perspectives on that age. When I'm 60, I'll know what 53 is. So, at the moment, I probably feel like I'm in my middle to late 40s. It's only natural.

I don't think I'm 25. I know plenty of people who are 25 and many remind me of myself at that age, but I am certainly not like them any more. However, whatever '53' is seems very alien to me. As I mentioned before, today's 50-year-olds are nothing like their parents at that age, but neither are they trying to be 25 again.

Back to women. Ask most 'baby boomer' women if they want to be 25 again and you'll hear a resounding 'No!' They like where they are now – just get rid of a few wrinkles and a few aches and pains, that's all.

IMPLICATIONS FOR THE MARKETER

Many views and opinions have been expressed in this chapter. Most of them agree with each other, but a few express opposing ideas. For marketers with an international remit, these global views and experiences are invaluable. Even for marketers working in a single country or region, it is useful to see how their markets compare with others in very different cultures. Some of these marketing implications are repeated in other chapters. Because they are so important, I make no excuse for stating them again.

The lack of focus on older consumers is common across all parts of the world.

! The problems and their causes are consistent across all areas of the world. Many of the solutions will be the same, but they must reflect local cultural differences. The starting point is to get senior management to take the issue seriously.

Asia is the same but different.

! Asia encompasses a huge range of peoples and cultures. Ageing has a different meaning for older people and their dependants, but things are changing. The trend is towards the Western mindset and values.

Myths about the effects of ageing on brand loyalty and the reaction to advertising have travelled well and have taken root in all of the geographies.

! The relationship between brand loyalty, the reaction to advertising and age does not follow some universal law. This is just as true in Sydney, Paris and Washington.

Advertisers are beginning to understand the value of older consumers. It is the advertising agencies that are reluctant to change from their youth-centric focus.

! Advertising is a tactical tool of marketing and must not define its strategy. Theoretically, advertising agencies, brand managers and senior management should have a common set of business objectives. This is not always true.

How women perceive ageing and its liberating effects is something marketers should understand.

! When researching the behaviour of older consumers, it is vital that the gender differences are understood.

The age profile of those working in the advertising industry makes it difficult for it to understand the over-50s' mindset.

! It is difficult, but not impossible, for advertising to reflect the experi-
• ences and attitudes of other people, not only those working in the industry. This should be remembered when reviewing creative and media planning proposals.

The over-50s are a complicated bunch of people. There is no simple, single way of segmenting them or predicting their behaviour.

! It is appealing to think that generations of consumers share similar
• values and these determine their behaviour, but it is not correct to do so. Older consumers are no different from any others in being influ-enced by multiple factors. Being labelled a 'leading-edge baby boomer', or any other generational term, says something about a person's behaviour, but not in enough detail to be used to define a marketing strategy.

Marketing communication is important, but it is only part of the marketing mix. The trap when defining a marketing strategy that is inclusive of older consumers is to focus on the communication aspect to the exclusion of everything else.

! Changing the priorities for product innovation, selecting different
• combinations of sales channels and changing the mechanisms of product support are as important as modifying the marketing communications.

SUMMARY

▌ Europe, Australia, Asia and the US have a few things in common. One of them is the lack of attention their marketers pay to the over-50s. Another, is the set of reasons proffered to explain why this should be.

▌ All the contributors had their stories about how marketers in their countries believe older consumers' lack responsiveness to advertising and are unwilling to change brands. It also appears that a lack of understanding about the over-50s' commercial importance has successfully spread itself around the globe.

▌ The contributors had similar views about the youthcentric nature of the advertising industry in their countries and the unwillingness of marketers and senior management to take the issue of the ageing population seriously. Both of these views are horribly similar to those expressed in the UK.

▌ On the positive side, companies' marketing departments are becoming aware of the need to do something about the increasing numbers of older consumers. Too often their response is limited to changes in advertising, whereas it demands a comprehensive reappraisal of the company's way of doing business.

▌ Several of the contributors believe that companies' short-term planning horizons are a significant factor that is stopping them changing their marketing focus on the 18–35-year-olds. It was felt that, unless senior management initiated a radical reappraisal of marketing direction, the middle layers of marketing management would keep targeting the same age groups.

▌ The consistency of the responses from the four continents shows how entrenched the marketing bias towards young people has become. It demonstrates how difficult an attitude – spanning diverse cultures and countries – will be to change.

5

What's different about being 'old'?

This chapter uses many different sources of information before reaching its conclusions. The most significant observations come from the research conducted by OMD, the media communications specialists. In support of this book, OMD researched different aspects of consumer behaviour and attitudes in Australia, the Czech Republic, France, the UK and the US. Details about the research methodology can be found in Appendix 4.

What is it that differentiates older people from those who are 10, 20 or 30 years younger? What are the characteristics of 'older' that are different from 'younger'? Are the differences so significant that they warrant changing what we sell and how we market? This chapter answers these questions using research rather than the normal collection of hunches and stereotypes.

HEALTH

How getting older affects people's health and physical condition has been well researched and is easy to understand. The results of ageing are ones that we observe every day in others and are almost certain to experience ourselves if we have not done so already.

According to the American Consumer Expenditure Survey, people aged 35–44 spend 46 per cent more on healthcare than 25–34-year-olds. The 65–74 age group spends a whopping 186 per cent more. Clearly, lots of things can go wrong with our bodies as we age, hence this increase in expenditure. It is a salutatory thought that even though life expectancy keeps increasing, the measure of 'healthy life expectancy' increases at a much lower rate. In the UK in 1981, the life expectancy of a woman was 77, but the age of healthy life expectancy was 67. By 2001, female life expectancy had risen to nearly 81 years, while healthy life expectancy had only increased by 2 years.

Unless you are in the health and beauty industry, which collates statistics on different age-related illnesses and forms of physical deterioration, there is little you can do with detailed information on what happens as you age and it makes deeply depressing reading! However, there are certain physiological factors that are relevant to most marketers as they affect everything from product design to building websites. However, beware: these comments come with their own health warnings. Much of the science of ageing is still hotly debated. The exact reasons for human beings experiencing these problems is not always known, but the end results are well understood.

Taste and smell

As a general rule, the sense of taste diminishes from around the age of 60 years. Older people need more intense concentrations of sweet and sour to achieve the same experience of taste as younger people. It is usually salty and sweet tastes that are the first to suffer, followed by the perception of bitter and sour tastes.

Smell is closely linked to the sensation of taste and this deteriorates at the same time. It is unclear if there is some innate reason for this or if it results from a lifetime of exposure to nasty substances in the environment. Smoking is the most obvious self-inflicted factor in damage to these senses.

Regardless of the cause, the type and intensity of enjoyment achieved from tasting and smelling changes. At a minimum, this might change people's product preferences. More seriously, it can remove a means of the body defending itself by reacting to unpleasant and dangerous substances.

Touch

Ageing results in a loss of tactile sensation due to the degeneration of the corpuscles in the fingertips. A measure of losing touch is that a 70-year-old might find it difficult to distinguish between a coin and a button in their pocket. A more serious example is reduced temperature sensitivity, leading to injuries such as hypothermia and burns. Losing sensitivity affects how we react to pain, vibration, cold, heat, pressure and texture. It is difficult know if these changes are related to ageing itself or to the disorders that are more common in older people.

Regardless of the cause, though, many people experience changes in touch-related sensations as they age. One of the most important implications of this for product designers is that it affects tactile feedback. This would affect older people's use of computer peripherals, in particular the mouse and keyboard, for example. Indeed, any device, especially if it has small buttons, becomes harder to use as we age.

Eyesight

From about the age of 40 onwards, our eyes start to their lose ability to focus. Reading small text without the aid of glasses becomes difficult, as does staring at a computer screen for long periods of time. To make matters worse, we suffer from declining colour perception and contrast sensitivity. As if these sight problems were not bad enough, ageing can also result in a degradation of peripheral vision and an increase in the level of illumination we need to see properly.

Deteriorating eyesight is not something that is generally considered in advertising, the web, packaging and product design. Most products and marketing media appear to have been designed for an 'average' user with 20/20 vision.

Dexterity

Older adults experience a reduction in their motor coordination. This creates difficulties when using pointing devices, such as a mouse, and small keypads. These problems are compounded by the onset of age-related illnesses that damage finger and wrist movement. Arthritis is the most common disease in this category, with over 15 per cent of the UK population suffering from health problems due to arthritis and related conditions.

Mobile phones are a perfect example of products that take little account of the physical limitations experienced by a sizeable percentage of the population. As phones become smaller, they demand ever-increasing levels of dexterity. This is fine if you are 18, but more testing if you are 68.

Cognitive skills

The effect of ageing on cognitive skills is a complicated issue, but there is general agreement that it does lead to reduced cognitive performance. Conducting multiple tasks becomes more difficult, as does undertaking a complicated process, as the slowing down of the speed of processing new information causes a tendency to lose attention.

This combination of factors has a major impact on the way older people use websites and is something that very few companies understand. However, the problems are not limited to websites but apply to all devices with complicated and poorly designed interfaces. An example of this is the home entertainment centre, containing TV, DVD, satellite receiver and a host of other components. For most people, assembling one of these systems is a new experience. Each component of the system has its own instructions that are written for the expert rather than novice user and each component has a unique interface. This combination of factors tests the cognitive abilities of all ages. Older people, who may also be new to the technical jargon, can find this type of task especially difficult.

Chapter 11 provides a more detailed description of the results of ageing on eyesight, dexterity and cognitive processes.

Hearing

The charts in Figure 5.1 show how closely hearing problems are associated with age and how men are more significantly affected by them than women.

Obviously, certain risk factors play a role in the onset of hearing problems, including chronic exposure to loud sounds and smoking. There has been a long-held suspicion that the first generation to experience highly amplified music would start to pay the price in the form of the early onset of hearing problems. At the end of 2004, the EAR Foundation and Clarity researched the extent of hearing loss in the 40–59 age group. Nearly half of the research sample said that they had difficulty hearing at least some of the time. About a third of the respondents had their hearing tested and 15 per cent were diagnosed by a medical professional as having hearing loss. Thus, this recent study showed a definite increase in hearing loss when compared with the results from a decade earlier.

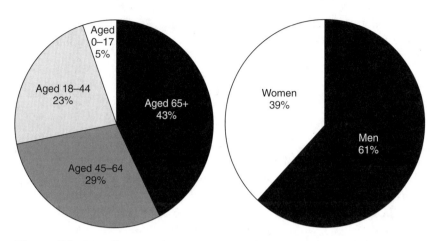

Figure 5.1 *Distribution of American population experiencing hearing loss (by age and gender)*
Source: National Health Interview Survey on Disability, National Center for Health Statistics, US, 1994

Physical capacity

Ageing is accompanied by a decline in muscle mass, flexibility and endurance. However, the extent and age of onset of this deterioration is governed by how much physical exercise a person takes. A fat, listless couch potato, aged 30 will be no physical match for an active 60-year-old who exercises regularly.

A visit to the popular retirement resorts of Florida or the southern coast of the UK shows how people who are serious about exercise and their diet stay in excellent physical condition, while others lose mobility, strength and endurance. The steep rise in obesity that affects much of the developed world is amplifying the differences in the physical condition of people as they age by causing the early onset of diabetes and cardiovascular problems.

Implications of the different effects of ageing

Even if the causes of these seven types of health-related ageing are debatable, the effects are well understood. There is no mystery about the numbers of people who experience these problems and how they will increase in the future.

As the population ages, so must the hypothetical user who is used as the basis for product and marketing decisions. It is pointless making decisions relating to the physical condition of your average 20–30-year-old when the majority of people suffer from some or all of these age-related conditions.

BRAND THEORY

There is no statement more likely to stifle a conversation about marketing to people over the age of 35, let alone those in their 50s, than 'The over-35s have fixed brand repertoires'. From this simple statement explodes a myriad of inferences about the cost and worth of targeting anybody outside the magical 18–35 age group. Various explanations are offered in support of this proposition, ranging from younger people's greater propensity for experimentation to the argument that with ageing come experience and self-confidence.

This latter argument sounds like it has a ring of common sense. It is reasonable to assert that those who are older become more their own people, have tried more brands and will make rational decisions about the ones they prefer. The flipside of this theory is the concept of 'naive consumers', who spend the first part of their lives bouncing around the great supermarket of life, prey to advertisers and fashion, experimenting with different brands and then exiting, aged 35, as self-assured beings with their shopping list for the next 45 years of life complete.

Before looking at the research evidence to support or destroy this argument, there are a few logical flaws and inconsistences that are worth considering.

New products

It is just possible that, after the age of 35, there are totally new products and services launched that did not exist during the 'naive consumer' period. One wonders how these now 50-year-olds are supposed to react to the internet, mobile phones, computers, economy travel, convenience foods and most electronic products that were introduced after their 36th birthdays.

According to McKinsey, in 1991 there were 15,000 brands on American grocery shop shelves. A decade later, there were 45,000. If the 'naive consumer' theory is correct, then people who were older than 35 in 1991 would be permanently less likely to buy these 30,000 new brands. What a terrifying prospect for the marketers responsible for these new brands?

Loyalty

A very simplified view of why consumers keep purchasing the same brands suggests that it is for one of the following five reasons:

I they really like the brand and are 'loyal';
I it's a habit, not a conscious decision;
I the risk of changing is not worth the potential benefits;
I it is difficult and a hassle to change;
I it is consistently the cheapest.

It is dangerous to group these together under a single title of 'brand loyalty'. The motivations behind these different reasons for sticking with the same brands are very different. For instance, changing electricity and gas suppliers, bank accounts, mortgages, ISPs and credit cards have historically been cumbersome things to do. These subscription-type products have experienced low levels of brand switching in the past. However, new technology and trading regulations make changing companies much easier than it used to be and millions of consumers now do so each year.

A decade ago, the reason for selecting a particular airline or holiday company was totally different from the rationale today. Not surprisingly, few of the companies of that era exist in their original form or with their original brand.

It is difficult to believe that the simple 'naive consumer' explanation has much value in the complicated and dynamic area of consumer loyalty.

New concepts

Branding theory and practice continually evolve to match the changes in the needs and behaviour of consumers and the potential of new communication channels. If the 'naive consumer' theory is to have any credibility, it must be robust enough to adapt to these changes.

Does the theory have any value in a world where, as consumers segment into smaller groups, brands are reacting and dividing into sub-brands? How does the theory explain the way in which consumers react to the new brands enabled by the web? What does the theory predict about consumer behaviour in an era of multicategory brands, such as Wal-Mart and Tesco? Then, the 'naive consumer' theory looks like a tired old marketing concept marooned in the fast-changing world of branding.

Brand valuation

The 'naive consumer' concept suggests that a good part of a brand's value is determined by the age of its customers. A brand with a customer base in their mid-30s should, theoretically, have the highest value. This is because customers still have a lifetime to keep purchasing the product and the investment has already been made in persuading them to adopt the brand. A brand with young customers would be valued less as they, theoretically, will keep changing until they 'mature' after the age of 35.

None of the brand valuation models I researched worked in this way, however. Research published in the *Harvard Business Review* showed that companies generate 80–90 per cent of their profits from fewer than 20 per cent of their brands. It is not surprising that companies such as Procter & Gamble and Unilever have been cutting brands. Unilever intends to reduce its 1,600 brands by about three-quarters. If the 'naive consumer' theory is correct, then these companies are destroying a huge amount of latent purchasing value. All the investment that went into persuading younger consumers to adopt these brands is being abandoned. Strangely, this argument is never mentioned.

Ehrenberg's theories

Dr Andrew Ehrenberg's theories of brand equity and the effect of brand size on purchase loyalty are well researched and considered to be robust and well proven. Perhaps his most profound conclusion is that loyalty varies little between competing brands. When there is a small variation, it is due to the respective sizes of the brands.

This theory was behind his famous 'double jeopardy law', which predicts that small brands not only have fewer buyers but these buyers are less loyal. Few marketers will not have heard the saying 'your customers are really other people's customers who occasionally buy from you'.

Strangely, Ehrenberg's theories about brand loyalty make no mention of the age of the customers. The NBD-Dirichlet theory, which predicts the patterns of brand competition, also makes no reference to the customer's age as one of its variables. The only relationship between age and purchasing that Ehrenberg's research discovered related to pricing elasticity. He found that the young (under 45) were consistently more sensitive to price changes than the over-45s. These results held true in the UK, Germany and the US. You would have thought that this result would have encouraged more targeting of the old.

If the argument that the over-35s have a fixed brand repertoire was a minor element of branding theory, then it would not matter if it contained some inconsistencies and contradictions. It is not a minor part of branding or marketing theory, though – it is critical to most of the big decisions that marketers make. This is despite the fact that even this cursory and somewhat tongue-in-cheek inspection of the theory, shows it to be highly suspect.

BRAND RESEARCH

In 2002, DDB/Accenture released the findings of its 'Lifestyle Study', which plotted the age distribution of people agreeing with the statement 'I tend to stick with well-known brands.' The research compared these findings with the results of a similar study conducted in 1975.

The conclusions were clear. In 1975, the numbers of people who agreed with the statement increased steadily with age. People aged 20–29 agreed, on average, 66 per cent of the time, rising to 93 per cent for those aged 70–79. The 2000 results were markedly different. There was virtually no difference for the age range 20–69 and then a slight increase for the 70–79 age category.

Between October and September 2004, OMD used its consumer panels in Australia, the Czech Republic, France, the UK and the US to research people's attitudes towards brands, technology, change and new experiences. The objective was to measure how reactions changed with age and nationality. The results of the research are intriguing. The details of the sample size and the questionnaire are provided in Appendix 4.

Before beginning the study, we had two abbreviations about the research methodology. First, we were measuring claimed rather than actual behaviour. Second, our research tool was the web and by only using internet users this might inject a bias into the results. Our main objective was to investigate the variations in responses for different ages and nationalities rather than absolute results. We believe that our methodology enabled us to achieve this objective. The research panels were selected to be as representative of the population as possible. The over-65s have the lowest levels of internet use, but in the countries researched, the penetration level for this age group is between 25 and 50 per cent of the population. The exception to this is the Czech Republic and there the interviews were conducted by telephone.

We wanted to understand how the age groups responded to the statement 'I tend to stick to well-known brands' to be able to compare our results with those of the Accenture study since the question has taken on something of a totem status.

The responses from each country are shown in Figure 5.2. In the US, Australia and the UK, the percentage agreeing with the statement declines with age, then increases and remains constant.

'I tend to stick to well-known brands'

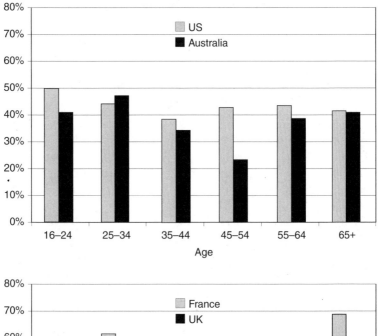

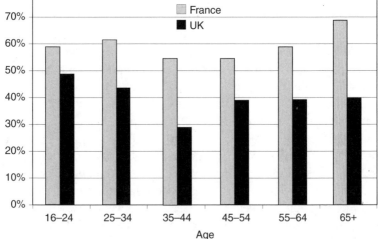

Figure 5.2 *Percentages of each age group agreeing with the statement 'I tend to stick to well-known brands'*
Source: OMD, 2004

France is the only country where the percentage of over-65s agreeing with the statement is greater than that for the 16–24 age group. In the Czech Republic, the number of people aged 60–79 who agreed with the statement was just 3 per cent higher than that for those aged 15–29 years.

The results of this quantitative research, with the exception of France, fail to support the premise that older consumers tend to stick to well- known brands. In fact, it shows the diametrically the opposite conclusion to be true.

To further probe the attitudes towards new brands, we also measured the level of agreement with the statement 'I am willing to try new brands.' This is a more positive, proactive statement than the 'passive' statement 'I tend to stick to well-known brands.' As expected, the question generated a more extreme set of responses. Figure 5.3 shows how each country group responded to this statement.

In France and the Czech Republic there was clear relationship between age and the level of agreement with the statement. In France, over 60 per cent of the 16–24 age group agreed with the statement, which fell to 40 per cent for the over-65s. The Czech Republic had an even greater decline in the numbers who agreed, falling by 30 per cent between the oldest and youngest groups.

The pattern of responses in the UK was far more varied. The over-65s were more in agreement with the statement than those aged 25–34.

In Australia, there was no clear relationship between the level of agreement and age. In the US, there were fewer older people agreeing with the statement than younger, but the percentage difference over the age range 16–54 was less than 6 per cent.

In Australia, the UK and the US, the agreement with the statement varied by just 7 per cent for the over-65s.

With the exception of France and the Czech Republic, there was no discernable relationship between age and the willingness to try new brands. In Australia, the UK and the US, the results for the over-65s was were very similar.

Finally, we combined the data for the two statements – 'I am willing to try new brands' and 'I tend to stick to well-known brands' – to create a single metric that represented how positive each age group was towards using new brands. Because older people's attitudes towards brands are invariably compared to the teenagers and people in their 20s, we normalized the data to the 16–24 age group. This was done by making the 16–24-year-olds' responses the datum line (100 per cent) and calculating

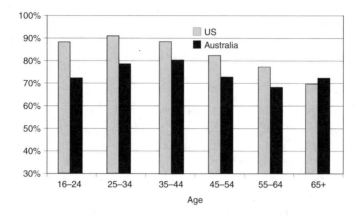

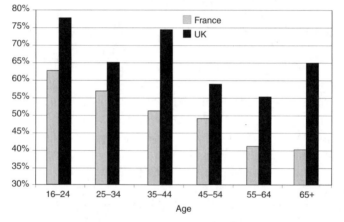

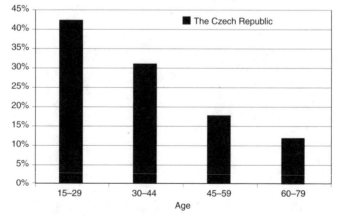

Figure 5.3 *Percentages of each age group agreeing with the statement 'I am willing to try new brands'*
Source: OMD, 2004

the variation of the older groups around this as the norm. This made it easier to contrast the variations of the different ages with what should, theoretically, be a group that is most receptive to trying new brands. The results of this analysis are shown in Figure 5.4. As the data for the Czech Republic were collected using a different set of age ranges to that of the other countries, they cannot be included here.

What does this research say about ageing and people's reactions to new brands?

I *France:* people's positive reactions to new brands declines with age;
I *Australia:* exhibits a diametrically different result, with older people being more positive about new brands than the young;
I *US:* shows a small decrease in positive reactions to new brands with age, a person aged 45–54 being 2 per cent less positive about new brands than someone aged 16–24, and somebody 55–65 being 9 per cent less positive;
I *UK:* has the most positive reaction to new brands among the 35–44-year-olds, but there is virtually no difference between the reactions of people aged 55–65+ and those aged 25–34;
I *The Czech Republic:* had an almost constant reaction over the age range 15–44 followed by a decline for older age groups.

These results show that the concept that people's propensity to change brands declines with age is hopelessly simplistic and misleading. France supports the argument, but Australia supports an opposite conclusion. In the UK and US, the level of positive reaction does decline with age, but it is neither linear nor significant.

TECHNOLOGY

Marketers often argue that they direct advertising at the young because 'older people don't like new technology.' If this premise is correct, then it follows that there is little value in optimizing interactive marketing channels to cater for older people or to target them as customers of high-tech products.

To research this topic, we asked for responses to the statement 'I really enjoy the challenge of keeping up with technology.' We then measured how each age group varied from the answers given by the youngest group. The results are shown in Figures 5.5 and 5.6.

As with the questions about brands, the responses showed significant differences between countries:

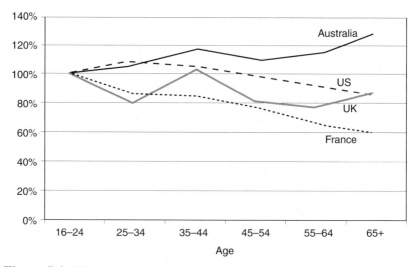

Figure 5.4 *Changes in positive reactions to using new brands, with the data normalized to the 16–24 age group*
Source: OMD, 2004

▌ *France:* for the ages 25–64, there was less than a 7 per cent difference in the level of enthusiasm for keeping up with technology than from those aged 16–24 – a trend that was reversed for the over-65s, who showed a greater desire to keep up with technology than those aged 16–24;

▌ *Australia:* the desire to be involved with technology increased with each age group, the over-65s responding 20 per cent more positively to the question than the 16–24-year-olds;

▌ *US:* older people were consistently less inclined to keep up with technology than the younger ones – over the age range 25–64 the level of decline was less than 10 per cent, but it fell rapidly for the over-65s;

▌ *UK:* exhibited a similar pattern to that of France, but with only a 2 per cent difference over the 25–64 age range and an increase in the level of interest from the over-65s;

▌ *The Czech Republic:* the results divided into two age categories in that there was only a 3 per cent difference between those aged 15 and 44, but then the interest in technology rapidly declined.

There is a more detailed discussion of ageing and technology in Chapter 11.

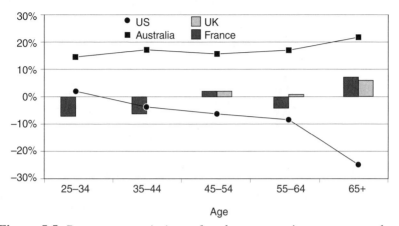

Figure 5.5 *Percentage variations of each age group's responses to the statement 'I really enjoy the challenge of keeping up with technology' from the responses of 16–24-year-olds*
Source: OMD, 2004

The enthusiasm for keeping informed about technology varies greatly by country. In Australia, ageing increases the desire to stay involved. In the Czech Republic, however, the results are diametrically opposed to this view. France and the UK have varying results, but the amount of variation with age is small. The US has a small variation up until the age of 64, then it rapidly declines. These results show that it is very dangerous to make any generalized comments about ageing and an interest in and desire to be involved with technology.

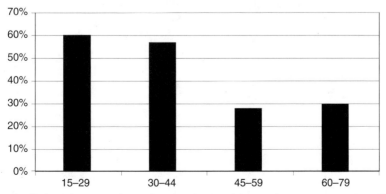

Figure 5.6 *Responses from the Czech Republic to the statement 'I really enjoy the challenge of keeping up with technology'*
Source: OMD, 2004

EMBRACING CHANGE

Another of the commonly held stereotypes of older people is that they 'don't want to change'. This assumes that mental agility and the desire to embrace change declines with age in a similar way to eyesight or dexterity. It is assumed that, in the same way that it gets harder to touch your toes by the time you are 60, the brain is no longer flexible enough to accept change and new ideas at this age.

We tested this assumption by asking for responses to two statements: 'Change is something that benefits us in our lives' and 'I don't understand why people want to keep changing things'. We combined the responses to derive a measure of how positive people are to change. To make comparisons between countries and ages easier, the data were normalized to the results of the 16–24 age group (that is, their response was set as 100 per cent). The results are presented in Figures 5.7 and 5.8.

As with the responses to the other statements, the results showed significant differences between the countries:

∎   *France:* increasing age had a small effect on the measure of positive reaction to change – over the age range 16–65 it showed a decline of 9 per cent;

∎   *Australia:* in keeping with the previous research results, the Australians' positive reaction to change increased with age;

∎   *US:* between the ages of 16 and 65 there was just a 4 per cent reduction in the positive response to change, while over the age of 65 there was a more significant decline of 14 per cent;

∎   *UK:* the positive reaction to change increased for the age range 16–44 and then declined, the average response from the 55–64 age group being 6 per cent below that of the 16–24-year-olds;

∎   *The Czech Republic:* this country exhibited the most marked reduction in the positive attitude to change with age, the oldest age group, on average, being over 30 per cent less positive in their response to embracing change than the youngest.

The results from Australia depict a country becoming more positive to change with age, which is totally opposite to the results from the Czech Republic. There is very little difference with age in the responses from the other countries. The over-65-year-olds in France and the UK show a slight increase in the level of their positive response.

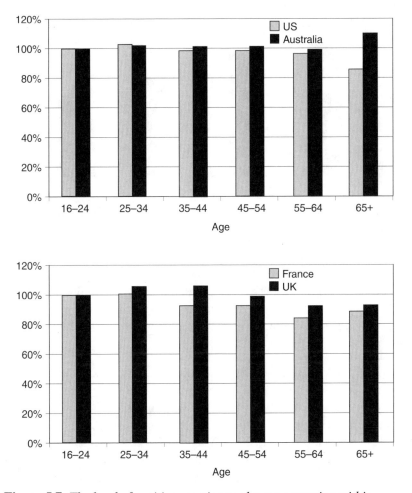

Figure 5.7 *The level of positive reaction to change occurring within respondents' lives, measured by age, in Australia, France, the UK and the US* Source: OMD, 2004

WANTING NEW EXPERIENCES

The final stereotype tested was the idea that getting older means people are less likely to want to try new experiences. We measured responses to this idea in a similar way to the method used for the statement about change. We asked respondents to give their answers to a positive statement and a negative one and then combined the results into a single measure of 'wanting new experiences'. The two statements were 'Life still holds new experiences for me to enjoy' and 'I prefer enjoying things that I am

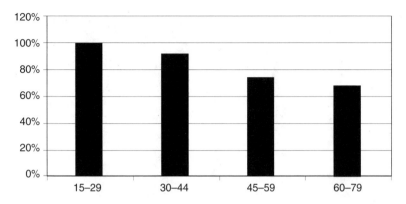

Figure 5.8 *The level of positive reaction to change occurring within respondents' lives measured by age in the Czech Republic*
Source: OMD, 2004

familiar with rather than seeking new experiences.' The results of the analysis are shown in Figure 5.9. As with the responses to previous statements, the data were normalized to the 16–24 age group.

The variations by country in the responses to these statements were similar to those for the desire to change:

❙ *France:* increasing age reduced the positive response to new experiences, but it did not happen in a linear way – the 45–54-year-olds gave almost the same responses as the 16–24-year-olds;

❙ *Australia:* the appetite for new experiences increased with age;

❙ *US:* between the ages of 16 and 65 the level of enthusiasm for new experiences was higher than or equal to that of the 16–24-year-olds, but after the age of 65 it showed a steep decline, yet even at the lower level it was only 20 per cent below the figure for the youngest age group;

❙ *UK:* the UK was the most positive regarding wanting new experiences, with the 65-plus even exceeding the enthusiasm of the Australians;

❙ *The Czech Republic:* showed a steep decline with age – the 45–59-year-olds having approximately 50 per cent of the enthusiasm for new experiences that the youngest age group had.

As with the results that measured the positive reaction to change, the Czech Republic showed a steep decline with age. The other countries gave totally different results. In the UK and Australia, getting older is accompanied by an increased desire for new experiences. In the US, this same pattern occurs up until the 55–64 age group, after which it rapidly declines. In France, there is an irregular but small decline with age.

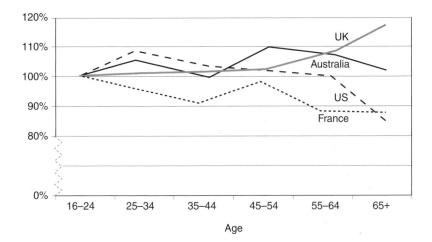

Figure 5.9 *Measures of the positive reactions to wanting new experiences, normalized to the 16–24 age group*
Source: OMD, 2004

FINANCIAL SECURITY

Are older people more or less confident about their future financial security than the young? One argument is that younger people give little thought to their long-term financial future. When they do think about the subject, they have the confidence and optimism of youth, believing that it 'will be all right' when they get old. An alternative argument is that the financial pressures on today's young people make them sceptical and anxious about the future.

Of all of the topics, the research results from responses to statements relating to this question produced the most significant variations by age. We asked people to comment on the two statements: 'I view the future with confidence, knowing I will be financially secure' and 'I am anxious about the future, especially my financial security.' As with the other questions, the responses were combined into a single measure, showing the level of confidence each age group had about their financial future. For each country, the data were normalized. The youngest age group – 16–24 – was set at 100 per cent and the other groups compared with the response of this age group. Figure 5.10 shows the profile of the responses for the US, Australia, France and the UK.

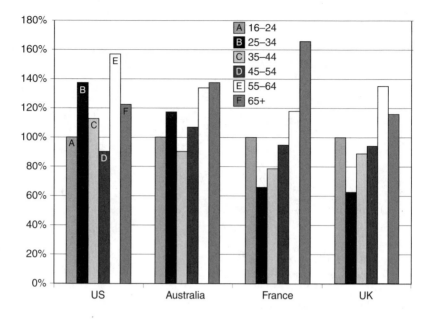

Figure 5.10 *How confident the different age groups are about their financially security*
Source: OMD, 2004

In France, there is a significant and consistent increase in confidence about financial security with age. In Australia, the confidence dips with the 35–44 age group and then increases. In both the UK and US, the 55–64-year-olds are the most confident, followed by the 65+.

These results show that older people are more confident, financially, about the future than the young. In the Czech Republic, the results are diametrically opposite to this view. Confidence in the future progressively declines with age and then shows a small increase in the 60+ age group.

In Chapter 2, it was argued that the younger people are exposed to financial pressures that were not experienced by many older people when they were that age. This is a conclusion that has been substantiated by this research.

THE AGE-NEUTRAL CONSUMER

OMD's research highlights three truths that should be emblazoned on the front covers of all books about marketing:

▌ *Truth 1:* there is no simple formula linking a person's age to how they behave as consumers;
▌ *Truth 2:* when age does appear to be linked to differences in behaviour, the variations are small;
▌ *Truth 3:* the behaviour of older people varies by their nationality.

Those people who took part in our research in the Czech Republic and, to a lesser extent, in France appear to be nearest to the classical marketing stereotypes of how older people behave. Older Australians have been issued with a different rulebook and behave in the opposite way. There are lots of reasons for this, but without more research, any discussion would be pure conjecture. The important point is that there is no simple rule that you can apply to the peoples of the Czech Republic and Australia. The responses of the French are also different from those of the British and Americans.

For most questions, the responses within each country were similar up until the age of 65 years. The change in responses from the over-65s was most pronounced in the US.

If you want to make a broad assumption about consumer behaviour, it is more accurate and safest to assume that it is age-neutral rather than that it is age-related. This simple assumption has profound consequences. If you accept it as a truth, then it changes the way that you approach marketing. Chapter 8 explains the new rules of age-neutral marketing.

There are many other pieces of research, published data and anecdotal evidence that support the view that the variations in the ways that people of different ages think and behave are not significantly different from each other. Let us look at a few examples.

The strategic consultancy and think tank Future Foundation researched how different age groups respond to a range of consumer decisions, such as the influence of men and women when choosing holidays, mortgages, cars and home audio equipment. The results show very little variation in the responses across the age range of 16 to 65.

Pew Research conducted a global study to measure how people's attitudes changed to political and social issues with age. Table 5.1 shows the results from five countries agreeing with the statement 'We are better off in a free market economy.' The reaction in the US was constant for the age range 30–50+, though the 18–29-year-olds were markedly less enthusiastic. In the

Table 5.1 *Positive responses to the statement 'We are better off in a free market economy.'*

Country	18–29 (%)	30–49 (%)	50+ (%)
US	54	74	75
France	62	67	55
Germany	60	69	72
China	75	67	71
Vietnam	96	96	94

Source: Pew Research, 2003

other countries, there was very little difference across the 18–50+ age spectrum. The agreement with the statement in China and Vietnam was surprisingly high and age-neutral.

In 2004, consumer research company TNS measured how much, on average, women in the UK spend on clothing. From women under-35 to those over-55, the difference in spend was just 17 per cent. Women in the age range 35–55+ spent almost exactly the same. Interestingly, most money was spent by women aged 35–54.

AARP measured how well people understand and cope with their personal financial affairs. The research showed that up to the age of 65 there were only a couple of percentage points difference between the measures of confidence for any of the age groups. Over the age of 65 the difference increased, but even then only by a margin of 10–12 per cent.

Neither these snippets of research nor the work done by OMD depict all age groups acting exactly the same. It would be crazy if they did. Instead, the question marketers must ask about age, or any other segmentation variable, is 'Are the associated differences large enough to warrant a different marketing approach?'

Is marketing to the over-50s that different from marketing to the over-40s? Is it that much different from marketing to people in their 40s or 30s? The evidence would seem to say that there are more similarities than differences.

THE MARKETING BOTTOM LINE

It is bizarre that marketers pay scant attention to the things that are known to be different for young and older people and yet are obsessed with the differences that research suggests either don't exist or are very small.

Young and older people differ physically. This fact should impact all areas of marketing. It does not; it is largely ignored.

The overwhelming balance of evidence shows that attitudinal differences between young and old are more akin to fairytales than the result of solid research. Even so, this myth dominates the way marketers think and act.

Marketers would improve their own effectiveness – and that of their companies – if they paid more attention to the physical effects of ageing and less to the behavioural ones. Most importantly, they would radically improve how they relate to and satisfy their customers.

So, what does it mean to be old? I cannot think of a better answer than one given to me by Robin Wight, Chairman of WRCS: 'It is a young mind, in an ageing body, with a maturing wallet.'

IMPLICATIONS FOR THE MARKETER

Ageing is accompanied by a decline in physical condition affecting taste, smell, touch, eyesight, hearing and cognitive abilities. Thus, if product design, packaging, communications and customer care decisions are based on the physical condition of your average 20–30-year-old, they will become increasingly at odds with the needs of the market.

! Review all areas of marketing and decide what changes need to be implemented in order to account for the physical condition of older consumers.

OMD's consumer panels in Australia, the Czech Republic, France, the UK and the US researched how ageing affects people's responses to new brands, technology, change, concerns about financial security and wanting new experiences.

! Study the results from this research discussed above. Decide the implications for your international marketing strategy and the assumptions you make about consumers of different ages.

Attitudes do not appear to change significantly over a large part of the age spectrum.

! Reconsider the age range of consumers for which the company's marketing is age-neutral.

SUMMARY

▌ In this chapter we have discussed the characteristics that distinguish an 'older' from a 'younger' person and whether or not the differences are so significant that they warrant changing what we sell and how we market.

▌ The most obvious and well-researched effect of ageing is the decline in physical condition. While there are disputes about the exact science of ageing, it is known that taste, smell, touch, eyesight, hearing and cognitive abilities all decline with age.

▌ As the population ages, so must the hypothetical user on which product and marketing decisions are based. It is pointless making decisions based on the physical condition of your average 20–30-year-old when the majority of people suffer from some or all of the age-related conditions.

▌ How ageing affects consumers' attitudes and behaviour is less well understood than its physical effects. Marketing has amassed a number of assumptions about how the over-35s respond to new brands, technology, change and wanting new experiences. These assumptions, rather than research, guide many marketing decisions.

▌ In 2004, OMD used its consumer panels in Australia, the Czech Republic, France, the UK and the US to research these attitudes. A key finding was that the concept that people's propensity to change brands declines with age is hopelessly simplistic and misleading. The research found that there was no simple formula for linking a person's age to how they behave as consumers. When age does appear to be linked to differences in behaviour, the variations are small.

▌ The most surprising result was how the responses differed by country.

▌ Marketers would improve their own effectiveness, and that of their companies, if they paid more attention to the physical effects of ageing and less to the attitudinal ones. Most importantly, they would radically improve how they relate to and satisfy their customers.

6

The strange world of segmentation

Every marketing textbook has as at least one chapter dedicated to the science – some might say art – of market segmentation. Rarely does the discussion of segmentation explore how it is applied to older people and, unfortunately, when it does, many of the conclusions reached are of dubious value.

All segmentation methodologies are built on a few basic assumptions. If these are wrong or questionable, then all of the charts, tables and diagrams constructed using them are not worth a jot.

This chapter discusses these assumptions and their validity in relation to improving the understanding of the older market. Hopefully, it distinguishes the fact from the hyperbole.

KEEP SIGHT OF THE OBJECTIVES

Market segmentation divides consumers into smaller groupings of like-minded individuals to create better consumer strategies, leading to better research, product development and communications. In short, all aspects of marketing improve by having a better understanding and more refined focus on the customer. What could be simpler?

Things go wrong when the segments are not created as a result of any research, but from guesswork and stereotypes. Even worse is constructing elaborate segmentation methodologies that are so unwieldy that they are useless in directing marketing activity.

The BBC provides a superb case study of how organizations can contract the all too common marketing disease of 'segmentation paralysis'. The cause of this disease is an inordinate amount of time and money being spent on the process of segmentation, resulting in it becoming too complicated and theoretical to implement.

In November 2004, Professor Patrick Barwise from the London Business School conducted a review of the BBC's digital television services at the behest of the UK government. Here is a quote from the report:

> The BBC is full of bright, enthusiastic people. Sometimes, it overcomplicates things.
>
> A few years ago, its planning and strategy group excelled itself with its notorious 250-page document, '100 Tribes'. This broke the UK population down into dozens of so-called 'smart demographic' segments defined by age, life stage, gender, attitudes and interests.
>
> In a market such as television, which is only weakly segmented, it is hard to see how '100 Tribes' could have encouraged clear and valid strategic thinking, intelligent resource allocation or programme-making creativity.

Needless to say, the BBC's digital television strategy is no longer attempting to use this kind of extreme segmentation.

The result of 'segmentation paralysis' is countless hours of marketers' time spent dissecting an infinite number of consumer variables, resulting in the creation of countless PowerPoint slides and Excel spreadsheets. Two things are often overlooked. Tactically, how the segments can be applied and what level of confidence can be attributed to findings. Beware, it is easy to become preoccupied with the process and lose to sight of applying the outputs.

So many marketing processes rely on the quality and usability of the segmentation model. If it is wrong or difficult to apply, it damages the business. Applying the simple set of guidelines shown in Table 6.1 will help avoid wasting time on useless segmentation exercises and making some of the common mistakes.

Segmentation methodologies come in all shapes and sizes and from lots of different sources. Some have their origins in sociology and psychology that has been adapted to explain consumers' behaviour. Others are the proprietary methodologies of research and consultancy companies.

Often a company's ability to use segmentation is limited by the fact that it only has small amounts of data for its customers. Worse, however, is to segment solely by the products and services the company sells.

When talking with marketing directors, the phrase I loathe hearing is 'I know we should focus more effort on older age groups, but we have already done our market segmentation.' This treats segmentation as a one-time

Table 6.1 *The rules of segmentation*

Rule of segmentation	Example
You must be able to apply the results of the segmentation.	Applying the segmentation strategy must lead to a better choice of channels, product design, pricing, advertising creative and so on.
Segment definitions must be based on evidence, not conjecture or stereotypes.	Too often, companies make statements such as 'Our prime segment is "baby boomers".' This is so vague as to be worthless.
Segments must be differentiated from each other.	Is the behaviour of the 50–55 age group that different from that of the 56–60 age group? Are the differences large enough to warrant different marketing campaigns?
A consumer must remain part of a segment for a sufficient period of time to have marketing value.	If a consumer is only a member of a segment for a transitory time period that is less than the marketing cycle, then it is of dubious worth.
Segments must be important enough to warrant marketing expenditure.	If you are a luxury cruise company, it is of little value to segment the part of the population incapable of affording your holidays.
The characteristics of segments change and must be regularly re-evaluated.	This is a common mistake with age segmentation. It is assumed that the characteristics of a 50-year-old are the same today as they were 5–10 years ago.
Segments must be defined in consumer, not company, terms.	It is common for segments to be created on the basis of how the company is organized rather than how its customers think and act.
The number of segments must be relevant to the company's marketing resources.	A large retailer may have the marketing and IT resources to manage tens or even hundreds of segments, but most smaller companies are lucky if they can cope with six or seven.

exercise that, when completed, cannot be questioned, even if it is plainly wrong. Markets evolve and so should the means of segmenting them.

50 IS JUST A NUMBER

Like all aspects of marketing, age-neutrality applies to the theory of market segmentation. Companies must fight the insatiable desire to consign customers and prospects to the 'over-50' ghetto the instant they depart their 49th year. Let's remember that the age of 50 is an artificially defined moment in time, with no significance other than that which society attributes.

As OMD's research has shown, the differences between people at the ages of 30, 40 and 50 can be insignificant. Why oh why do we have methods of segmentation that insist on enforcing demarcations where none exist? Note that all the means of segmentation described in this chapter have the potential to fail if they reinforce such artificial age boundaries.

Age-neural marketing means assuming people's behaviour is the same unless the evidence shows it to be different. Remember this when reading the rest of this chapter.

SEGMENTING BY AGE

The great attraction of using age as a means of segmentation is that it is simple. The trouble is that it is also simplistic.

Andrew Walmsley, the Managing Director of the media agency i-level, identified a fundamental problem with using age to segment a market: 'Age is an imprecise proxy for targeting consumers' interests.' He went on to say that it introduces 'two sets of rounding errors'. First, you have to make the assumption that people of a certain age want certain products. Second, you must make assumptions about different age groups' media habits.

During our interview with Robin Wight, the Chairman of WCRS, he observed, 'Everybody in their head is 25.' He was forcefully making the point that perceived and actual ages are different things. The first is defined by the date on our birth certificate; the second is a state of mind. Much research has been done to try and establish the relationship between these two ages. In the US, a person of 80 is thought to feel 60, while at 70 the perceived age is 55 and at 50 the age in the person's mind is thought to be 42. It is unlikely that such a mechanistic relationship exists, but it does illustrate the fact that the age that appears on a customer and prospect database has to be treated with care as a means of driving marketing decisions. Any segmentation process that uses age must take account of the large differences in the age profiles of different ethnic groups. Figure 6.1 shows the age profiles of some groups in the UK derived from the 2001 census. The proportion of older people in the black African, Bangladeshi, Pakistani and Chinese groups is significantly lower than for the white

British group. 'Ethnicity' is even more important when targeting specific towns and regions as the concentrations of ethnic groups can have significant effects on their age profiles. All countries with significant levels of ethnic mix show similar variations in their age profiles.

The final – and possibly most important – weakness of using age to determine market decisions is the increasing trend for consumers' behaviour to be age-neutral. As OMD's research has proved, there are significant bands of age where age is of no use in determining how people think and act.

Despite the caveats relating to the value of age as a way of understanding consumers, it is still widely used. There are five main variants of age segmentation, each of which is discussed below.

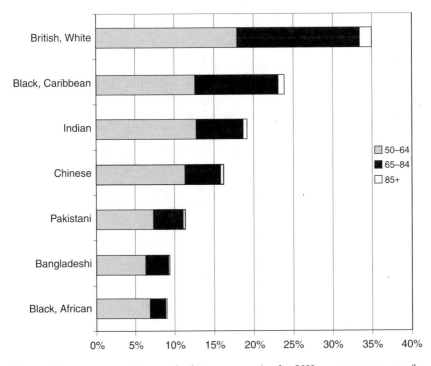

Figure 6.1 *Age breakdown of ethnic groups in the UK as percentages of the population*
Source: 2001 census

Age ranges

This involves dividing a market into age groupings, such as younger than 18, 18–21 and 21–25. Invariably, when older the age groups are included, the range of years is wider – 36–45, 46–55 and over 55, for example. Very often, the top age mentioned is 60 and, in many cases, all people over the age of 50 are grouped into a single category called 'the 50-plus'.

One of the many weaknesses of this approach is identifying market-related factors that directly attach to specific age ranges. Another problem is that a period of 10 to 15 years covers a vast slice of somebody's life. For example, the period between 50 and 60 could include both the time of an individual's maximum earnings and when they stop working, which makes defining the characteristics of the segment extremely difficult.

If the age ranges are closely correlated to consumer behaviour, then they have some value. If, as is more often the case, they are selected for arith-metical convenience, then they are next to useless.

Different variations on 'old'

Rather than simply using the term 'old', it is often subdivided into groups with titles such as the 'young-old', 'middle-old' and the 'old-old'. Because these terms are not universally defined, it is necessary to state the age range relating to each segment. So, the 'old-old' might be people aged 75 and over.

The same reservations about the value of such segments apply as for age ranges. Because these terms have arbitrary definitions, there is the added potential problem of creating confusion. I might think that the 'young-old' relates to 40–50-year-olds, whereas you might believe it is those who are 55 to 60.

Generational age groupings

If there are two words that should be jettisoned from the English language they are 'baby' and 'boomers', closely followed by 'silver' and 'surfers', 'Millennials' and, while we're at it, 'Generation X' and 'Generation Y'. More recently, another term entered the marketer's lexicon: 'generation Jones'. This should receive the same treatment. All of these names are shorthand for age-defined segments.

Because these terms are so widely used, it is necessary to spend some time making sense of this sea of silly names that masquerades for a scientific method of age segmentation. The birth of the latest generation – 'generation Jones' – provides us with a good illustration of the weaknesses of this technique.

Generation Jones – often referred to as 'genJonesers' – were born between 1954 and 1965. Like all of the other groupings, the dates have been arbitrarily specified. In 2004, this generation were aged between 39 and 50.

The question that everybody asks is 'Why Jones?' Apparently, it has nothing to do with Tom Jones or Catherine Zeta-Jones or Indiana Jones but is because it is an anonymous generation and a matching nondescript name was wanted.

The biggest gripe the proponents of this group has is about its identity – or, to be more accurate, its lack of one. Are those in it really the last stages of the boomers or the first gasps of Generation X? Come to that, does it matter?

Sociologist Jonathan Pontell, who has promoted the adoption of this new generation, has always felt like he was trapped inside a boomer's body: 'I can remember first hearing the words "baby boomer generation" as a high school student', muses Pontell. 'The whole class burst out laughing when the teacher told us we were baby boomers. It was so obvious we weren't. ... I wasn't spending sleepless nights obsessing over the fact that I'd been mislabelled, but in the back of my head, I never identified with the boom.'

Pontell's support for the genJonesers grouping has been added to by others in the marketing industry. The media agency Carat, for example, issued the results of its study into genJonesers and determined that they are 'realists with a social conscience'. They believe that they are 'A generation that views itself as more lateral thinking, creative, energetic and politically active/aware than the generations around them.' These are bold, if not a tad bland, statements about a group that represents 20 per cent of the UK's population.

Determining where one such generation stops and another starts seems to be as much of an art as a science. How are marketers supposed to categorize the dispossessed born at the point between one generation and another? Do we have millions of people, whose birthdays come at the boundaries of the generational divides, spending their lives in a perpetual state of confusion about where they belong?

Discovering a new generation is a bit like finding another planet in the solar system. Astronomers debate whether the thing is an asteroid, a planet or a speck of dust on the end of the telescope and then some bright spark comes along with 'new research' that proves categorically that it is a planet. Well, some research carried out by the University of California (UCLA) is marketing's equivalent of the astronomer finding a new planet as it claims to prove that a new generation has been discovered. We can officially declare that the genJones is an age group in its own right.

UCLA has conducted an annual poll of 350,000 college freshmen since the mid-1960s. One of the questions in the poll concerns students' ranking of two different life goals: how important is it to develop a meaningful philosophy of life' and 'be very well off financially'. Table 6.2 shows the percentages of freshmen agreeing on the importance of the two statements for the period 1966 to 1990.

This analysis shows that genJonesers have a distinctly different view of life from the generations on either side of their age cohort.

Most of the justification for considering 39–50-year-olds as a separate group is along the lines: 'How could it make sense that a 36-year-old, who was raised during Watergate and who is now entering the workforce after just finishing her doctorate, would be in the same cultural generation as her 55-year-old father who was raised during the Fifties and who is now considering his retirement years?'

UCLA's analysis has a far more interesting conclusion than the one offered as proof of the genJones. Figure 6.2 shows a graph of the responses to the two questions on life goals asked of each year of students since the research began. The startling conclusion is that very little change in attitudes has occurred since the early 1980s, as shown by the horizontal lines in the graph.

If the definition of a radical change in life goals marks the birth or death of new generation, then for the past quarter of a century we have had a single generation holding similar life goals. Perhaps I have accidentally discovered 'generation boring'?

The arguments for generational segments are predicated on the concept that we see ourselves as belonging to one of these groups. As most people haven't the faintest idea if they are a boomer, Xer, Yer or Zer, it seems a totally false, and useless, concept.

There is some logic supporting the definition of the 'baby boomer' generation, even though the birth rate in the US started to climb in 1940. In 1945, the full effect of the hoard of sex-starved men returning from World War II was felt as the birth rate shot up. The birth rate in the US then declined from the late 1950s onwards.

Table 6.2 *UCLA poll of college freshmen's attitudes showing percentages agreeing importance of life goals*

Life goal	1966 (median year of baby boomers)	1977 (median year of genJonesers)	1990 (median year of Generation Xers)
Develop a meaningful philosophy of life	85%	61%	42%
Be very well off financially	44%	60%	76%

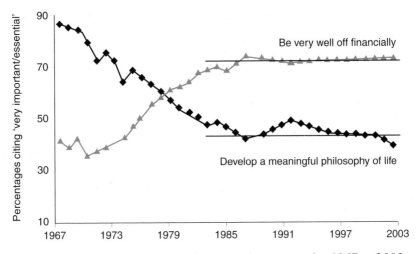

Figure 6.2 *UCLA's analysis of the life goal questions for 1967 to 2003*

In the UK, the birth rate increased after the World War's end, too, but declined earlier, in the late 1940s early 1950s. In the mid-1950s, it suddenly started to rise again, reaching a peak in 1964. The UK therefore had a two-stage baby boom, peaking in the decade after the boom in the US. Figure 6.3 shows the different 'booms' and 'mini-booms' in the US and the UK.

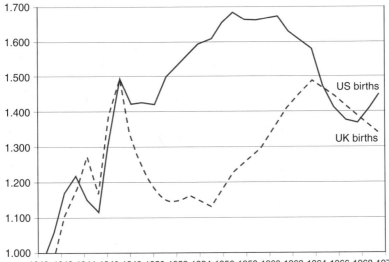

Figure 6.3 *US and UK birth rates, normalized to 1940 for comparison*
Source: Census Bureau, Department of Commerce, US, 2004

So, as American baby boomers pass through their mid- to late 50s, the UK variety are still in middle age. If you are confused, you are not alone! After the baby boomers, the generational divisions are even more artificial. The term Generation X – loosely referring to people born in the 1960s and 1970s – is a cultural idea rather than a demographic term.

Generation Y – loosely referring to people born in the 1980s and 1990s – beats all records for having lots of other silly names. Here are a few: the 'Millennial generation', 'Millennium generation', 'Net generation', 'N-gen', 'generation NeXt' and 'generation 2000'. The list goes on and on and on.

The usefulness of these age groupings, cohorts, generations or whatever you want to call them relies on a single, tenuous, assumption – namely, that the shared experiences of a cohort influence the type of people they become and the way they behave as consumers. That is one hell of a big assumption.

It is common for marketing books to have a diagram showing the events occurring at different times in an age cohort's life. For instance, the Vietnam War was raging as the first waves of baby boomers were in their formative years. Watergate, the stock market collapse and Nixon's resignation all occurred as a large group of Americans were in their teens and early 20s.

Events in the US were also experienced in the UK, along with local social and economic upheavals. The demise of trade union power and the Labour Party and the rise of Margaret Thatcher created massive disturbances. Even today, the name 'Margaret Thatcher' engenders either rage or adulation.

Surely such huge events must leave lasting scars on our psyches that determine our future behaviour? The answer must be 'Yes, yes, yes.' There cannot be any doubt that a person born during the hardships and horror of World War II will have a different perspective on life from somebody who bathed in the hedonistic self-indulgence of the 1960s. The huge problem is turning this statement of the obvious into something of value to a marketer.

The difficulties start with questions about the existence of universal sets of experiences that affect a whole generation. Karl Mannheim, social theorist, is attributed with establishing the academic basis for this theory in the early 1900s.

When experiences of the 1960s are recounted, they are invariably described with the sounds and images of 'flower power', demonstrations, music festivals, liberated youth and unbridled sexual freedom. Was life really a wild round of 'sex, drugs and rock 'n' roll' or does this represent a romantic view of reality that was only experienced by a small sector of society? We are talking about events that took place 30 years ago and no doubt our memories of this period have become distorted a jot? Maybe there has been some substitution of the archetypal images of the time for what really happened?

What if we reverse the theory and look at what is happening today and conjecture how it will impact teenagers when they reach their 60s. Surely if we understand how events that occurred 40 years ago influence today's 60-year-olds, then working them out the opposite way round should be easy.

We can't yet know the relative historical importance of 9/11 2001, the Iraq War and the fissure in American society caused by the second term of the Bush presidency or the disaster of the tsunami in the Indian Ocean in 2004. These events are certainly of significant importance, but how will they influence the behaviour of today's 18-year-olds in 40 years' time?

Nobody has the faintest idea. Equally, others share doubts about the homogeneous nature of the boomer generation. A study, published in late 2004, conducted at Duke University and using the 2000 census for the US came to the following conclusions:

> Baby boomers were not all political radicals: even for those boomers who were young adults during the late 1960s, opposition to the Vietnam War was far from universal, for example. One-third of the early boomers served in Vietnam, and younger voters were more likely to support conservative candidates.
>
> Given that the baby boomer generation is now more unequal than others at the same ages, we can expert them to be more unequal in old age than previous generations.
>
> We all fall into talking about the baby boom as if it was a homogeneous group, but it's a very heterogeneous group.

Uncertainty about the existence and predictability of this age cohort is trivial compared to the question of how early life experiences relate to all of the other things that determine our behaviour. Figure 6.4 shows some of the influences contributing to how we think, act and consume. Our family background, education, health, work experience, relationships, gender, ethnicity and the big unknown of life's random experiences all aggregate together to determine who we are.

What is the relative importance of our cohort experiences to where we live and work, our income and how our relationships work out? There is no theory or research that begins to answer this and similar questions with any degree of confidence. Any connections found between our early life experiences and the types of consumers we become are very tenuous.

Unfortunately, names like boomers, Generation X and Millennials are now well-embedded words in the marketing vocabulary. As shorthand for

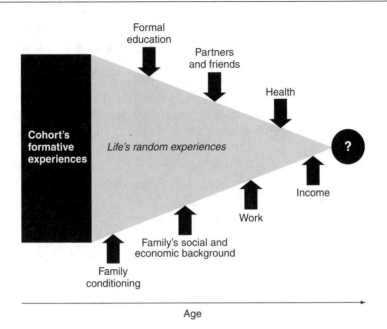

Figure 6.4 *Influences on behaviour after cohort's formative experiences*
Source: 20plus30, 2004

the different age groupings they have some value, but extreme care must be taken in using them as predictors of consumer behaviour. I shall say that again. Be extremely careful about using them as predictors of consumers' behaviour.

Age related to life stage

As we age, we move through different stages of life. Tweens grow into young adults who suddenly awake in middle age and then finally find themselves inhabiting old age. Theoretically, consumers' behaviour should correlate closely with these life stages. Obviously, the arrival of children generates demand for a raft of new products and services that the parents barely knew existed 12 months earlier. The transitions from being a dependant to an independent adult and from having a household with children to one where they have left are accompanied by different purchasing patterns.

If a consumer's life passed through an ordered number of life stages, at predictable ages, then the technique of life stage segmentation would be a winner. By understanding the different life stages of older people and how they determine consumer behaviour, marketing could create the most appropriate marketing strategies.

McKinsey, a strategy consultancy, researched the variables that most affected the viewing preferences of pay-TV audiences and found that age, employment status and family role were the dominant factors.

From this analysis, it constructed the life stage decision tree shown in Figure 6.5. If this is to be believed, somebody over the age of 35 who is the household breadwinner with no children at home is likely to be in a 'mature family'. An under-35-year-old who is not the breadwinner, employed with no children at home is likely to be an 'independent adult'.

For this model of segmentation to have any general applicability, it must cope with the trend for people's lives to follow less predictable paths. For example, women have children later in life, dual-income families are the norm, children leave home and come back again, and marriages break up. In the UK, the average age of women giving birth continues to rise and, at the time of writing is just under 30 years, and over 40 per cent of births are outside marriage. Now, one in five women are childless when they reach the end of their fertile life compared to a figure of one in ten for women born in the mid-1940s.

These headline numbers hide a wide diversity of behaviour by ethnic and social groups. In the past, for example, unmarried men and women in their midlife and beyond were thought to be mostly widows and widowers or spinsters and confirmed bachelors. In the US in 2004, however, most single people between the ages of 40 and 69 were divorced, followed by those who never married. Widows and the separated were a small minority. In the UK, the over-35 age group represents three-quarters of all

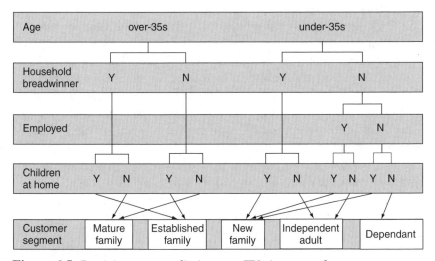

Figure 6.5 *Decision tree predicting pay-TV viewer preferences*
Source: McKinsey, 'Simplifying Web segmentation', *The McKinsey Quarterly*, 2001

divorces. Two decades ago, they accounted for only half. The patterns of marriage and household composition have changed and continue to do so, making age life stage prediction increasingly difficult.

Even if it were possible to take account of these variations in behaviour, it still leaves the problem of understanding the marketing characteristics of the different life stage segments. Groups with names such as 'mature family' and 'independent adult' are far too nebulous to be of very much use to marketing.

A variant of life stage segmentation is using age to predict life events. Examples of this are marriage, birth of the first child and ownership of a first home. For older people, the most important life event, from a financial perspective, is retiring. This might trigger moving home, taking the 'holiday of a lifetime' and using the new-found free time to travel and enjoy hobbies and interests.

Using life events, however, is prone to many of the same problems that plague life stage segmentation. For many people, the time when 60 or 65 marked the point of retirement is fast disappearing. Seeking re-employment post-50 can be very difficult, resulting in an early, enforced retirement. Other people have no need or intention of stopping work at 60 or any other age.

Depending on the value of a person's pension provision, retirement can be the fun-filled time of their lives or a nightmare of dwindling savings and a reduced standard of living. Early economic inactivity for men aged 55–59 is concentrated in the lowest two and the highest wealth groups, with a large percentage of the poorest groups describing themselves as 'sick' or 'unemployed'. The richest earners who have left the labour force describe themselves as 'retired'. There is a broadly similar picture for women aged 55–59. Figure 6.6 shows this relationship between wealth and inactivity.

Historically, the period prior to retirement was one when mortgages were paid off and other household debts minimized. Even this characteristic of the retirement life event is changing. Indeed, research by the UK's Consumer Credit Counselling Service showed that people in their 50s borrow more than younger age groups. In 2002/2003, the average unsecured debt for those in their 50s was approximately £20,000, compared with just under £15,000 for those under 50. Also, in the five years to 2003, the debt–income ratio for people in their 50s had leapt by more than 20 per cent, while that for the under-50s had risen by less than 4 per cent.

There are similarities between the segmentation techniques of age grouping, life stage and life events. At face value, they are appealing. They are simple and mechanistic to use and their predictions about consumers and how they are grouped appears to have a strong vein of common sense. Who can believe that baby boomers, who have always broken the rules of

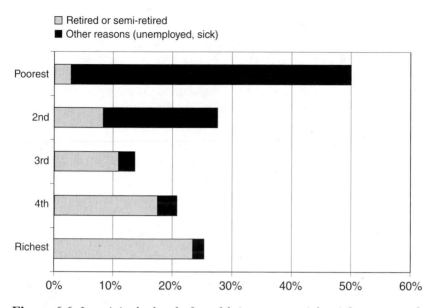

Figure 6.6 *Inactivity by level of wealth (poorest to richest) for men aged 55–59*
Source: Pensions Commission, 2004

society, will not keep doing the same in their 60s and 70s? Surely it is not unreasonable to believe that somebody over the age of 35 and working will have a family? We can also all think of examples of people moving house the instant they retire and taking a long-cherished holiday.

Doubts about the value of these age-based methods of predicting consumer behaviour, however, start once you look at the supporting evidence. Baby boomers are an incredibly heterogeneous generation, spanning the very rich to the desperately poor. 'Retirement' now encompasses everything from a life taking luxury cruises to an existence of low-paid part-time work, attempting to survive on State handouts. 'Mature families' can mean anything from a husband and wife living alone, after the children have left, to grandparents living with their unmarried children, helping to bring up their grandchildren.

Perhaps a decade ago, maybe two, it was possible to use age as a good predictor of consumers' needs and behaviour. Those days are long gone.

Age related to geographical location

By using a combination of a national census and neighbourhood statistics it is possible to classify consumers according to the type of residential neighbourhood they live in. By combining information about a person's age and address (such as by postcode or zip code), you can get an insight into the type of consumer he or she is.

Strictly speaking, this technique – called geodemographics – does not require age data to be effective as just knowing somebody's postcode is valuable marketing data. Because this method of segmentation is based on residential data, it is easy to apply as a direct marketing tool.

Geodemographics is such an important technique for marketing to older people that it warrants its own chapter, so it has one. Professor Richard Webber describes in detail how the technique can be applied in Chapter 7.

How to use age

Should marketers use the factor of age as a means of predicting behaviour and segmenting their markets for older people?

For certain groups of consumers, age will remain a predicting and targeting factor – especially at the extremes of the age spectrum. Companies with a good understanding of their markets and customers may well find, therefore, that age is a good method of segmentation. What is wrong is to assume that age is applicable to all markets.

It is a depressing thought, but ageing is a good predictor of physical and cognitive decline and the onset of certain illnesses. In the fullness of time, the wonders of genetic engineering might halt this relationship, but for now the effects of ageing can be universally applied. It is the relationship between age and people's behaviour that is far more problematic. Even the enthusiastic proponents of using the age demographic admit that it is a good place to start segmenting a market, but not to finish.

Most of the broad-brush descriptions of what different generations think and how they behave make good tabloid press reading but are difficult, if not impossible, to apply. Even worse, they distil the compli-cated factors describing older people into a few sound-bite terms that are factually wrong and misleading. Similar concerns apply to using age as a proxy for predicting life events.

A simple summary of the many pros and cons of using age are listed in Table 6.3.

Table 6.3 *Benefits and dangers of using age as a marketing variable*

The benefits of using age
There is a strong relationship between health and age. The onset of many illnesses is linked to age.
Cognitive, eyesight, hearing and dexterity deterioration are related to age. This creates product and service opportunities and also affects the design and use of marketing channels, especially those using technology.
A person's age is a guide to the images and sounds they experienced during different phases of their life. Although TV has somewhat blunted this effect with its recycling of old content, it is still useful.
For certain markets, life stages and life events might be related to age. This is not true for all markets. The techniques should only be used after the relationship has been established by research.
There is a strong base of research showing the relationship between age, residence and consumer behaviour. This technique, geodemographics, is particularly relevant to older people and provides marketers with contact data to drive direct communications channels.
Age is central to predicting macroeconomic-level developments. The effects of the ageing population on the demand for healthcare and pensions funding, for example, are well understood. The cynic could say that possessing the knowledge is useless unless it is accompanied by the political will to act on it!

The dangers of using age
Age segments based on age ranges, age groups, life stages and life events are appealing because they are easy to understand and seem well founded in our Day-to-Day experiences of older people.
They create a false confidence that a market can be segmented into homely sounding groupings that are often no more than caricatures and stereotypes.
Chronological age is a good predictor of our physiological condition, but it is the age we perceive ourselves to be that determines how we act as consumers. Unfortunately, the latter cannot be calculated from our birth certificate. All age segmentation models are based on chronological age.
OMD's research showed that, in some country markets, consumers' attitudes, especially about brands, do not vary over large parts of the age spectrum.
Just because age is a good way of segmenting customers in one market, it cannot be assumed that it will be equally successful in another, even if the customers are the same people.
Age segments that are meaningful for the indigenous population might be useless when applied to ethnic groups. In many towns and regions of the UK, Australia and the USA, the ethnic minority is close to becoming a majority, making the 'ethnic factor' vitally important. The attitude towards older people varies greatly between the Western world and the Middle and Far East. For markets with a high proportion of non-indigenous peoples, these differences need to be recognized.

SEGMENTING BY CONSUMER LIFESTYLE (PSYCHOGRAPHICS)

Dividing markets into segments on the basis of consumer lifestyles is sometimes known by its grander title of 'psychographics'. It is a segmentation technique that groups consumers on the basis of their beliefs, values, interests, ambitions, fears and numerous other 'soft' factors. In common with a great deal of theory regarding age-based segmentation, many of these techniques gain their legitimacy from academic research, much of it in the area of psychology.

There are three different types of lifestyle segmentation models used to categorize older consumers, described below.

Stereotypes

A marketing agency with the unusual name The Fish Can Sing published a report entitled 'Class of 2004/05' that examined people's purchasing habits and attitudes, then used the results to segment the UK's 'middle class' into 10 groups. This type of analysis is a perfect example of lifestyle segmentation using 'stereotypes'.

In the report, the older market was divided into lifestyle segments with names such as 'The Saga Louts', 'The Fair-to-Middlings' and the 'alt-middles'. Each segment definition was a thumbnail sketch describing the likes and dislikes, ambitions, hopes and hates of each group. 'Saga Louts' (named after SAGA, the best-known company providing travel and other services to the retired) are described as people in their mid-60s who are having the time of their lives. They boast how their pensions let them live a good life and they have never been so wealthy. Typically, they live in a suburb of expensive houses, located near to their relatives. The description goes on to say how they decorate their houses, where they go on their holidays, what furniture they buy – in fact, everything you could want to know about them.

The 'Fair-to-Middlings' are a more refined group of people. They are less garish in their tastes and altogether a more respectable type of person. The 'alt-middles' can be of any age. They are cynical about most aspects of modern life, which they perceive as offering little of value.

These segment descriptions make amusing reading and have an uncanny resemblance to one's acquaintances. They are, as the dictionary definition of stereotypes says, 'An image of a person or groups based on superficial observations and experiences which reflect preconceived ideas.' Rarely is this type of segmentation accompanied by any quantification, measures of confidence or any other form of qualitative evidence. Thus, unless they are used as a starting point for a market research exercise that then validates their accuracy or otherwise, they are a potentially dangerous way to describe the older market.

Life values based on psychological models

Datamonitor, an international research company, talks about Erik Erikson's theory of the eight stages of psychosocial development when describing the marketing context of senior consumers.

This theory calls the period between 40 and 65 'middle adulthood' and it is supposedly a time when 'each adult must find some way to satisfy and support the next generation'. The final phase of life – 65 until death – is labelled 'late adulthood' and thought of as being 'The culmination in a sense of oneself as one is and of feeling fulfilled'. It is very difficult to understand how these abstract concepts become translated into factors that marketers can understand and act on.

Research company TGI, part of Millward Brown, uses the theories of Shalom Schwartz, who postulated a model of 'life values' that determine behaviour. These values can be neatly plotted in two dimensions and have abstract names such as 'benevolence' and 'hedonism'. By questioning consumers about their values and beliefs, their responses determine in which segment they belong.

TGI has translated this model and used terminology that marketers have some chance of understanding. In TGI's model, 'benevolence' becomes 'virtuous' and 'hedonism' translates to 'experiencers'. The original Schwartz and the TGI-modified models are shown in Figure 6.7.

TGI has added a ninth segment to the model (not shown) called 'Indifferent' – a group of people who are neutral about many of their values. I can think of many acquaintances who fall into this group!

The strength of this segmentation methodology is that it is based on an academically robust set of theories. What makes it relevant as a practical marketing tool is that it has been translated and extended by research, providing conclusions appropriate to the 21st-century consumer.

In his testimony to the US Senate Special Committee on Aging, the senior partner from JWT's Mature Market Group gave a succinct and powerful endorsement as to why his organization believes values are a powerful way to segment older age groups:

Schwartz's model of universal human values

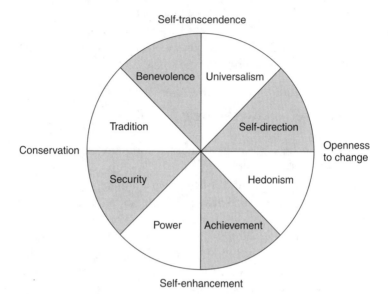

Schwartz's model of universal human values adapted by TGI

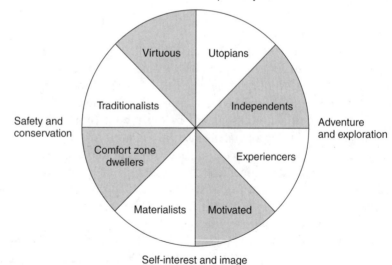

Figure 6.7   *Schwartz's model, as modified by TGI*
Source: Scwartz, 1992; TGI, 2004

Values are not held distinctly or separately, but as part of an integrated belief system, according to Schwartz. Values guide actions and judgments across situations. Attitudes and opinions, on the other hand, are 'domain specific' (beliefs about a particular object within a particular context).

Although attitudes and opinions affect behaviour, they are likely to change throughout one's lifetime. Values, on the other hand, are deeply engrained, remarkably stable, and change slowly, if at all, over the course of life. Moreover, values constructs are relatively few in number and are largely universal.

Values can be defined as (a) relatively stable thoughts or beliefs, (b) about desirable behaviours or ways of living, (c) that transcend situations, (d) guide decision making, and (e) are ordered by relative importance.

JWT has also used the concept of 'values' to derive a different set of segmentation groups. These have names such as 'Hearth and Homemakers' – people who keep their family and friends at the centre of their lives. 'In-charge Intellectuals' are people who are lifelong readers and thinkers, who keep up with change and are secure in their abilities, opinions and perceptions.

Many other research and advertising agencies have based their segmentation groups on models developed in the social and psychology departments of academia. For this research to be valid and useful, however, it must also be well founded on consumer research. The only way to judge the relative merits of these competing segmentation techniques is to look at the details of the research on which they are based and how well the techniques work in practice. There is no guarantee that a segmentation technique working in one market is proven to work in others, even though, in theory, 'values' should be market independent.

A few research companies use the respectability of academic research as a fig leaf to disguise the absence of reputable market research. A set of intriguing and exotic-sounding segment names is no substitute for demonstrable market research.

Lifestyles based on cluster research

The final method for analysing the older market using lifestyle segments is that of market research to identify clusters of consumers with similar behaviour, beliefs and attitudes. This approach does not rely on any psychological or sociological models, but is driven by the factors that determine modern consumer behaviour.

In 2004, a lifestyle research project won all of the UK's major marketing awards, including *Campaign*'s Media Award for Best Use of

Research and *Media Week*'s Research Project of the Year. What made this research project so unusual is that it was about the segmentation and behaviour of older people.

This research, 'Understanding Fifties and Over' (UFO), was a large-scale research investigation into the UK's 20 million-strong over-50s population. It involved 1,700 people aged between 45 and 89 taking part in a quantitative study. Qualitative clinics were conduced with a 100 people to understand their thoughts about brands, lifestyles and advertising. In addition, participants kept photo diaries to provide a rich insight into their lives and what they consume. The research was conducted by the media agency OMD UK in partnership with SAGA, *The Daily Telegraph* and Peugeot and was led by Jo Rigby, who contributed this book's chapter about media planning. A brief study of this project provides an excellent insight into the theory and practice of this technique of lifestyle research.

The objective of the study was to review the many beliefs about marketing to the over-50s and evaluate whether they are based on reality or simply myths and stereotypes. A subsidiary result was to create the definitive guide to the over-50s market in the UK.

Figure 6.8 shows how the UFO study was divided into seven phases of work. The output from the study was an understanding of the lifestyles and behaviour of the 1,700 people who took part in the research group and this was then related to how these affected their use of media and attitudes to different brands. After having established the outputs from the study, it

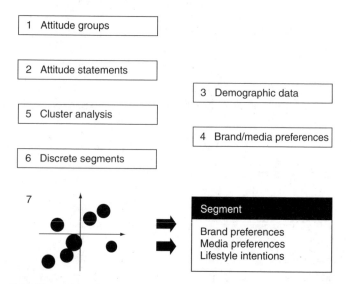

Figure 6.8 *How the UFO study was divided into seven phases of work*
Source: 20plus30, 2004

was a logical process to identify the topics that required researching. What follows is a very brief description of each of the study's phases.

Phase 1: attitude groups

A total of 30 'attitude groups' were defined to understand the beliefs and behaviour of the 1,700 research sample. These covered topics such as the attitudes to technology, holidays, fashion, brands and health. Table 6.4 shows a sample of the kinds of topics and attitudes researched.

Once these topics had been identified, it was a relatively simple job to define the details of which statements to research.

Phase 2: attitude statements

From the 30 attitude groups, 80 detailed statements were devised that formed the basis of the questionnaire. Examples of these questions, for five of the topics, are shown in Table 6.5.

The final step in the pre-research phase of the study was to expand these statements into the actual statements used in the questionnaire. So, for instance, when researching the use of technology, this topic was subdivided into different types of electronic devices. For the mobile phone, the question asked was, 'Which of these describes the way you use your

Table 6.4 *A sample of the 30 'attitude groups' tested in the UFO study*

Topic	Attitude being researched
Technology	Perception of the value of technology and readiness to use it
Internet	Levels, reasons and confidence of using the Internet
Perception of retirement	The benefits, opportunities and concerns about retirement
Role of the home	The position and pride the home occupies in their lives
Holidays	Type, regularity and importance attached to holidays
Fashion	Willingness to spend money on fashionable items
Social life	The importance and format of their social life
Brands	Importance of branded goods and their reaction to specific brands.
Politics	Views about UK politics and the country's relationship to Europe
Health & exercise	Views about health and fitness and the importance of diet and exercise

Table 6.5 *The statements used as the foundation of the UFO study's research questionnaire*

Topic	Question asked
Technology	▌ Being able to use computer technology gives me a feeling of empowerment
	▌ Technology is moving so fast I don't even bother to try to keep up
Brands	▌ It's always worth spending a bit more for the brands I want
	▌ There are not enough brands that are geared towards people like me
Holidays	▌ I like to take a risk on a new place when choosing a holiday destination
	▌ I like adventure holidays where you never know what's going to happen next
Fashion	▌ Fashion brands and labels don't really interest me
	▌ I would rather buy lots of inexpensive clothes than one expensive item
Social life	▌ I enjoy entertaining friends or family at my home
	▌ I have a very busy social life

mobile phone?' This was followed by a list of options, such as for emergencies only, work only, to help organize my social life, and so on.

The important thing about the pre-research phase was to continually refer to the desired outputs from the study to ensure that the appropriate questions were selected.

Once the research results had been collected, the next three phases of the project were conducted simultaneously. To help in explaining their purposes, they are divided into the two parts.

Phases 3 and 4: demographic data and brand preferences

The demographics of the group were analysed. Among other things, they showed that:

▌ the majority of the respondents were married (63 per cent);

▌ nearly 20 per cent of the people were in second marriages, with just over half (51 per cent) in double occupancy households and 24 per cent living alone;

▌ over 80 per cent described themselves as generally or very fit and well;

▌ data were collected on each person's brand preferences, which were aggregated together after the different lifestyle clusters had been defined.

Phase 5: cluster analysis

The research was analysed to identify clusters of responses with similar lifestyle values. From the 1,700 research sample, seven discrete groups of people were identified. Coincidentally, each cluster was approximately the same size.

Phase 6: discrete segments

The two attitude factors that best represented the differences between the groups were their degree of positive and progressive outlook to life. A matrix was constructed using these factors as the vertical and horizontal axes. Figure 6.9 shows the relative positions and sizes of the groups plotted on these two axes. The diameters of the circles indicate the relative sizes of each group.

The groups in the upper right-hand quadrant represent people with positive and progressive approaches to life – the Happy and fulfilled and Live Wires. The lower left-hand quadrant indicates a negative and conservative outlook – Anchored in the Past, for example. The Living Day-to-Day group is the largest and has a slightly negative and conservative view of life.

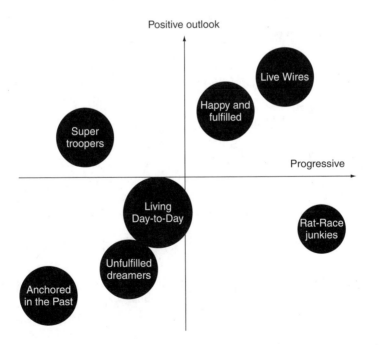

Figure 6.9 *The seven groups of people plotted according to their outlook on life*
Source: OMD, 2004

Segment descriptions

A highly abbreviated description of the characteristics of each lifestyle group is given in Table 6.6.

Details of two of the groups – the Live Wires and Anchored in the Past – are expanded and contrasted in Table 6.7. This illustrates the differences between these two very different lifestyle groups.

Anybody who lumps together the over-50s into a single homogeneous group should be forced to study the striking differences between these two groups of people. The Live Wires are positive about change and enjoying their lives. Technology is perceived as something that adds to their lives, holidays are to be planned and enjoyed, the modern world is seen as positive and not a threat. The Anchored in the Past are diametrically opposite in their views. They look back rather than forwards. Yesterday was better than today and tomorrow is expected to be even worse. They feel dislocated from technology, advertising and current fashions.

Phase 7: the results

The study's prime focus was to understand how the different groups respond to brands, technology, change and the media. Outputs from the study describing the differing media preferences of the lifestyle groups form an important part of Chapter 12.

Table 6.6 *The names and descriptions of the seven lifestyle groups*

Segment name	Description
Live Wires	Busy, health-conscious, financially sound. Enjoy holidays, cars, gadgets, clothes.
Happy and fulfilled	Financially secure, take lots of holidays. Anti-change, read broadsheets. Least influenced by ads.
Super troopers	Often lost a partner. Watching TV has become an important source of companionship.
Rat-race junkies	Still working and likely to have a second family. Financially anxious, but won't compromise on buying large ticket items like holidays.
Living Day-to-Day	Low-paid, can't afford luxuries. Are fashion-conscious and buy well-known brands.
Unfulfilled dreamers	Mixed views on advertising. Have loans, receive benefits, don't take many holidays, and are tabloid readers.
Anchored in the Past	Risk-averse, income from pensions/benefits, Little interest in holidays.

Table 6.7 *Comparison of the Live Wires and Anchored in the Past lifestyle groups*

	Live Wires	Anchored in the Past
'Pen sketch'	Have busy and fulfilling lifes. Enjoy using technology and keen to keep up to date with the latest developments. Socializing and taking holidays are very important things in their lives, as is maintaining a healthy lifestyle.	Not interested in technology, travel, fashion, decorating and healthy living. After retirement they are watching more TV and take little interest in their health. Have contempt for the active and prosperous lifestyle that others of their generation are portrayed as enjoying. In many ways have 'given up on life'.
Most likely to be:	Artistic, assertive, creative, energetic, organized, talkative and focused	Bad-tempered, miserable, moody and traditional
Least likely to be:	Bad-tempered, lazy	Artistic, assertive, flexible, spontaneous and talkative
Wishes	To be able to afford a house in South of France or a cottage by the sea, with a boat attached. To take lots of holidays and walks with spouse and friends.	That the world was a safer and better place but they are apprehensive. Having worked hard throughout their life they want to enjoy good health to make the best of their retirement.
Reaction to advertising	They have grown up in a consumerist world and are well equipped to decode rational and emotional messages. They enjoy advertising as part of the UK's creative output.	They are dislocated from the world of advertising and ill equipped to comprehend subtle messages and the emotional content of ads.
Percentage of research base	14%	13%

The variations in the responses of the groups to specific brands are illustrated in Figure 6.10. This shows the differing levels of use by the different groups of the Nokia brand. The Super troopers' reactions were the least positive and so their ranking was taken as the datum value against which the others were measured. As can be seen, the levels of use varied widely from group to group.

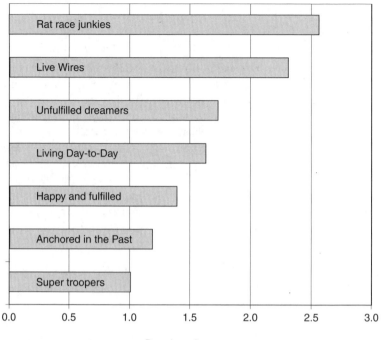

Brand use by group

Figure 6.10 *Reactions of the lifestyle groups to the Nokia brand*
Source: OMD, 2004

The groups' different responses to brands and media gives marketers vital information for improving the effectiveness of their marketing expenditure. This type of lifestyle segmentation has two great advantages over other lifestyle segmentation techniques. First, it is designed specifically for use with older consumers. Second, it has been created to deliver detailed insights into older people's attitudes to a limited number of factors, such as brands, media and technology. It is not a consumer research study that has been customized for use with older people; it has been designed with them as the focus from the start.

There are other lifestyle segmentation models. In the UK, Age Concern, working with the advertising agency TBWA, devised a system of six groups for 45–69-year-olds.

UFO was a generic study of the older age group, but the same methodology can be used to research specific industry sectors, such as finance, travel and cars. Having established the lifestyle clusters, the market research process can concentrate on establishing a detailed understanding of marketing variables such as advertising, media preferences and the dynamics of the opinion-forming process.

A significant danger of this segmentation methodology, however, is that it becomes too mechanistic and dominated by the requirements of the research company. If care is not taken, the research questions are formulated in isolation from the research sample. In simple terms, the over-50s are asked questions that the research company thinks are important. These may be very different from the issues of concern to the respondents. To ensure that this doesn't happen, it is important to conduct sufficient qualitative research to really understand how the different respondents think and behave.

Another potential weakness is that by only researching older people, you conclude that the lifestyle groups are specific to them. It may be that, for certain lifestyle groups, people aged from 30 to 60 years all share the same characteristics.

OTHER SEGMENTATION FACTORS

In addition to age and lifestyle, income, gender, geography, education and health are other ways of segmenting the over-50s market.

The same principles apply to using these factors as to any age group, but there are some special considerations to take into account with the over-50s.

Income

As discussed in Chapter 2, the difference between pre- and post-retirement income can be significant. For segmentation purposes, it is people's post-work, disposable income that is the important factor. The relative spending power of consumers is liable to be subject to significant change when work income ceases and they become reliant on pensions and savings.

Geography

A consumer's geographical location is an important element of information for the marketer. How this information is used is covered in detail in Chapter 7, which is about geodemographics.

Health

Health is a segmentation factor that has some linkage with age, lifestyle and geography. In addition to influencing a consumer's overall behaviour, it determines their demand for products and services related to the health industry. It is a notoriously difficult element of consumer information to collect.

Education

The level of formal education influences people's consumer behaviour. For example, it is one of the most important factors in determining the level of internet use. It is a difficult consumer characteristic to identify, although there is some relationship between income, geography and education.

Gender

How the ageing process affects men and women's consumer behaviour is vitally important and little understood. The common wisdom is that women have become more self-assured and positive in the way they embrace ageing. These types of observations have a horrible ring of being simplistic stereotypes, however, which they are.

There are snippets of information about older women's behaviour and attitudes that provide a patchwork of disjointed research. For instance, the Henley Centre measured people's feelings of 'well-being' and found that women from the age of 30 to 60 recorded a higher level of this feeling than men. We also know that women in their 50s are significant purchasers of consumer electronics, are more likely to holiday alone or with girlfriends than with a spouse and they use the web more than men. Unfortunately, there is little research that gives a comprehensive view of these gender differences.

For companies where older women represent an important group of customers, it would be prudent to conduct bespoke research to understand their consumer behaviour. It would be a disaster to think that today's 50-year-old women have much in common with their counterparts of two decades ago.

HOW WELL DO YOU SEGMENT THE OVER-50s MARKET?

A few simple questions are not going to reveal all the issues about how well a company segments its over-50s market. What the five questions in Table 6.8 provide is a first-level estimate. They indicate whether the segmentation model is in desperate need of attention or passes the first level of tests.

Table 6.8 *Questions for evaluating the quality of a segmentation model*

Segmentaton questions	☺ Well Done	☹ Beware!
Where age segmentation is used is the:		
oldest age category "the 50-plus"?	**NO**, the top age is when there is little further change in customers' behaviour.	**YES**, but it wasn't set at 50+ for any particular reason.
'grey market' market defined as starting at 50?	**NO**, we do not make a distinction between old and young markets.	**YES**
number of years in each age range set arbitrarily?	**NO**, they are set as the result of market research.	**YES**, they were set in 10-year increments.
Does the market segmentation drive all of marketing's activities?	**YES**, our segmentation drives all aspects of our marketing.	**NO**, we only use it to guide our use of creative and media planning.
Do you have a high level of confidence that the characteristics of the segments represent today's over-50s?	**YES**, we regularly check the behaviours we attribute to our segments are correct.	**NO**, they have not been re-evaluated since originally established.
Are segments adequately differentiated from each other?	**YES**, segment differences justify separate marketing campaigns.	**MAYBE**, they haven't been researched or tested to know for certain.
Are lifestyle segments are arbitrarily defined by the age of the people researched.	**NO**, our research covered a full range of ages and did not start at 50.	**YES**, we assigned life-style segments after just researching the age range of 50 and above.

The final statement about the subject of segmentation is important, obvious and too often ignored. For market segmentation to deliver value, it must be accurate, usable and be used. This applies to every age group.

IMPLICATIONS FOR THE MARKETER

A segmentation model is only of value if it can assist marketing decisions and drive marketing activities.

! Whatever type of segmentation is being used, two things are of para-
* mount importance. First, tactically, how can the segments be applied, and second, what level of confidence can be attributed to findings.

Irrespective of the segmentation theory and the definitions of the segments, they must be based on evidence, not conjecture and stereotypes.

! There are numerous market segmentation models aimed at the older
* market. They all attribute amusing and exotic-sounding names to the segments and paint convincing thumbnail sketches of the segment types. The thing that differentiates the models is the extent of current market research that supports their conclusions.

The characteristics of market segments change and must be regularly re-evaluated.

! When comparing competing segmentation models, check how
* frequently the segment characteristics are re-evaluated using marketing research.

The age 50 is an artificially defined moment in time with no significance other than what society attributes. It has no value in defining the demarcation between different groups of consumers.

! Any segmentation system that uses the age of 50 to determine the
* boundary between different groups of people is suspect.

Cognitive, eyesight, hearing and dexterity deterioration are related to age. The effects of ageing should determine the design and use of marketing channels, especially those using technology.

! Interactive channels, particularly the web and e-mail marketing,
• must be designed to take account of age-related deterioration and
health issues.

Cognitive, eyesight, hearing and dexterity deterioration are related to age.
Age is also associated with a range of illnesses. The effects of ageing
creates the need for new products and services to meet the requirements of
older consumers.

! Products and services should be designed around the physical capa-
• bilities of their users.

Geodemographics is the study of the relationship between age, household
address and consumer behaviour. It is a powerful technique for
segmenting markets and driving direct marketing campaigns.

! Geodemographics should be investigated as a means of segmenting
• and directing communications to older people.

Perceived – rather than chronological – age determines consumer behaviour.

! There are no scientific ways of determining the differences between
• perceived and chronological ages, but the idea of the two ages is an
important marketing concept, especially when considering an advertising creative.

Because age is a good way to segment customers in one market, it cannot
be assumed that it will be equally successful in another, even if the
customers are the same people.

! The safest approach is to assume that segmentation models are not
• transferable between markets until proved by research.

Age segments that are relevant to the indigenous population might be
useless when applied to ethnic minority groups.

! When a market has a significant number of ethnic groups, the
• difference this makes to the age profile and the assumed behaviour
of the segments must be evaluated.

The only way to judge the relative merits of competing segmentation techniques is to look at the details of the research base and how well the techniques work in practice.

! Does the segmentation model work in practice? This is the only
● determining factor when evaluating different models. The academic
   pedigree of the model is a secondary factor.

All segmentation techniques risk becoming too mechanistic and unduly
influenced by the requirements and mindset of the company rather than
the consumer.

! Any segmentation model must be based on a qualitative research
● exercise to understand the issues, language, behaviour, priorities and
   concerns of the older audience.

All segmentation techniques risk defining segments as being specific to
'older people' when, in fact, the same behaviour applies equally to young
age groups.

! When reviewing lifestyle segmentation models, find out whether the
● lower age of the research sample was set for a market-related reason
   or one of convenience.

The relative spending power of consumers is liable to significant change
when work income ceases and they become reliant on pensions and
savings.

! When using income as a segmentation factor, it should be the level
● of disposable income after retirement that is the starting point.

There is anecdotal evidence and piecemeal research to suggest that
women's behaviour changes more during their 50s and 60s than that of
men.

! If older women represent an important group of customers, it is
● prudent to conduct bespoke research to understand their consumer
   behaviour.

SUMMARY

▋ Rarely do textbooks about marketing segmentation explore how it is applied to older people. Unfortunately, when they do, many of the conclusions reached are of dubious value.

▋ Market segmentation divides consumers into smaller groupings of like-minded individuals to create better consumer strategies, leading to better research, product development and communications. In short, all aspects of marketing improve by a better understanding and focus on the customer.

▋ The exercise of segmenting the market creates significant traps that marketers must avoid. It is easy to become preoccupied with the process of segmentation and lose sight of applying its outputs. The characteristics of segments are often treated as being fixed and unchanging. They are not.

▋ The differences in consumers' behaviour that determines market segments should be based on evidence rather than myth and stereotypes. Too often it is not.

▋ There is no magical significance to the age of 50 as the demarcation point when a company's market is defined as 'grey', 'mature', 'senior' or whatever other name you care to apply. The age 50 is an artificially defined moment in time, with no significance other than what society attributes.

▋ The great attraction of using age as a means of segmenting the over-50s is that it is simple. The trouble is that it is also simplistic. Some of the problems of basing marketing decisions on a consumer's age are that there are:
- differences between actual and perceived age – older people make decisions based on the age they feel rather than the age on their birth certificates;
- doubts that it has value in predicting peoples' behaviour as consumers;
- distortions created by the different age profiles of ethnic minorities.

Age is used in half a dozen ways to relate a person's age to behaviour. All of these variations rely on 'knowing' that a consumer in age range X has Y-type behaviour.

▌ Defining different kinds of behaviour might result from bespoke research. It might result from referencing academic models that link age with types of behaviour, such as generational segmentation – for example, baby boomers, Generation X and so on.

▌ Another popular technique is to relate age to the major events in the older person's life – most importantly, when they retire.

▌ Age might be problematic as a predictor of behaviour, but it is useful in understanding both the physical and cognitive problems associated with getting old. It is important to understand the decline in eyesight, dexterity, hearing and mental processes, especially when designing interactive marketing channels.

▌ It is the tenuous relationship between age and behaviour that makes age segmentation so problematic.

▌ Grouping consumers by their lifestyles and behaviour is the other main method of segmentation. There are three ways in which this is achieved.

  – The least useful is when segments are defined according to popular myth and stereotypes without reference to any market research. They create caricatures of people that make amusing reading but are next to useless as a means of driving marketing activity.

  – Another form of lifestyle segmentation is one based on the theories of sociologists and psychologists such as Shalom Schwartz, Erik Erikson and Abraham Maslow. The concepts of the 'hierarchy of needs' and 'universal values' are translated into 21st-century marketing-speak and supplemented by consumer research.

  – The final type of lifestyle segmentation is one that is based on classical market research that investigates specific aspects of consumer behaviour. The objective of this research is not to uncover any universal truths, but to answer questions about the ways in which older people behave in relation to today's marketing issues. Subjects such as brand preferences, the use of different types of media and attitudes to using technology are the kinds of areas that are researched.

▌ In addition to age and lifestyle, the traditional forms of segmentation also apply to the over-50s market. Segmentation factors such as income, gender, geography, education and health are used. The same principles apply to using these factors as would to any other age group, but there are some special considerations to take into account with the over-50s. For example, when segmenting by income, there is little point in using the pre-retirement income, as once people are reliant on pensions and savings, their relative wealth levels can change radically. As people get older, their household location is more important as a means of predicting their lifestyle than income alone.

▌ How the ageing process affects men and women's consumer behaviour is vitally important and little understood. The anecdotal evidence suggests that the women experience a greater degree of change than men. Certainly, if older women represent an important group of customers, then their consumer behaviour should be researched.

▌ The final statement to make about segmentation is important, obvious but too often ignored. For market segmentation to deliver value, it must be:
  – accurate;
  – usable;
  – used.

The value of geodemographics

Geodemographics allows marketers to use a person's postal address to predict their consumer behaviour. The technique is especially applicable to the over-50s and provides marketers with a means of both segmenting their markets and driving direct marketing campaigns.

Because of the subject's importance and specialist nature, I wanted a world-class authority to write this chapter. Richard Webber is a visiting Professor at the Centre for Advanced Spatial Analysis at University College London. He is one of the world's leading experts on the theory and application of geodemographics and kindly agreed to share his knowledge in this chapter.

QUALITATIVE RESEARCH AND GEODEMOGRAPHICS

Qualitative research provides marketers with valuable insights into how the over-50s are likely to respond to specific product propositions or styles of communication. Marketers use its findings when developing new product and service strategies, deciding which communication channels to use and considering their overall advertising strategy. Qualitative research is equally relevant to the design of direct marketing copy and the scripts used in telephone call centres. Data collected on media preferences are valuable in the media planning process.

Where qualitative research has less value is in determining a segmentation strategy to be used with an address file of prospects or existing customers. This section explains how geodemographics can extrapolate the findings of research based on a very small number of representative consumers across the universe of all households. This provides marketers with the means for using a geographically based segmentation strategy to guide their use of local communication channels.

For organizations targeting the over-50s, it permits using postal addresses to determine the probability that each consumer on a prospect and customer list or each website visitor or each caller to a call centre is likely to be aged over-50 and belong to a particular segment. How is it possible to know if he or she is a professional, on the cusp of retirement, one of a retired couple living on a modest pension in a seaside community, a wealthy person who lives in the country or a poor and frail tenant living in sheltered accommodation?

Developed simultaneously in the US and the UK in the late 1970s, geodemographic classifications use a combination of census and other neighbourhood statistics to classify every consumer into a market according to the type of residential neighbourhood in which they live.

Such classifications have been commercialized in some 20 countries around the world, mostly by specialist international operators such as Claritas in the US and Experian in Europe. In larger markets, such as the US, they place consumers in as many as 60 different types of neighbourhood. In smaller markets, such as New Zealand or the Republic of Ireland, only 30 neighbourhood types are used. These categories are given labels to describe the prevailing demographics and attitudes. For example, the UK's Mosaic category J51 is titled 'Sepia Memories' and consists of postcodes containing very old but wealthy people living alone in private apartments. The US's PRIZM category 'Hard Scrabble' consists of zip+4 codes that contain low-income farmers, predominantly in the southern states.

Although the classifications are customized to the specific demographics of each market, it would be surprising if there were not a number of types of neighbourhoods that occur in more than one country. For example, estates of large, new, privately owned detached houses that are attractive to young families, rural areas and coastal retirement communities are three types of neighbourhood that occur in almost every country.

This has led Experian, the coordinator of the international network of the Mosaic geodemographic classifications systems, to establish 'Global Mosaic'. This is a common set of 11 general geodemographic classifications that provides a framework into which the detailed geodemographic classes specific to each national market can be placed. Global Mosaic reserves specific classifications for neighbourhoods of both high- and low-income elderly.

The purpose of a geodemographic classification is both to profile and to reach target markets. For instance, when conducting a market survey, the classification that best describes a respondent's neighbourhood can be added to the survey database. This enables the results of the survey to be cross-tabulated by types of neighbourhood. For instance, if the survey is researching consumers' attitudes to a company's brand, then it is possible to identify the types of neighbourhood – and hence, by implication, the postcodes throughout the country – where consumers' attitudes towards that brand are most likely to be favourable.

Alternatively, the type of neighbourhood where a customer lives can be inferred directly from the postcode of their address and can be added as an extra field within the customer database. This allows companies to identify the types of neighbourhood that generate their largest numbers of customers and produce the most profit. The same principle applies to analysing the costs of service, loyalty, credit and insurance risk by neighbourhood.

Reader's Digest and American Express are examples of international companies using geodemographics to improve response rates to cold prospect mailings. Most major UK high street banks also use geodemographics as one of the many inputs for the statistical models that evaluate the creditworthiness of potential new clients. It is also used to set credit limits for existing customers. Telecommunication companies use geodemographics as a factor in calculating the potential lifetime value for both new and existing subscribers. Political parties in both the US and the UK are heavy users of these segmentations systems as a means of targeting key voters at election time.

Irrespective of whether or not an organization uses external survey data or internal behavioural information to profile its market, geodemographics provides a highly effective way in which to augment its segmentation strategy.

SEGMENTING OLDER CONSUMERS

Geodemographic classifications often highlight subtle but important distinctions within the older consumer community. Table 7.1 defines the nine distinctive types of residential environment where older people are disproportionately concentrated together that are used in Experian's UK Mosaic classification. Also shown is the size of each segment in the UK

Table 7.1 *Examples of Experian's UK Mosaic consumer segments with a high proportion of older people*

% of UK pop.	Aged 65–84	Aged 85+	Aged 65+	Mosaic's segment definitions
0.51	35.6	11.6	47.7	*J51 Sepia Memories* – Sepia Memories accommodates very old people living in private flats, often by the seaside. Most have enough money to be able afford most of the products and services that they need or would like. At this stage in life, personal contact and the trustworthiness of contacts take precedence over impersonal forms of advice.
1.14	35.3	4.3	39.6	*J54 Bungalow Retirement* – Bungalow Retirement tend to be older married couples who have retired to seaside bungalows from metropolitan suburbs. Postmodern advertising is seen as being irrelevant and few can be bothered with the sophisticated lifestyle nuances that appeal to younger conspicuous consumers or inner-city singles. This population likes advertising to be factual statements with clearly explained benefits.
1.08	28.8	4.9	33.7	*J53 High-spending Elders* – High-spending Elders tend to be fit and wealthy married couples who have retired to the seaside or country. They have conservative values but, in their professional lives, have often had to learn the art of compromise with people of different opinions in order to secure advancement or agreement. While meticulous appearance and good order are key values, the modern generation of wealthy pensioners is not averse to adventure or risk and many still enjoy active sports.
0.22	25.2	5.3	30.5	*J56 Tourist Attendants* – Tourist Attendants tend to be older people who live in areas of high landscape value, many of whom run tourist businesses. They assume the values of their clientele and many small proprietors may have moved to these neighbourhoods in middle age to set up their businesses, perhaps because they have enjoyed visiting the area in earlier years.

% of UK pop.	Aged 65–84	Aged 85+	Aged 65+	Mosaic's segment definitions
1.08	21.3	5.4	26.7	*J52 Child-free Serenity* – Child-free Serenity contains a mix of very old and younger people living in smart, urban, private flats. They share a common preference for planning, good order and smart appearance. Residents are not necessarily concerned about the personalization of the products that they buy, but are prepared to pay premium prices for brands of higher quality.
2.42	20.9	3.6	24.5	*J55 Small Town Seniors* – Small Town Seniors are mostly older people who live close to the centres of small market towns. With their low earnings and older age profiles, these neighbourhoods attach a lower priority to material possessions than to satisfying social relationships within the local community. People find it particularly difficult to relate to the more sophisticated nuances of lifestyle imagery that they associate with big cities, which they rarely visit.
0.43	43.7	10.1	53.8	*I48 Old People in Flats* – Old People in Flats live on little money in social housing, often in inner cities. They cannot afford to buy the products they see advertised on their televisions, which they watch for much of the day. They do not belong to the generations who have been able to determine their own destiny. Few have had the opportunity to save.
1.13	28.1	5.5	33.6	*I49 Low-income Elderly* – Low-income Elderly tend to live in low-rise estates of social housing. They mostly share conservative values, with an emphasis on sobriety, self-reliance and careful spending. These are not people who are in a position to take risks and few would wish to do so if they could.
1.02	23.0	4.5	27.5	*I50 Cared for Pensioners* – Cared for Pensioners tend to live in sheltered accommodation maintained by local councils. They contain a population that is old-fashioned in its attitudes and conservative in its tastes. Most people of this generation have memories of the hardships associated with the inter-war Depression and are understandably cautious spenders of what little money they have.
9.03*	14.7	2.1	16.8	Total/average for the UK

*The percentages these segments represent are of the total UK population.

population, plus the percentages of their population aged over-65 and over-85.

These segments are of two broad kinds. First, they identify, housing specifically built for the elderly by local authorities, whether in the form of sheltered homes, bungalows or flats in small developments (Types I48–I50). Second, they identify neighbourhoods that are especially popular with retirees. Typically, these are private flats in managed developments in cities, coastal retirement communities and environmentally attractive, semi-tourist locations favoured by the wealthier and fitter newly retired (Types J51–J56).

The statistics for the number of over-85s in the 'Sepia Memories' category show the concentration of older people present in these neighbourhood segments. At the time of the 2001 census, this age category represented 2.1 per cent of the UK population, yet it accounts for 11.6 per cent of the population in this neighbourhood segment.

A great many of the elderly geodemographic segments are found in coastal locations. This is can be seen from the maps in Figure 7.1, which show the locations of the parliamentary constituencies (electoral divisions) in England and Wales that have the highest proportions of their populations living in the 'Sepia Memories' and 'Small Town Seniors' neighbourhoods. These are shaded according to the percentages of their populations falling into each type of neighbourhood. The darker the colour, the higher the density of the population in this category. The southern coast of England, from Plymouth to Southend-on-Sea, shows a high concentration of both types of neighbourhoods.

It is relatively easy to see how this segmentation technique can be used to target different types of products and services. For example, the segment 'Bungalow Retirement' is a better prospect for cruises than it is for chair lifts. 'Sepia Memories', because of its very elderly but wealthy widows living in leasehold flats, is a better prospect for investment advice than for holidays. 'High-spending Elders' are particularly good prospects for home improvement products, as well as independent overseas travel. Such differences in opportunities are the result of differences in factors as varied as household income, house tenure, level of infirmity and building type.

People in each geodemographic segment vary not just in terms of the value of their assets, the level of their expenditure and how they spend their money, but also exhibit very different channel preferences. While, on average, those aged over-50 are less likely to use a personal computer, 'High-spending Elders' are much more active users of the internet than those in the 'Bungalow Retirement' segment. By contrast, residents in 'Bungalow Retirement' are heavy users of mail order, while 'Small Town

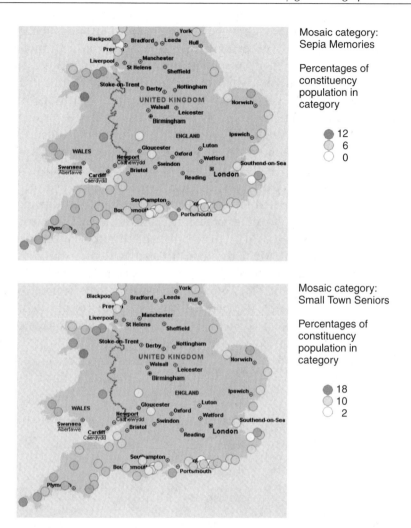

Figure 7.1 *Density of 'Sepia Memories' and 'Small Town Seniors' in UK parliamentary constituencies*

Seniors' attach a particularly high importance to personal contact and consider visits to local, well-known shops to be as much social as economic transactions.

A key factor when selling to the upmarket 'Sepia Memories' and low-income 'Cared for Pensioners' is that they have reached a stage in their lives when key decisions are often made on their behalf, whether by wardens in their residential homes or sons and daughters.

Although neighbourhood classifications, by their nature, are not built on attitudinal data, they often identify important attitudinal differences between the clusters. Research suggests that a major motivation for people moving to 'Bungalow Retirement' from their homes in metropolitan suburbs is their lack of engagement with their local community and even with their immediate family. Motivations for the move are to spend time with people of a similar generation who share the same social and political views. An additional motivation is the desire to escape the confusion and diversity of 'big city living'. By contrast, 'High-spending Elders' and 'Tourist Attendants' are motivated to move to places that exhibit stronger community ties and deliver high landscape or environmental quality. Such people often become local leaders in their own community and seek to engage across both age and income groups, deliberately not wanting to live in a retirement 'ghetto' or be treated by marketers as 'old people'.

Figure 7.2 illustrates the differences in the age distributions for two of Mosaic's types – 'Sepia Memories' and 'Bungalow Retirement'. In this figure, the horizontal axis measures age in five-year bands from 20–24 on the left to 90+ on the right. The vertical axis represents the extent to which each age group is more or less concentrated in that type of neighbourhood compared with the country as a whole. A level of 100 indicates a concentration of the group equivalent to the average for the UK.

As the line rises, the neighbourhood becomes a net importer of that age group. By contrast, a downward-sloping line indicates either a net

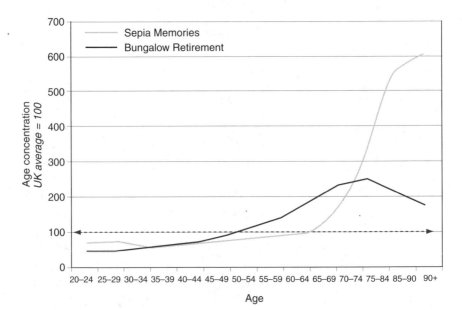

Figure 7.2 *Age distribution of the Mosaic 'Sepia Memories' and 'Bungalow Retirement' neighbourhood types*

migration of that age group or a higher than average level of mortality. In both neighbourhood categories, there is a positive gradient after the age of 50, indicating a net inwards migration above that age. It is interesting to observe that for 'Sepia Memories', the steepest gradient of the line, where inward migration is the greatest, is over the age of 70. By contrast, the steepest gradient for 'Bungalow Retirement' is around retirement age. Indeed, there seems to be a net outward migration from 'Bungalow Retirement' at the very oldest age bands as they move home when they reach really old age, often migrating to 'Sepia Memories' neighbourhoods.

Many residents in the cluster 'Small Town Seniors' perceive living in a socially mixed community as a positive benefit. These tend to be people who have lived in their homes for very many years, are well known to many in their local communities and appreciate the physical proximity of where they live to shops, churches, community centres and other places of social interaction. By contrast, the motivation for many of those living in 'Old People in Flats' neighbourhoods is simply to survive. These are areas where old people are poorly integrated into the local community and most dependent on support from local government care services.

The descriptions of people in all of these neighbourhood clusters are, in the language of sociology, 'ideal types'. Not everyone in these neighbourhoods is aged over-50 and of those who are, not all will conform to these stereotypes. Indeed, the majority of people aged over-50 live in neighbourhoods where older people are not in a majority. Nevertheless, the range of consumers who are covered by these segments helps marketers to avoid the trap of thinking that all older people are essentially similar in needs and attitudes. Likewise, when applying targeting to direct channels, it is possible to select prospects for a campaign according to the probability of the message being relevant to its recipients. There are few certainties in marketing, but this technique helps increase the probability of success by targeting the right type of older person.

A measure of the potential savings from using geodemographics is illustrated the following two statistics. Divide the UK into two markets of equal population size. One group contains postcodes in geodemographic clusters with above average proportions of the over-65s. The other contains clusters with below average proportions of the over-65s. The first group would contain two-thirds of all the UK's over-65s – twice that of the second. Alternatively, if a marketer ranks the geodemographic clusters by percentages of people aged over-65, then they can reach 50 percent of those aged 65+ by targeting only one-third of the country's population. This level of targeting effectiveness increases considerably if the target market is restricted to people aged over-75 or if additional segmentation factors are added, such as wealth or income.

THE FORMATION OF 'GREY' NEIGHBOURHOODS

These UK differences match up to a greater or lesser degree with the patterns evident in other countries. Indeed, one of the strengths of geo-demographic classifications is that they reveal how much more dependent on cultural factors some patterns are than others. The US, Australia and New Zealand are examples of other markets where there is a strong tendency for older people to segregate themselves geographically. In these markets, where the ties of the extended family are relatively weak, retirement is an opportunity to relocate to one's 'ideal' community, whether by the ocean, in the green mountains or, indeed, in age-based gated communities built around physical security and common lifestyle interests.

Table 7.2 shows the different types of neighbourhoods in the US containing high concentrations of elderly people. These have been provided by Claritas and illustrate the US PRIZM consumer segments. There are some similarities and some differences between the US and the UK. For example, the segment 'Sunset City Blues' is very similar in character to the UK type 'Small Town Seniors'. As in the UK, there are both upmarket and downmarket neighbourhoods of old people. There are two big differences, however, between the two markets in terms of where old people concentrate. First, despite the attractions of Florida and California, the coast is much less of a magnet for affluent retirees in the US than it is in the UK. In the US, prosperous pensioners, seeking to live among similar people, are much more likely to seek out suburban neighbourhoods than in the UK. The second big contrast is in the circumstances of the poor elderly person. In the UK, many of these people live in sheltered or purpose-built accommodation rented from their local State authority. Their American counterparts are more likely to rent private apartments from private landlords in downtown areas.

In these markets there is a strong link between fashions in tourism and retirement. In the UK, most coastal retirement resorts lie close to what, in earlier times, were the principal destinations for holiday travel. As cars liberated holidaymakers from locations served by coaches and railways and as self-catering holidays increased in popularity, rural destinations became attractive alternatives to classic seaside resorts. This was especially true for the more affluent. Retirement flows soon reflected this change, with country cottages in areas of high amenity value replacing bungalow estates as sought-after retirement destinations.

Today, as cheap flights and rented cars open up mainland Europe as a holiday destination, people who have regularly holidayed in rural and

Table 7.2 *Examples of Claritas' PRIZM® NE consumer segments with a high proportion of older people*

% of US pop.	Aged 65–84	Aged 85+	Aged 65+	US's PRIZM segment definitions
0.87	21.05	4.17	25.22	*Grey Power* – The steady rise in numbers of older, healthier Americans over the past decade has produced one important byproduct: middle-class, home-owning suburbanites who are ageing in place rather than moving to retirement communities. Grey Power reflects this trend – a segment of older, midscale singles and couples who live in quiet comfort.
2.25	19.73	3.04	22.77	*Simple Pleasures* – With more than two-thirds of its residents over 65 years old, Simple Pleasures is mostly a retirement lifestyle: a neighbourhood of lower-middle-class singles and couples living in modestly priced homes. Many are high-school-educated seniors who held blue-collar jobs before their retirement. A disproportionate number served in the military – no segment has more members of veterans' clubs.
1.15	14.26	2.48	16.74	*Close-in Couples* – Close-in Couples is a group of predominantly older, African-American couples living in older homes in the urban neighbourhoods of mid-sized metros. High-school-educated and empty nesters, these 55-year-old-plus residents typically live in older city neighbourhoods, enjoying secure and comfortable retirements.
1.54	16.77	2.79	19.56	*Sunset City Blues* – Scattered throughout the older neighbourhoods of small cities, Sunset City Blues is a segment of lower-middle-class singles and couples who have retired or are getting close to it. These empty nesters tend to own their homes, but have modest educations and incomes. They maintain a low-key lifestyle filled with newspapers and television by day and family-style restaurants at night.

% of US pop.	Aged 65–84	Aged 85+	Aged 65+	US's PRIZM segment definitions
0.86	16.62	4.05	20.67	*Old Glories* – Old Glories are the nation's downscale suburban retirees, Americans ageing in place in older apartment complexes. These racially mixed households often contain widows and widowers living on fixed incomes and they tend to lead home-centred lifestyles. They're among the nation's most ardent television fans, watching game shows, soaps, talk shows and news magazines at high rates.
1.14	22.41	4.14	26.55	*Golden Ponds* – Golden Ponds is mostly a retirement lifestyle, dominated by downscale singles and couples over 65 years old. Found in small bucolic towns around the country, these high-school-educated seniors live in small apartments on less than $25,000 a year; one in five resides in a nursing home. For these elderly residents, daily life is often a succession of sedentary activities, such as reading, watching TV, playing bingo and doing craft projects.
0.93	16.06	4.18	20.24	*Park Bench Seniors* – Park Bench Seniors are typically retired singles living in the racially mixed neighbourhoods of the nation's satellite cities. With modest educations and incomes, these residents maintain low-key, sedentary lifestyles. Theirs is one of the top-ranked segments for TV viewing, especially daytime soaps and game shows.
1.19	14.59	2.64	17.23	*City Roots* – Found in urban neighbourhoods, City Roots is a segment of lower-income retirees, typically living in older homes and duplexes they've owned for years. In these ethnically diverse neighbourhoods – more than a third are African-American and Hispanic – residents are often widows and widowers living on fixed incomes and maintaining low-key lifestyles.
1.07	16.12	2.96	19.08	*Hometown Retired* – With three-quarters of all residents over 65 years old, Hometown Retired is one of the oldest segments. These racially mixed seniors tend to live in ageing homes – half were built before 1958 – and typically get by on social security and modest pensions. Because most never made it beyond high school and spent their working lives at blue-collar jobs, their retirements are extremely modest.
11.27*	1.07	1.07	1.07	Total/average for the US

*The percentages of these segments are of the total population of the US.

coastal Europe are now increasingly retiring to France and Spain. By contrast, in Mediterranean countries, where it is the family that has traditionally played a more important role in supporting older people than in the UK or the US, there is less house movement on reaching retirement. Neighbourhoods of old people – in particular of people aged over-50 – are less associated with the coast and more with the depopulated countryside, from which the young have migrated to urban centres. Likewise, in much of southern Europe, as well as the parts of the UK where coalmining was the principle occupation, concentrations of old people are associated with declining communities that historically were dependent on heavy industry.

In Third World countries, where geodemographic classifications are available, the person's wealth is the most important factor determining their geographical distribution.

APPLYING GEODEMOGRAPHICS

Geodemographic classifications are used to improve marketing decisions about target audiences and drive local media channels. For example, in the 1970s and for much of the 1980s, most national retail chains adopted a similar trading model across the country – stocking a uniform set of products, selling at the same prices and promoting in the same way. Current retail practice, however, is to apply geographic segmentation to determine what products to stock and optimize the prices charged. Today, most major supermarket chains, banks, pharmacies, department stores and motor distributors use data about their geographical catchment areas to determine their merchandise and local marketing strategies. The presence of the over-50s in these catchment areas is a key consideration when customizing retail outlets, whether in terms of how customers are served, promotions, prices, pack sizes and brands stocked.

The neighbourhood cluster can be further divided into 'bricks', which are units in the hierarchy of postal geography. These can be used to determine the household locations for door-to-door leaflet distribution. An example would be a campaign to sell car insurance to people over 50. A 'door drop' can be delivered by national distribution companies exclusively to those 'bricks' containing the highest proportions of households owning a car and people of the right age.

Political parties, cable TV operators and catalogue mail-order companies have all successfully used geodemographic data to create 'canvass guides' for their door-to-door salesforces or, in the case of political parties, canvass teams. These 'guides' list the streets and the house ranges to include and those to exclude from a campaign. They are organized to include those streets with the highest proportions of households conforming to types of behaviour known from analysis to generate the best response.

The media that can target households includes direct mail, telephone selling and leaflet distribution. SAGA, the UK's best-known company targeting the over-50s market for its travel and insurance products and its magazine, is one of Britain's largest users of direct mail, contacting many millions of people each year. Although SAGA is able to access precisely by name many millions of respondents to lifestyle survey questionnaires, these names represent only 25 per cent of its target population defined solely by age. In order to contact people who fall within its target age group most efficiently, SAGA uses the Mosaic geodemographic classification to focus on those Mosaic neighbourhood types most likely to be aged over-50.

Privacy issues are deterring companies from communicating with customers and asking for personal information. Many businesses, such as banks and credit card operators, have already captured the ages of their customers. Many have not. Appending a geodemographic classification to a customer's record provides an inexpensive, efficient and unobtrusive way to increase knowledge of their likely life stage and level of affluence. This is done without having to contact the customer and ask for sensitive information.

SYSTEMS FOR PREDICTING AGE

In the UK, it is possible to statistically predict the ages of people by using publicly available sources of information. The UK is divided into geographic regions for the purpose of political elections. Each region has an electoral register that contains information about the people in that region who are eligible to vote. This information includes the first (given) name of the elector and their partner and the number of years that they have been recorded on the electoral roll at their current address. It is possible to predict the person's age using these two pieces of information.

There are some first names, such as John, that never go out of fashion. There are many more that have been fashionable for only a limited period of time. People with the name 'Percy' or 'Jean' are most likely to have been born in or around the 1920s, so their most likely age in 2004 was around 80. By contrast, people called 'Kevin' are mostly aged under 50 and those named 'Jason' are mostly aged under 30. In general, the fashion for girls' names is more volatile than it is for boys' names.

The reliability of the age estimate can be improved by taking into account both male and female names where both occur against the same surname at the same address. For example, a 'John Smith' living with a 'Jean Smith' is much more likely to be aged over 50 than one living with a 'Jade Smith'. Further improvements in the reliability of the age prediction can be achieved by taking into account the number of years the person has been included on the electoral roll at that address. Given that people cannot be registered on the electoral roll until they are 18 and young people are more mobile than old people, it is likely that a 'John Smith' who has been living with a 'Susan Smith' for 11 or more years at the same address will be older than two people with the same names who have just appeared on the roll living at that address. It is equally the case that a John Smith living alone is, on balance, likely to be younger than the John Smith living with Susan Smith.

Table 7.3 illustrates the level of accuracy that can be achieved when predicting a person's age from this information alone. The table was constructed by comparing the actual ages of over 1,000,000 respondents to UK lifestyle surveys with the estimates of their ages generated by the predictive model. The figures on the diagonal show the percentage of respondents in each band whose ages were correctly predicted by the model.

Table 7.3 *Matrix showing how knowing a person's first name assists in predicting their age*

		Actual age					
		18–24	25–34	35–44	45–54	55–64	65+
Estimated age	18–25	78%					
	26–35		61%				
	36–45			60%			
	46–55				70%		
	56–65					53%	
	66+						71%

Combining the items of information – a person's name, a partner's name, years at address and household composition – with the type of neighbourhood they live in enables suppliers of geodemographics services to provide a surprisingly accurate tool for applying segmentation strategies to the media that operate at the level of the individual person. It is this technology rather than neighbourhood classification alone that is at the heart of SAGA's targeting success.

GOVERNMENT – THE FINAL FRONTIER?

Traditionally, government has been slow to recognize the merits of applying segmentation to its own communications, relying instead on either broadcast media or direct mail.

A good example of how geodemographics could improve the way in which government communicates with older people is provided by the work one of the UK's police regions. Devon and Cornwall police is responsible for policing a number of affluent coastal retirement communities, many of whose residents are recent migrants from other parts of the UK. A continuing problem in these retirement areas is the activity of burglars masquerading as meter readers working for the gas and electricity utilities. To counter this threat, the police originally mounted a series of promotional campaigns to inform residents of the potential threats. These involved the use of poster sites, selected at random, and press coverage in regional newspapers.

Subsequently, local police analysts recognized that a far better way to reach those at risk was to use geodemographics to target their communications. The households at greatest risk reside in 'Bungalow Retirement' neighbourhoods. They found that a far more effective way of reaching this vulnerable group than the previously used methods was to use a combination of door-to-door canvassing, leaflet distribution and direct mail – all driven according to this single geodemographic cluster. A classic case of the rifle being better than the shotgun!

THE CHANGING PROFILE OF GEODEMOGRAPHIC CLUSTERS

Clearly the pattern of residential segmentation among older people is not fixed but subject to a number of social and economic trends. It is difficult to forecast the overall effects of these changes, but easy to identify the factors most likely to have an impact.

Perhaps the most predictable is the declining status of traditional coastal retirement neighbourhoods. A combination of cheap travel, familiarity with overseas tourist destinations and the improved health of early retirees reduces the attraction of urban seaside resorts as a location for retirement.

In the US in particular, but to a significant though lesser degree in the UK and Australia, retired people will increasingly be attracted to developments specifically created for their needs, whether gated communities, lifestyle or resort communities or even urban developments designed specifically for older people.

The falling birthrates and increasing proportion of older people in Mediterranean and Central Europe may well diminish the strength of extended family networks and lead to a greater willingness of older people to migrate shortly before or after retirement, as in the US and the UK. This is likely to be encouraged by the growth of multicultural populations, congestion and crime in Europe's larger cities.

Patterns of movement on retirement will also inevitably be affected by changes in the relative affluence of older people relative to those of working age. Factors contributing to this change are, in Australia and the UK, rapid increases in residential property values and, throughout all industrialized nations, the declining value of pensions resulting from a period of lower interest rates and increased life expectancy.

IMPLICATIONS FOR THE MARKETER

Geodemographics can be used to describe the characteristics of consumers in the catchment areas of retail outlets. The promotion and merchandising of retail outlets can be optimized for the types of consumers in their local market. The accuracy can be enhanced by combining trading data from other outlets with similar geodemographic segments.

! There is a global set of geodemographics segments that apply to older people. If a marketing strategy extends over multiple countries, there is the potential to use the same global geodemographic segments.

In some countries, peoples' ages can be predicted by combining geodemographic segmentation with publicly available information. In the UK, this data can be gleaned from the electoral register. If the age of consumers is an important marketing factor, then this technique provides a powerful way to predict its value.

! Geodemographics segmentation improves the accuracy of commu-
• nication channels that target individual households, such as direct mail, mail drops, telesales and so on. For direct marketers, geodemographics is a powerful tool for creating a household-based communication strategy. It can be used for both the planning and the implementation of the strategy.

Geodemographics improves the quality of the knowledge about people by using their postal addresses to predict their life stage and style of consumer behaviour. Postal addresses can be used to provide a simple way of predicting the behaviour and life stage of older consumers. Its great strength is that it is not invasive of people's privacy.

! Further, the value of qualitative market research can be extended by
• using the respondents' postal addresses. Having identified their geodemographic segments, these can be used to extrapolate more from the research findings.

As the age of people increases, so does the accuracy of using geodemographic forecasting. There is not a direct correlation between age and accuracy, but the older a person is the more likely it is that their household address will correctly predict their geodemographic segment behaviour.

! The changing patterns of behaviour of older people are reflected in
• the definitions of the geodemographic segments. This is because the definitions are periodically redefined to reflect the changes in people's behaviour. Monitoring the segmentation definitions over time therefore provides an insight into the changing behaviour of older people.

SUMMARY

▌ Geodemographics uses a combination of census and other neighbourhood statistics to classify every consumer in a market according to the type of residential neighbourhood in which they live. It was developed simultaneously in the US and the UK in the late 1970s and is now available in over 20 countries. A set of 11 global geodemographic classifications has been created, enabling cross-country comparisons of national segments.

▌ The segmentation data are mostly provided by specialist international companies, such as Claritas in the US and Experian in Europe.

▌ The descriptions of neighbourhood clusters are, in the language of sociology, 'ideal types'. They are descriptions of the types of consumers who are more common in these segments than they are in other segments. The segments are given names, such as 'High-spending Elders', 'Bungalow Retirement', 'Small Town Seniors' and 'Child-free Serenity'. Not everyone in these neighbourhoods is aged over 50 and those who are do not all conform to these stereotypes. Nevertheless, the range of consumers covered by the segments helps marketers avoid the trap of thinking that all older people are essentially similar in their needs and attitudes.

▌ In the UK, the segments applying to older people fall into two main groups. First, there is housing specifically built for the elderly by local authorities, whether in the form of sheltered homes, bungalows or flats in small developments. Second, there are neighbourhoods that are especially popular with retirees. Typically these are private flats in managed developments in cities, coastal retirement communities and environmentally attractive, semi-tourist locations favoured by the wealthier and fitter newly retired. Together these segments represent approximately 9 per cent of the UK population.

▌ The purpose of geodemographic classifications is both to profile and to reach target markets. It enables the:
  – value of qualitative consumer research to be extended by extrapolating its results using data about the respondents' geodemographics segments;

– value of customer and prospect data to be improved by using their postal addresses to predict their life stage and behaviour
– effectiveness of retail outlets to be improved by matching their format to the local catchment area;
– age of consumers to be predicted when combined with other publicly available information;
– effectiveness of communications campaigns to be improved by targeting households more effectively.

The pattern of residential segmentation among old people is not fixed but subject to a number of social and economic trends. Perhaps the most predictable is the declining status of traditional coastal retirement neighbourhoods. As a new generation of people with decades of experiencing overseas holidays reaches retirement age, the trend is for more people to move overseas or to country areas rather than coastal areas. This is especially true of the UK. In the US in particular, but to a significicant though lesser degree in the UK and Australia, retired people are increasingly attracted to developments that have been especially created for their needs.

■ The patterns of residential movement on reaching retirement are also affected by changes in the relative affluence of older people compared to those of working age.

■ The greatest strength of geodemographics is that it is simple to use and provides a direct link between the theory of the segmentation categories and their application in driving a communication strategy.

8

The rules have changed

We are over halfway through the book and it is a good point to step back from the intricacies of demographics, brands, consumer behaviour and geodemographics and ask the question 'What does all this knowledge about older people mean to the fundamentals of marketing?'

A quarter of century ago, the first article appeared in the *Harvard Business Review* explaining the business implications of the increasing number of older people. Much has changed since 1980. As predicted, the population has aged. In addition, life expectancy has increased, along with the economic power of older consumers. Most importantly, the mindset of today's 50-, 60- or 70-year-old has changed beyond recognition compared with their counterparts of 25 years ago.

Few would argue that marketing has adapted to these changes. Instead, the gap between marketing's perception of the world and reality has steadily widened. The remaining chapters of this book explain how to narrow the gap – how marketing's vision of the world and reality can be realigned.

This chapter begins this journey by summarizing what we know about older consumers and the consequences for marketing. However, understanding these truths and what to do about them is not enough – they have to be acted on. Unless the way in which marketing perceives and reacts to people's age is permanently changed, it will continually revert back to its youth-obsessed ways. In this chapter, I propose my solution to stopping this from happening. Marketing must become age-neutral. Before discussing what this means, however, it is useful to summarize our journey so far.

THE MARKETING LANDSCAPE IS CHANGING

When marketers consider this strange race of people aged 50 and over, they must feel like a sports car driver who has been merrily racing along a smooth road but now finds that the surface is getting bumpy, the signposts have disappeared, it's getting dark and the car's steering is failing. Convinced that he is heading in the right direction, he drives on, ignoring all evidence to the contrary. Instead of stopping and reading the map he keeps on driving. For reassurance he plays the same, familiar music, louder and louder. He is getting lost and he knows it.

The old map of consumer marketing was exquisitely simple. It had a single road, leading to metropolis '18–34-year-olds'. Now the landscape has changed, dissolving into a myriad of side turnings and lanes. New signposts appear with names such as 'the over-50s'. Some of these go nowhere but some lead to six-lane motorways. Marketing needs a new map – and maybe a new car, too.

The Western and much of the Eastern world is institutionally ageist. Youth, youthfulness, vitality and modernity always trump age, maturity, wisdom and experience. It is not surprising that living in a culture where young is good and old is boring, marketers behave as they do. This is not a value judgement; it's a fact of life.

Another fact of life is the relentless shift in the economic centre of gravity towards older people. Each day, there are more, better-off oldies and fewer, increasingly indebted youngsters. Our culture faces 'young', while the economic reality is pointed towards 'old'.

These opposing forces are creating strains and conflict. Attempting to make sense of this dilemma is the archetypical 'thirtysomething' marketer. Every so often they hear the media screaming 'the future is grey' and blaming young marketers for their insipient age-phobia. All of the time, fellow marketers whisper to them not to worry, that it doesn't really matter and, anyway, we all know that 'the future of a brand is the young'. Senior managers look down from their offices on the top floor, seemingly unconcerned about the commotion.

SIMPLISTIC AND CONFLICTING ADVICE

There are two opposing arguments vying for the marketer's attention. On one side are those demanding that the marketing world stops its obsession with youth and takes the over-50s seriously. Many of these people claim to have unique insights and knowledge of the older mind. Often they are obsessed with the cultural upheaval of the 1960s and how it determined the collective behaviour of the older generation. To strengthen their arguments, they mix in a dose of sociology and psychology thoroughly and distil the concoction into a set of simple rules about pre- and post-baby boomers and other strange-sounding generational groups. Their rules are touted as helping marketers do everything from writing advertising copy to launching new products. All of this advice is accompanied by a bombardment of facts, figures and examples of the new, financially liberated oldie that are designed to frighten the young marketer into action.

The other side of the argument is driven by a potent combination of apathy, laziness and marketing soundbites. Why bother to change when life seems just fine? Why suffer the aggravation of working outside your comfort zone and trying to get inside the minds of people like your mum and dad? Anyway, we all know that older people don't try new brands, use technology or want to change. Best to ignore the fuss and it will go away.

Whenever the subject is discussed or reported, these opposing arguments are regurgitated. It is like Bill Murray's experience in the film *Groundhog Day* – a ceaseless round of identical arguments, quotes, examples and unresolved questions.

THE REALITY OF THE SITUATION

With the right map, the new marketing landscape is simple to navigate. The challenge is leaving behind the contours, legend and landmarks of the old one!

Alternatively, marketers can keep using the old '18–35' view of the world. At some stage, however, reality has to be confronted. It is not a matter of if but when.

What follows are observations and conclusions about the new marketing reality. They have already been discussed in previous chapters, but this is the first time that they have been combined and presented as a set of simple rules. The danger in summarizing what are complicated issues is that it is impractical to mention all of the associated caveats and conditions. Such is the impact of the issue, I am taking this risk.

The research and evidence collected in writing this book suggests that marketing thinking needs to change. This new marketing reality can be grouped into the categories behaviour, segmentation and marketing constructs.

Behaviour

Evidence, logic and common sense scream the obvious truth: 'Don't assume or make generalizations about the ways in which older people behave'. OMD's research and that from other sources shows that the magnitude of the behavioural differences resulting from ageing appear to be small and different in each country. The rules that result from these conclusions are shown in Figure 8.1.

Segmentation

The analysis in Chapter 6 showed that, in most instances, chronological age is an unreliable way of segmenting the older adult market. Treating somebody aged 50 differently from a 40- or 60-year-old makes little sense, apart from where a product is only applicable to certain ages of people (certain types of financial services are age-specific, for example). As was also shown in Chapter 6, segmenting people in terms of their 'life stage' and 'generation' is equally dangerous. Mistaken assumptions about age and behaviour are at the centre of both these ideas.

For certain market and product combinations, chronological age might be a valid segmentation technique. It is safer to assume that age is not a valid way of segmenting a market and to make the exception only when a clear link between age and behaviour can be proven.

Segmentation by lifestyle is a safer technique, but it is only as good as the quality of the research on which the segmentation categories are based. The research must be both current and conducted in the country where the segmentation is being used.

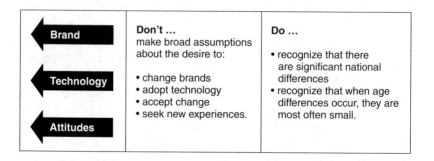

Figure 8.1 *How consumer behaviour changes with ageing – the dos and don'ts*

The previous chapters showed that, by studying the details of the economic, regional, ethnic and geographical distribution of older people, rich insights into the dynamics of this market can be derived. A combination of economics, demographics and good luck has created a subset of the 50-plus age group with a level of spending power that it is hard to see being repeated. This group – the 'charmed generation' – presents a one-time opportunity for marketers.

How the ageing population affects the spending power of those in their 20s, 30s and 40s is rarely discussed. As was noted in Chapter 2, there is strong evidence to suggest that young peoples' spending power will be adversely affected. Already, the 18–35 age group is showing signs of financial strain caused by high levels of debt, the irregular patterns of employment and the sky-high costs of accommodation. Having to fund their own and their parents' and grandparents' pensions will exacerbate the problem.

The rules that result from the conclusions drawn about market segmentation are shown in Figure 8.2.

Marketing constructs

Marketing's instinctive approach is to be youthcentric. This might be disguised as being 'youthfulcentric', but it invariably results in an irrational targeting of the sub-35-year-olds.

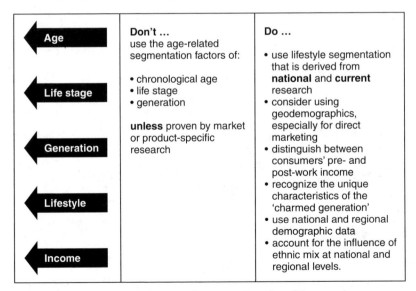

Figure 8.2 *The dos and don'ts of segmenting the older market*

The constructs that marketers use to guide their approach to older markets include how stereotypes are used, which factors of ageing are deemed to be important (and those that are ignored) and the assumptions about how ageing affects consumers' behaviour.

It is bizarre that marketers pay scant attention to the real differences between young and old people (physiological), but are obsessed with the variations that might not exist. Far more attention should be given to the marketing implications of physical ageing and far less to hypothetical behavioural differences.

The discussion that does occur about marketing to older people focuses almost exclusively on marketing communication, especially advertising. While communication is vital, it is only one of the marketing dimensions. As with all audiences and markets, new product development, marketing channels and customer support are equally important. The rules that result from these constructs are shown in Figure 8.3.

There are four ways in which marketers can react to this last list of dos and don'ts. My preferred reaction is for them to be accepted and applied. The second best outcome is for them to be disputed, on the basis of evidence. This at least indicates that the issues are being taken seriously. The most probable outcome, however, if history is any guide, is for them to generate agreement and then for nothing to happen. What is unforgivable is for them to be ignored.

	Don't ...	Do ...
Complexity **Stereotypes** **Instinct** **Physical**	• confuse 'youth' and 'youthfulness' • look for, or believe, any simple 'rules' about the older market – there aren't any • be influenced by the appealing simplicity of stereotypes of older people • ignore the age-related physical differences.	• resist the instinctive reaction to target the 18–35 age group • evaluate all aspects of marketing – not just communications.

Figure 8.3 *Marketing's assumptions about ageing – the dos and don'ts*

AGE-NEUTRAL MARKETING

Jeremy Bullmore is the past Chairman of both J. Walter Thompson and the UK's Advertising Association, as well as a non-executive director of WPP. When he was asked, 'How should communicators approach the 50-plus market?' he gave a disarmingly simple and brief response. He said he believed that there were four things to get right:

▌ select the right media;
▌ see the world through their eyes;
▌ treat them as people;
▌ don't be surprised if they don't differ too much from other members of the human race.

What an elegant and precise explanation. He is suggesting that you consider older people in pretty much the same way as you would any other. Age-neutral marketing says something very similar.

> The *principles* of marketing to a 30-year-old are the same as to somebody age 75 years. Marketing theory is intrinsically age-neutral. It should be unbiased, dispassionate and make no assumptions about the implications of age.

but

> The *application* of marketing is instinctively youthcentric and requires continual interventions and effort to remain age-neutral.

Here is the conundrum: marketing theory is unaffected by age, but marketers are. The way most companies practise marketing is not neutral – it is contorted by years of age bias. If marketing is to align itself with the real rather than its imagined world of older consumers, it must return the practice of marketing to a neutral state.

An insight into marketing's problems comes from understanding what the Alexander Technique is and why it works. The Alexander Technique is used to improve body posture. A body that is balanced works a lot better than one that is not. How most adults sit and move their bodies looks nothing like the beautifully coordinated, relaxed movements of a child. The ravages of everyday life take their toll and the natural poise of childhood contorts under the ravages of stress and hours sitting staring at the TV and PCs.

It is easy to identify what is wrong. The head doesn't balance correctly on the spine, which distorts the angle of the shoulders, resulting in poorly aligned hips, causing stress on the knees and ankles. The mechanics are obvious and you would think it would be simple to realign our posture. Unfortunately that is not so simple. Most of us are unaware that we are using our bodies in a contorted way. How we move and hold ourselves feels normal to us. Even when we try to sit up straight and pull back our shoulders, we forget and our posture returns to 'normal' moments later. The unnatural movements have become instinctive and habitual.

The way the Alexander Technique works is by permanently changing these ingrained habits. It achieves this not by a series of treatments and exercises, but by returning the body's balance to its truly natural state. I wish I could invent a marketing equivalent of the Alexander Technique – a collection of exercises, processes and therapy allowing marketing to correct its instinctive and habitual bias towards youth. The closest I can come is to define a set of age-neutral rules that marketers should use, continually, to ensure that they are not returning to their contorted, youth-centric ways. These are set out in Table 8.1.

The rules defined in Table 8.1, combined with the two core propositions mentioned earlier, represent the ten tenets of age-neutral marketing. They are simple and easy to understand, but unless they are ingrained in the culture of marketing, the tendency will be to drift back towards an irrational youth bias. How age-neutral marketing is applied in practice is the subject of the next chapter.

It is vital to understand that age-neutral marketing does not propose or assume that age is dismissed as a marketing variable. There are many good reasons for targeting children, tweens, teenagers, twenty-, thirty-, forty- and fiftysomethings, pensioners or any other group. Age-neutral marketing does not propose a 'one size fits all' approach to marketing that ignores age. Such a suggestion would be daft.

What it does mean is that marketing principles are applied unencumbered by bias, and when decisions are made about different ages, this is done for rational reasons rather than ones tied to fads, habits and convenience.

Table 8.1 *The rules of age-neutral marketing*

Consumer behaviour
Assume consumer behaviour is age-neutral unless there is convincing evidence to the contrary.
Forget the assumptions about the effect of ageing on consumers' reactions to new brands, technology, change and new experiences unless there is convincing evidence to the contrary.
Plan how to exploit the changes to consumer markets created by changes to the population's age and economic structure.
Remember the importance of country and ethnic differences for the behaviour of older people.
Scope
Apply an age-neutral approach to all areas of marketing, not just communications.
Incorporate the physiological effects of ageing into all aspects of marketing.
Resist limiting the use of age-neutrality to 'niche' and 'project' marketing. It should be central to the way a company markets everything.
Segmentation
Forget using chronological age as a primary means of segmenting adult markets unless there is evidence proving its validity.

IMPLICATIONS FOR THE MARKETER

This chapter contains only two implications for marketers, but they are the most important in the book.

All of the research and evidence collected in the process of writing this book points to a single conclusion. Marketing's perception of older people is seriously flawed. Marketers need to close the gap between reality and their perception of it. This chapter contains a set of guidelines to help in this reorientation.

! Consider each of the dos and don'ts that are associated with behaviour, marketing segmentation and marketing constructs. What are the top five issues that need your attention?

The practice of marketing is under continual pressure to be youthcentric. If marketing is to function properly, it needs to be age-neutral.

! What rules do you already follow? What rules will require a change in your approach to marketing? What actions need to happen if your company's marketing is to become age-neutral?

SUMMARY

▌ The Western and much of the Eastern world is institutionally ageist. Youth, youthfulness, vitality and modernity always trump age, maturity, wisdom and experience.

▌ It is not surprising that, living in a culture where 'young' is good and 'old' is boring, marketers think of their youthcentric ways as being normal. They are not.

▌ The principles of marketing work just fine, irrespective of the age of the customer. The problem is that marketing decisions are made in an environment that is inherently age-biased. Marketing theory doesn't need to change, but it does need to become age-neutral. To do this, marketers need to rethink their approach to the effects of ageing on market segmentation, consumer behaviour and marketing practice. To achieve this objective, this chapter contained a list of dos and don'ts associated with each of the three factors.

▌ It is not difficult for marketers to adapt to the changing age composition of the market. All they need to do is apply the rules of marketing minus the age assumptions.

▌ The final part of this chapter discussed the concept of age-neutrality and listed the 10 rules that must be followed if it is to be achieved.

▌ Age-neutral marketing does not imply that age is dismissed as a marketing variable, so that there is a 'one size fits all' approach. It means that marketing principles are applied, unencumbered by bias, and when decisions are made about different ages, they are for rational reasons rather than driven by fads, habit and convenience.

9

From theory to practice

Unless marketers and other corporate managers take the increasing economic power of the over-50s seriously, then all the facts, research and theory discussed in this book are worthless. The sad reality is that most companies do not feature this subject in their strategic and tactical priorities. If it does appear in a company's business plan, it is most likely hidden away in the section entitled PEST (Political, Economic, Sociological and Technological factors) and then as a byline in the list of sociological facts, along with things such as 'ethics and religious' and 'changing regulations'.

Marketers and corporate managers are not stupid people, so why don't they do something about exploiting the business potential of this opportunity? How can this matter get on to the Board's agenda and marketing director's action list? Answering both these questions is the objective of this chapter.

Once the subject has attracted sustained corporate attention, then formulating and implementing tactical marketing actions is a relatively straightforward matter.

CONSTRAINTS ON CHANGE

Understanding why there is such a reluctance to think and act on anything to do with the rising numbers of older people and their effect on consumer markets is the starting point for changing the situation.

When I look at the marketing world, I see nothing short of a comical farce. I see a highly conservative world that is frightened to act outside a narrow track of accepted behaviour. I see clients and agencies focusing the majority of their marketing resources on an age group that is shrinking in relative importance. I see people in their 50s, 60s and 70s who are nothing like their media and marketing stereotypes.

I know that this is not the way the world appears to the majority of marketers. Looking through their eyes, the focus on the 18–35-year-olds is perfectly normal and correct. Most of the faces they see are young. The reason they are working in the profession is because it is 'young'. What incentive do they have to step outside the accepted norms of thinking? They don't expect to be around in the same job that long, so why change what seems to be working? Given the option of working on a marketing campaign promoting products used by their friends or ones by their parents and grandparents, it's a no-brainer as to which they choose. Anyway, nobody in senior management seems concerned, so why should they be?

Both these visions of the world are oversimplifications, but they do illustrate the gulf that exists between most marketers and those who are passionate about registering older people on the marketing agenda.

There are other factors preventing marketers from broadening their focus away from 18–35-year-olds. Some of these are specific to the managers responsible for deciding business strategy and others to the tacticians who implement the strategy.

Strategists

During 2004 both *The Economist* magazine and McKinsey, a management consultancy, published surveys listing senior corporate managers' most important issues. Strangely, there was not a mention of demographics, the ageing population or anything remotely connected with the subjects discussed in this book.

The closest *The Economist*'s survey got to the subject was in its statement about the importance of the customer:

> The customer remains king. Increasing customer satisfaction is once again respondents' top strategic priority. Building closer relationships with existing customers is regarded as the best way to maximize growth opportunities.

This is an admirable objective, but there is little evidence that companies are attempting to do this with customers who happen to be 'old'.

In June 2005 McKinsey published a research paper entitled 'What global executives think about growth and risk.' Amazingly the ageing of the population in the developed world was voted the fourth most important factor. Even more astonishing was that it was seen as leading to more positive than negative outcomes.

When the issue of ageing does make it to the Board's agenda, it is most likely to be about the consequences of the costs to the company's pension scheme or the effects on manpower planning as the 'baby boomer' generation retires. Rarely is the subject raised as a positive issue associated with business opportunities rather than problems.

Charles Roxbourgh, a director in McKinsey's London office, wrote an article entitled 'Hidden flaws in strategy'. In it he identified how behavioural economics explains why good executives back bad strategies. Three of the flaws he identified go a long way to explaining why senior management consistently ignores the marketing upside of an ageing population.

- *'The status quo bias.'* Rather than make significant changes, managers have a tendency to leave things as they are. An explanation of this attitude is that most people have an innate aversion to loss. The potential excitement of the gain doesn't outweigh the risk of loss. Certainly, most managers have a status quo bias when it comes to adapting their marketing to embrace older customers. The thing they most fear losing is their brand's appeal to the young, should it appear that they are also trying to engage the old.
- *'The herding instinct.'* Conforming to the behaviour and opinions of others is a fundamental human trait and an accepted principle of psychology. Warren Buffett, the investment guru, once said, 'Failing conventionally is the route to go.' He went on to say, 'As a group, lemmings may have a rotten image, but no individual lemming has ever received bad press.' For many years, it was common to hear the statement 'Nobody ever got fired for buying IBM.' It just goes to prove that even unwritten sayings such as 'Nobody ever got fired for targeting the 18–35s' will not last for ever.
- *'False consensus.'* Managers overestimate the extent to which they share the same opinions and beliefs as their peers. This is reinforced by the way that they select the facts and opinions supporting their existing beliefs and give them more weight than inputs that might challenge their thinking.

These flawed types of behaviour go a long way to explaining why senior managers have been so slow to react. However, there is another, more powerful, reason.

The annual changes in the age profile of the population, like its economic consequences, are small. If the changes are viewed over a 10-year period, the results are significant. During a company's annual planning timetable, the age composition of its market will only alter by a small amount. In the same time period it is inevitable that a more pressing issue will arise that demands it be given higher priority. Another year passes and nothing is done. Coincidentally, the current management team is unlikely to be around then to deal with the consequences of their inertia.

The danger of not acting when major change takes place very slowly is illustrated by the story of frogs and boiling water. In case you've forgotten how this works from earlier in the book, I'll tell you it again here as its lesson is an important one.

If frogs are put into a container of cold water and it is then slowly heated, the frogs die. Why don't they jump out? Because the temperature increases so slowly that they fail to notice their changing (and dangerous) environment before it is too late to act. The ageing population is equivalent to the water that is being heated. It is not yet boiling, but it is getting very hot!

When the e-business phenomenon surfaced in the late 1990s, it immediately grasped the attention of senior managers and made it to the top spot on most Boards' agendas. The business use of the internet created an intoxicating mix of the fear of being left behind and the tantalizing potential of gaining huge competitive advantage. Arguably the issues in this book and their business consequences are of greater significance than e-business. The trouble is, they have been a long time coming, contain little mystery and don't result in anything as tangible as a website.

Tacticians

The reason most quoted for marketing being youthcentric is that most marketers are young (sub-35) and so more likely to be influenced by and interested in their own peer group. So, the argument goes, young marketers are only interested in talking to young consumers.

The observation is correct, but the conclusion is not. To suggest that marketers are unable to think outside their own generational cohort is simplistic and insulting.

The marketing profession is forever bemoaning its lack of influence in determining corporate strategy. If this is true, and I think it is, then it is ludicrous to suggest that youthful marketers are single-handedly responsible for their companies ignoring such an important customer group as the over-50s. The culprits are the people who make the rules, control the agendas and establish the business priorities. The rules of the game that marketers play by are set by senior corporate managers. If the rules were altered to become age-neutral, then, begrudgingly, those responsible for marketing tactics would also change.

At the moment the rules are the same as they have been for the last couple of decades, so it is no mystery that so are the marketing tactics.

One of the fundamental rules for creating change is that you first have to convince the person that change is necessary and then provide them with a process to take the first steps in the new direction. The remainder of this chapter explains how both of these tasks can be achieved for senior corporate managers and those implementing the marketing strategy.

ACHIEVING CHANGE – CORPORATE MANAGERS

Something that nobody likes, especially senior managers, is being asked a simple question that they cannot answer – especially if it is about a subject that is their responsibility.

The annual shareholders' meeting is an event that most directors dread. It is when they are put on the spot and have to answer all of the questions that they wish went unasked. To help directors prepare for this ordeal, PricewaterhouseCoopers creates a list of the possible shareholders' questions that might be asked. Some of the questions are general – 'What is the Board's role in the company's strategic planning?' for example. Other questions are specific, such as 'Does the company have sufficient resources in place to ensure compliance with Section 404 of the Sarbanes-Oxley Act?' The document lists well over 500 questions, but none makes mention of demographics, the ageing population, older customers or any subject related to this book.

When PricewaterhouseCoopers' document does contain questions associated with the effects of the ageing population, what will they be? The questions will probably be something like the following.

▌ What percentage of the company's advertising spend is targeted at the 18–35 age group and how does this compare with the age profile of the company's customer base?

▌ How does the company's marketing strategy reflect the increasing business importance of older customers?

▌ What specific actions are planned by the company's HR, product development, R&D, customer care, marketing and sales groups to respond to the changes in the population profile in the company's main markets?

▌ Is the value of the company's brands increased or diminished by the age and income demographic changes in its markets?

▌ What are the major risks resulting from the changing population profiles and how are these being minimized?

Confronted with these questions, most managers would be able to give a 'politician's' type of response along the lines of 'We ensure our strategic and marketing plans address the needs of all of our customers, irrespective of their age.' Few would be able to give an informed and detailed response. These, though, are not unreasonable questions to ask. Senior managers should be able to answer them with conviction borne out of understanding the facts.

What follows is the next level of questions (see Table 9.1) that a company's Board should be able to answer. Companies operating in multiple markets, selling multiple brands, should be able to answer for their primary product and market.

It could be argued that directors should be involved in this level of detail and in most instances this would be right. However, these are not ordinary questions – they are a core component of a company's marketing strategy.

For companies confident about answering these questions already, my sincere congratulations. You are, without question, in a minority.

If the questions highlighted doubts and uncertainties, then you are not alone and the following options are some of the ways in which they can be resolved.

Options for action

It may sound obvious, but it cannot be stated too strongly:

Table 9.1 *The primary and secondary questions a company's Board of Directors should be able to answer*

Primary questions	Secondary questions
How is the age composition of our markets changing?	What effects does this have on our marketing strategy?
What is the target age range of our customers? How has this changed in the past five years and is it anticipated that it will change in the next five years?	What research and assumptions are used in reaching these decisions?
How is our media spend allocated over the age profile of the market? Will this change?	What was the basis for deciding how we apportion the spend?
What account is taken of the needs of people aged 50 and over in our new product development?	To what extent do we research the needs of older customers?
Is our marketing age-neutral?	What are our responses to the 10 tests of age-neutrality? (See Appendix 3)

adopting an age-neutral approach to marketing is a strategic, not a tactical, decision and can only be achieved with the full support of senior management.

The first step towards changing the assumptions and strategies that have become ingrained in the corporate culture is to use one or all of the following textbook approaches.

▋ *Ask the difficult question* 'Explain to me, from first principles, why we spend the majority of our promotional and new product development expenditure on people under the age of 35?'

▋ *Test the contrarian approach* 'What would be the effect if we were to apportion our marketing spend in the same proportions as the age profile of our customers?'

▋ *Generate tension* Create a team to produce a marketing strategy based on age-neutral principles and have it evaluated against the present strategy. This type of approach was adopted by GE when it formed its 'destroy your business' teams to test the effects of e-business on its traditional ways of doing business.

▋ *External evaluation* Have the marketing arguments and market research that determines the marketing strategy validated externally.

Testing the company's instinctive assumptions creates the right environment for considering change. The next step is to decide what actions to take. Figure 9.1 shows the four main options available to the Board. Each

Figure 9.1 *Options for 'next step' actions based on the magnitude and scope of change required*

segment of the matrix holds an action with a different scope and magnitude. What next step is appropriate will be determined by the change required.

Experiment

The most common approach companies adopt towards an older market is to treat it as a niche or a 'project'. This normally takes the form of a promotional campaign targeted at the older demographic. Often the campaign retains the same creative, but just broadens the media selection.

The risk of using the 'projects' approach is that such initiatives are insufficiently resourced and given too little time to prove their worth. Too often, companies fund a limited promotional campaign for a product that was initially designed, packaged and promoted to 18–35-year-olds and then wonder why it didn't work. The mistake can then be compounded by treating the target older market as a single entity.

The worst thing that can occur by adopting the experimentation approach is that it confirms the ingrained prejudices about older consumers. If a poorly funded and managed project fails, the company can rightly claim that it has 'tried marketing to the over-50s, but it didn't work'.

Experimentation is a valuable tool, but it does need to be fully resourced for a period that is long enough to provide accurate results. The 'campaign for real beauty' that was launched by Dove, the Unilever cosmetics brand, is an excellent example of a significant and prolonged campaign that generated tangible results. This campaign is discussed in detail in Chapter 13.

Viewing older people as a 'niche' might be a valid approach, depending on the relative size of the group to the total market. When this technique is used and older people comprise the numerical majority of the market, it does strain the meaning of the word 'niche'.

The most important factor to remember – irrespective of experimentation as a technique – is to use it as means of gaining information and experience that can be applied in the wider context of the company.

Realign

Rather than just mounting a project and altering the age focus of marketing communications, this approach involves changing multiple parts of the marketing mix.

Building the requirements of older people into the new product development (NPD) process should be a standard procedure. Unfortunately, it rarely happens. It is so exceptional that whenever the subject is discussed, the same examples are always quoted:

▐ Ford's use of inclusive design to create the Focus model;
▐ BT's Big Button telephone;
▐ OXO's range of age-friendly kitchen tools;
▐ NTT's 'easy-easy' mobile phone.

When evaluating how to adapt to the ageing population, the NPD process is at least as important as marketing communications, closely followed by customer support.

Obviously, conducting multiple projects increases the company's financial and manpower commitment. It also increases its chance of success. The obvious explanation for this is that they receive more resources, but equally important is that they attract more boardroom attention and commitment. This in itself sends a message to the rest of the company about the level of importance the Board attributes to this subject.

Commit

The immediate result of adopting this approach will not necessarily lead to a great deal of visible change, but, potentially, it will have a greater and longer-term impact on the company.

This approach treats the issue 'What do we do about the ageing population?' as something warranting Board-level attention. It raises the profile of the issue from being one of many marketing activities to something that has and retains the highest level of management focus.

The outcome of this attention may well result in activities that are identical to those already discussed in the sections on the experiment and realign options. What is important about this approach, however, is that the initiatives are part of the strategy agenda rather than being isolated marketing activities.

The starting point for the 'commit' approach is for the company's Board to confront the issues discussed in this book and then decide how to respond. A first step is for directors to put one of the following questions on the Board's agenda:

▐ What is our strategy to exploit the ageing population and the change in consumer power?
▐ How are the different functions within the company planning to respond to the changing age composition of our markets?
▐ Is our marketing age-neutral – should it be?

Big bang

E-business, total quality management (TQM) and corporate social responsibility (CSR) are examples of developments that resulted in companies adopting a 'big bang' approach. In a short space of time, these issues went from relative obscurity to being something that companies needed to understand and do something about.

In hindsight, many businesses wished that they had not been so eager to embrace the concepts in such an uncritical way and be swept along with the tide of corporate conformity.

I would like to think that the concepts in this book are so obvious and worthy of attention that they create a sea change in executive attitudes. In reality I know that this is most unlikely. What is more likely is that new companies will have as a core element of their strategy the exploitation of older consumer markets. Rather than radically change their core businesses, larger companies will respond by creating their own 'older-facing' subsidiaries.

As long as companies *seriously* consider the issue of the ageing population and its implications, it doesn't matter if none of the four options is adopted. Once this subject receives even the most cursory attention, it cannot help but result in a change in strategy. It is not hyperbole to claim that any company that doesn't consider this issue is risking its shareholders' interests.

ACHIEVING CHANGE – MARKETING

In a similar way, to achieve change with corporate managers, the starting point for the marketing group is to ask a simple question such as 'Is the company's age targeting determined by using market research that is both current and comprehensive?' Hopefully this question is easy to answer and it is a yes.

To give a more detailed understanding of how marketers perceive the value of older consumers, three simple tools have been created that test their thinking.

▮ *Are decisions made based on facts or stereotypes?* The questionnaire in Chapter 3 (see Table 3.2) provides a set of questions that allows marketers to evaluate the extent to which their decisions are determined by age stereotypes.
▮ *Is the company's marketing age-neutral?* This can be measured by answering the questions in Appendix 3, which test the 10 factors of age neutrality.
▮ *Can the allocation of marketing resources by age of consumer be justified?* If a marketing strategy is well conceived, it should be possible to substantiate why the allocation of marketing resources

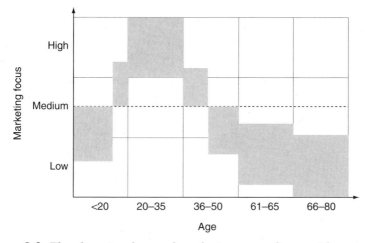

Figure 9.2 *The changing focus of marketing expenditure with age*

varies with the target age of the customer. As an example, Figure 9.2 shows a typical profile of marketing expenditure when the focus is on the 18–35 age group – the width of the 'line' indicating the approximate range of spending for the different age groups. The dotted horizontal line represents an age-neutral marketing position. It is a good test for marketers to plot their company's marketing resource profile and justify when it varies either side of the age-neutral line.

The purpose of these three simple tests is to highlight when decisions are made on the basis of myth rather than evidence. If, having completed the exercises, it is decided to modify the strategy relating to consumer age, then read the following section, which discusses the available options.

Options for action

When a marketing group is at the point of realizing that something should be done, the next step is deciding what that 'something' might be. No simple formula exists that determines the correct approach, but the possible options are limited to five main strategies (see Figure 9.3).

The diagram shows the different options for adapting and re-positioning a youth-focused product. In this context, the terms 'young' and 'old' are intentionally vague as they vary from company to company. For most organizations, the 18–35 group represents 'young' and anything older is 'old'. Likewise, there is no absolute definition of what constitutes a new or modified product. For some companies, it might involve significant change, while for others, a minor modification to the packaging may be all that is required.

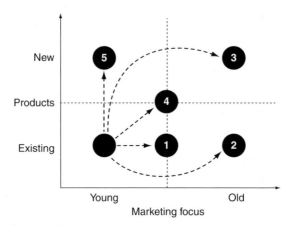

Figure 9.3 *Options for changing the product and marketing focus combinations*

Option 1: same product, broader age focus

This is the easiest option to implement. There is no change to the product – the only thing that alters is the marketing focus. Most of the time, this means broadening the media brief to include older people.

Option 2: same product – focused on old

This approach is likely to use a different communication channel. For example, a number of companies have used direct marketing to target the older demographic. The rationale for this choice is that it might be the most appropriate channel but it also minimizes 'diluting' the mainstream media coverage that remains targeted at the young.

Critical to this, and the previous option, is identifying the right segment of the older market to target.

Option 3: new (or modified product) – focused on old

In this instance, a totally new or highly modified version of the product is targeted at the old market.

The implementation of this option can take the form of a new product that is overtly targeted at the 'old', such as the range of age-friendly mobile handsets that are entering the market. Alternatively, the product can be based on behaviour and attributes most likely to be found with older people. A good example of this is the new car and home insurance products that are only available to people with low insurance claims – a characteristic more likely to be found with older people. The attraction of this 'indirect' option is that the market becomes self-selecting and it is not necessary to present the product as being for old rather than young people.

Option 4: modified product – neutral age focus

With this option, the product is modified so as to be applicable to all ages and the focus of the marketing is unbiased by age. For most consumer products, this will mean only minor product changes as most of them will be in the packaging, sales channels, creative and media selection.

This option is the most radical. Both Options 2 and 3 consign the product to an age ghetto that can be insulated from the rest of marketing's activities. With this option, however, the risk calculation is that, by broadening the product's age appeal, it generates a net increase in business. Most companies make the instinctive decision that the potential gain is outweighed by the risk of negatively affecting the product's appeal to the younger audience.

The only way to make a reasoned decision is to expose the option to an unbiased appraisal using the normal marketing techniques.

Option 5: New product – focused on young

Finally, there is the option of retaining a focus on the young age group, modifying or creating new products based on their requirements.

The purpose of the five options

These five options are a very simple representation of what is a much more complicated process. My objective in formalizing and simplifying the process is to force people to think about *all* of the options that they could pursue. Also, if any option is rejected, for this to be done on the basis of understanding rather than hunches.

Remember, doing nothing is making a decision. It is deciding that all of the evidence provided in this book does not justify making any changes to the existing marketing approach. I cannot think of one company to which this applies.

OBJECTIONS TO CHANGE

It doesn't matter how much evidence demonstrates why companies should reappraise their approach, there will be many, maybe the majority, who will not be convinced. It will not be because they have research to dispute the facts, but because they will hold on to a few specific examples that they believe prove their case. For example, the slow adoption by older people of texting 'proves' that they are technophobic. The perceived tendency for showing off declining with age 'proves' that older people are not fashion-conscious.

The only way to contest these arguments is to separate the facts from the myths. Within this book are the facts that counter the most common arguments.

There is a final group of objections that don't rely on any arguments related to age. Normally, they are bold assertions that are presented as factual claims. The following are the most common arguments together with the appropriate responses.

▊ *If this is such a great idea, why aren't others doing it?* This argument is based on a logical inconsistency, as if it were true, then change would never take place. There is also the assumption that 'others aren't doing it', which is not necessarily correct. Just because companies are not shouting about their experiences does not mean that they are not occurring. Most amusingly, this is the very same argument that was put to me in the late 1990s when I was talking to companies about incorpo-rating web-based channels into their business models.

▊ *Who is making money out of the older market?* The response to this question is simple. Most consumer goods companies already generate a sizeable proportion of their business from older people – many without trying. In some cases, this happens in spite of them being as unfriendly as possible. Just think how much more business could be generated if, instead of a neutral or antagonistic approach, we focused on this group? Certainly the owners of SAGA – the holiday and finance company for the over-50s that was sold for £1 billion – are examples of those who have made money from this market.

▊ *Youth is the engine of change.* This is a difficult one to argue against because its meaning is so imprecise. In some industry sectors, such as consumer electronics, the influence of young buyers is undoubtedly important. In the travel and automobile industry, this is not the situ-ation. Even if it were generally true that younger people are early adopters, this does not mean that they are the group that delivers the greatest profit.

▊ *We live in a culture that is centred on youth. All we are doing is reflecting society.* The observation is true, but – and it is a very big but – is the conclusion the sensible business decision? There is a building tension between the value our society places on youth and the declining economic importance of the young. Blindly aping society's values may not be the most sensible marketing approach.

IMPLICATIONS FOR THE MARKETER

Deciding how companies react to the issues raised in this book is an important decision for senior managers.

! Earlier in this chapter a series of techniques were described that tell managers if their assumptions and strategies relating to the age of their customers are well founded.

Companies should know if their tactical marketing decisions are age-neutral. Are they driven by facts or stereotypes?

! To answer this question, marketers should complete the set of exercises described earlier in this chapter.

Five options for adapting a marketing campaign for a product that is designed and focused on a young market were described earlier in this chapter.

! Marketers should consider the business value of each of these five options to their own products and markets.

SUMMARY

▌ How do you get the question of marketing to the over-50s on to the Board's agenda and the marketing director's action list? The first step is to prove that it is an important issue and one about which they are ill informed.

▌ The youthcentric mentality is deeply entrenched in management thinking. To change it requires a company to re-evaluate its most basic assumptions about why and how it determines its marketing focus. If senior managers are forced to justify, from first principles, their youth-focused strategies, it becomes clear whether their plans are based on hard research or result from following the generally accepted wisdom. This chapter contains a series of techniques to reveal the depth of real understanding.

▌ It is vital that senior managers are convinced of the need to change. These are the people who determine the business culture, control the agenda and establish the business priorities. They set the rules of the game that marketers play. If the strategy is altered and becomes age-neutral, then the marketing tactics will follow.

▌ Senior managers must decide the scope and magnitude of change that they want to achieve. It might be to conduct an experiment in a single market or with a limited range of products. Alternatively, it could be to totally reorientate the company's approach to the market.

▌ The decisions marketers must make concern the extent of change necessary to the products and the marketing focus on the young and old sectors.

▌ The main objective of all the ideas and techniques discussed in this chapter is to get senior managers and all marketers to seriously consider the implications of the ageing population on their business. If this is done, the result will invariably be that they adapt their strategies and plans.

10

Interactive channels – myths, facts and unknowns

Life was so simple when communicating with customers was limited to advertising, direct mail, the phone and face-to-face meetings.

During the last decade, the number of communication channels has mushroomed with the widespread adoption of e-mail, mobile messaging, interactive digital TV (iDTV), instant messaging and the multitude of services delivered via the web. It is vital, therefore, that marketers understand how older people react to these new channels and why the ageing process makes special demands on implementing these technologies.

This chapter discusses how ageing affects people's use of technology and the implications this has on designing technology-dependent marketing channels.

WHAT IS AN INTERACTIVE CHANNEL?

Before discussing how ageing affects the use of interactive channels, it is best to be clear what is meant – or at least what I mean – by 'interactive channels'.

There are two factors that distinguish an interactive from other types of communication channel. First, the individual has the ability to control, in real time, the information that they receive. Second, it is a two-way channel, so, as well as receiving information, the individual can interact and feed back their responses.

Interactive channels provide many more and richer ways for organizations to interact with their markets. But they do have a very big downside: they can be very difficult to use, especially for older people.

The following are the main interactive channels in the marketer's armoury.

▮ *E-mail* marketing needs little introduction. Anybody with an internet connection knows the annoyance of receiving unsolicited e-mails attempting to sell the exotic, obscene and illegal. Mixed in among the unwanted e-mails are the newsletters and e-zines from organizations that we have asked to send us material. The simple e-mail has evolved to include images, sound and controls that enable us to link and interact with the sender. With the widespread introduction of broadband, e-mail will advance even further to include sound and video.

▮ *Instant messaging* lets people who are connected to the internet 'speak' to each other in real time. Simple text was the initial method of communicating, but now instant messaging includes speech, image and video. In 1996, when it was first launched, it was the plaything of young people. Eight years later, the corporate world is the primary user. Over a quarter of companies in the US use it as an officially supported service and well over half of companies acknowledge that their staff uses the service.

▮ *Mobile phone messaging* has followed a similar path to instant messaging. Initially it was the province of the young, who discovered short messaging service (SMS), now known as texting. This unwieldy, difficult to use way of sending messages is one of the biggest and most unlikely channel success stories of all time, with a quarter of the world's mobile users sending a text message more than once a day. It has developed out of its origins as the province of the youth and is now used by all ages and has been adopted as a mainstream commercial communications channel. The new generation of networks and phones enables images and video to be added to the simple text message.

▮ *Interactive digital TV (iDTV)* transforms the television from a device where channel selection is the only option available to the viewer into one that is more akin to a computer. Channels are expandable, letting the viewer select their own preference for viewing, and, most importantly, they provide a two-way dialogue between viewer and channel owner. So, as an advert for a pizza brings my tastebuds to life, I can use my TV to place an order for a home delivered pizza. To give a measure of the importance of iDTV, in 2002 the amount spent on digital and interactive services in the US was $24 billon. Europe spends approximately half this amount. In May 2004, the BBC's interactive service was used by 50 per cent of the available audience, which equates to 10 million viewers. The UK advertising figures for the first quarter of 2005 indicate that the iDTV advertising channel will achieve an annual growth of over 30 per cent.

▌ *The web* is the last in the list but most certainly not the least important. I long ago gave up plotting the worldwide number of web users, but it is well over half a billion people. The web is used for everything from a simple information source to something enabling consumers and companies to complete most of their routine transactions. The web can be a radio, television and means of searching billions of pages of information.

These are the communications channels of the present and future. They can be used for every form of marketing activity, from brand building to one-on-one customer interactions. As computing and networking technologies continue their relentless increase in performance and decrease in cost, the potential of these channels can only grow.

In the UK, online presence represents about 12 per cent of consumers' media consumption, but accounts for less than 3 per cent of advertising spend. There is a simple message coming from these statistics – online advertising is set to rapidly increase.

In an interview in August 2004, Sir Martin Sorrell, Chief Executive of WPP, commented on the forecasts that in the US interactive advertising would be more important than magazine advertising by 2007: 'I think the challenge facing paper publishers – newspapers and magazines – is getting greater and greater. I read less weeklies and less fortnightlies. I don't get my "market close" from the FT any more – I get it from Bloomberg the night before. Can I wait for *Fortune* or *Business Week* or *The Economist*? The answer is probably no.' Sir Martin Sorrell is not your average 59-year-old, but he represents a large and growing group, of older people who instinctively use interactive media.

Interactive marketing is the most youth-focused of all the marketing disciplines. Marketers must understand why ageing affects the way people use these channels. Older eyes, hands and heads are different to those of the young. Once this simple fact is understood, then the task is to make interactive marketing channels neutral to the user's age.

MYTHS ABOUT TECHNOLOGY AND AGE

The young are 'good' with technology and the old are 'technophobic'. This sentiment summarizes the commonly held view on the relationship between age and technology.

There are undoubtedly snippets of evidence that support this idea. For example, '55 per cent of worldwide mobile phone owners, who use SMS more than once a day, are 18 years old or younger'; 'the internet usage levels of the 18–24-year-olds has reached a saturation level'. Added to these random facts are the anecdotal stories about parents' problems using DVD players and mobile phones that are solved in an instant by their 10-year-olds.

There can be no doubt that young people who have spent a large part of their early years gazing at computers, video games, mobile phones and TVs are going to be at ease with the digital world. Does this early immersion in the world of screens, menus, keyboards and technical jargon imply ever-lasting generational differences in terms of reactions to technology?

Like most areas of marketing, when you probe a little deeper, the link between age and technology is a little more complicated than this. For instance, the most frequent players of computer games are not teenagers but those over 35 years old. Householders in the US aged 45 to 54 spend more than $2,000 a year on televisions, mobile phones and computer online services, making them the biggest spenders on every type of information product except radios, where householders aged 65 to 74 spend the most. Thus, a 50-year-old is as likely to be using the internet as somebody aged 30.

In 2005, the Nielsen Norman Group studied the way that teenagers use the web. Instead of finding a bunch of fluent users, they were substantially less able than adults. Their success rate in completing a set of standard tasks was 55 per cent, compared with 66 per cent for adult users.

There were three reasons for their poor performance:

I   they had insufficient reading skills;
I   the way that they researched using the web was poor;
I   they had dramatically lower patience levels.

The consultants wryly commented that the reason for teens having the reputation for being techno-whizzes is that the 'Teens who don't volunteer to fix your VCR when it's blinking "12:00" are not the ones you remember.'

We still tend to refer to interactive channels as 'the new technologies' even though most of them are now far from new. It is often forgotten that today's 50-year-olds pioneered most of the major technical innovations of the web and mobile phone. Three of the most influential people in the history of IT – Tim Berners-Lee, inventor of the web, Jorma Ollila, the long-time Chairman and CEO of Nokia, and Bill Gates, of Microsoft fame – have all had or are very near their 50th birthday. It was the bright young teenagers of the 1970s, now in or approaching their 50s, who created the high-tech world we inhabit.

The young have undoubtedly driven the adoption and use of SMS. It seems that they are likely to do the same with the multimedia messaging service (MMS) – the mobile phone technology that transmits sounds, images, and video. We should be careful about extrapolating that the young will always be technology's early adopters from the experience of messaging and applying it generally when this is one small part of the picture.

There are special reasons for SMS being so youth-dominated. SMS (texting) was introduced in 1995 and remained a little-used service until teenagers discovered its potential and made their own ways of communicating. The fact that it was a complete mystery to the older generation was its great attraction. Once a critical mass of users was achieved, it became the 'must have' product to use.

The new waves of technology are not following this youthful route. Wireless technologies such as WiFi and Bluetooth are being driven by the older, corporate world. Products using G3 are likely to be used by an older age group who can afford their high cost. The latest gizmos for PCs, PDAs and notebooks are as eagerly awaited by the middle-aged geeks as their youthful counterparts.

When a product with a new technology becomes a fashion accessory and a means of retaining status with your peers – such as the latest release of a mobile phone – then the young will be the first into the shops. It would be very misleading to extrapolate from this example that this is the case for all forms of technology-based products.

Looking back over the last decade, it's easy to see why being young correlated with being the first adopters of a technology. However, there is no evidence to suggest that it will be the same in the future. For the first time in history, older people will be an identifiable and an important market for high-tech products and services. Businesses and young adults will remain important market sectors, but older people will become an increasingly vital segment. Indeed, for some types of products they will be the primary market.

The special needs of older people will be a significant factor in making suppliers improve the design of their user interfaces. The incentive to capture a large and wealthy market will make designers of electronic devices take account of the ways in which age affects customers' abilities to use their products. A generation of people weaned on the notebook computer and mobile phone are not going to reach their 70s and abandon these devices because of failing eyesight and clumsy fingers.

Product designers at Microsoft, Nokia and Intel must learn to satisfy the requirements of a generation of 50-year-olds who have grown up with the PC, mobile, PDA and all things internet and value these products just as much as 30-year-olds. The techno-savvy 50-year-olds represent a market opportunity for technology-based products that improve the quality of their lives as they age.

We are just beginning to see the emergence of a new range of products, referred to as 'pervasive computing'. The combination of inexpensive computer processing linked to sophisticated sensors can continually monitor people's movements and actions. This technology will assist with a whole range of age-related problems, doing things such as reminding people to complete tasks and watching for sudden behavioural or physical changes.

Technology's centre of gravity is moving towards satisfying the demands of older age groups, driven by their spending power and age-related needs.

FACTS AND FIGURES

There is an immense amount of data detailing the numbers of people who use the internet, mobile phones and iDTV. This data is segmented by age, race, income, education and just about any other criteria you can imagine. While the fine detail of the analysis is interesting, it's the 'big picture' messages that are most important for marketers.

Technology is important to older people

The data from the US's Consumer Expenditure Survey (see Figure 10.1) shows the astonishing growth in purchases of computer products by the 55–64 age group.

The rapid growth can be partly explained by this group's historically low level of PC ownership, but cannot explain on its own a growth rate that is nearly four times that of the national average.

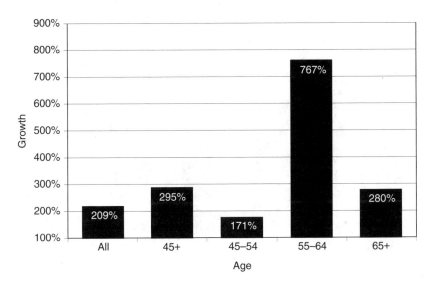

Figure 10.1 *Growth in expenditure on PC products for the period 1990–2001*
Source: Consumer Expenditure Survey 1990–2001

Use of the internet

Data about older peoples' adoption of the internet and mobile phones is a good measure of their use of interactive channels and its importance to their lives. Figure 10.2 shows the level of internet use for adults in the US. Nearly 50 per cent in each age range are connected to the internet, with the exception of the over-70s.

The important message for marketers is the relatively small difference in internet penetration – just 16 per cent – for the age range 30–58. All the indications are that this difference in internet usage is diminishing.

Jupiter Research, an American interactive channels consultancy, believes that the over-65s will increasingly go online. Table 10.1 shows that, by 2006, nearly 40 per cent of this age group are expected to be internet users.

All of this analysis demonstrates the relentless rise in the numbers of those over-50 in the US using the internet. For a marketer, it is important to know how this trend relates to the total numbers of consumers who regularly spend time online.

The data shown in Figure 10.3 is from International Demographics (December 2004), a consumer research company, and shows the percentages of the total adult online audience in the US in each age group. The right-hand axis plots the cumulative percentage numbers of people online, starting with the oldest group – shown by the dotted line.

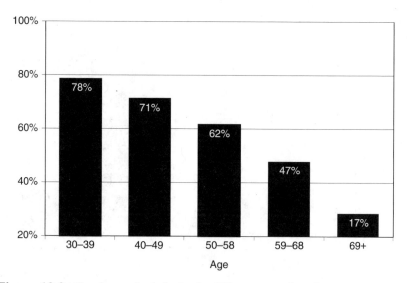

Figure 10.2 *Numbers of adults in the US connected to the internet*
Source: Pew Internet and American Life Project, April 2004

Two vital conclusions come from this analysis. First, the 18–24 age groups are relatively small. Second, the population of regular online users in their mid-40s and older represents over 50 per cent of all internet users. The internet is ageing along with its users!

Data for the UK's adoption of the internet by age group, shown in Table 10.2, delivers the same core message. Over 50 per cent of each adult age group, with the exception of those older than 64 years, are connected to the internet.

Countries that have been leading users of the internet – Australia and Japan, for example – have all followed the same age distribution pattern as the US and the UK.

China is an excellent example of an 'emerging' internet nation, with a young population. China's median age is 31.8 years, compared with Japan's 42.3 years, and its internet population is dramatically skewed to

Table 10.1 *Forecasts for online audiences in the US by age*

Year	50–64-year-olds online (%)	65+ online (%)
2003	50	23
2004	55	28
2005	61	33
2006	65	37

Source: Jupiter Research, 2003

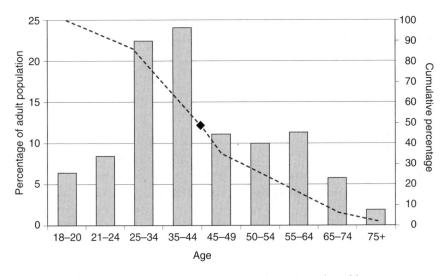

Figure 10.3 *Total adult online audience in the US analysed by age group*
Source: International Demographics, December 2004

the younger age groups. Adults aged under 30 account for 62 per cent of its population of internet users and those over 35 a mere 17 per cent.

China's use of the internet has increased by a factor of 140 in the past 6 years, mainly driven by young people. It will be fascinating to see how, and when, this profile changes to reflect the age mix of the country's population.

Europe has a significant 'north/south divide' in the numbers and age of people going online. For instance, an older person in the Netherlands is five times more likely to use the internet than their Portuguese counterpart.

Older people are emerging as the leading users of some types of internet services. The Pew internet report (2004) researched the growth in personal content creation – blogs, websites and file sharing, for example – and found that the over-50s were among the three main users of these types of features.

Table 10.2 *Numbers of users of the internet in the UK*

Age	Using the internet (%)
25–44	83
45–54	69
55–64	51
65+	21

Source: National Statistics Office, October 2003

All of these words, tables and charts convey one simple message: older people are a significant and growing proportion of internet users and must be taken seriously.

Mobile phones

The pattern of mobile phone use is similar to that shown for the internet. Between the ages of 35 and 64, the level of penetration is nearly 70 per cent and there is only a relatively small difference between any of the age groups in this span. Over half of the 65–74 age group own mobile phones and it is only at the age of 75+ that adoption rates decline. Figure 10.4 shows the level of mobile phone usage in the UK in August 2003.

The evidence suggests that while there is not that much difference in the age profile of mobile phone use, there is a significant difference in the rate of uptake of the devices' more complicated features, such as making video calls and taking and sending photo messages. This is not surprising as features of handsets – the screen size, keyboard, menu structure, volume levels and so on – have been optimized for a younger generation, who are assumed to be dexterous, with 20/20 vision and perfect hearing.

From the marketer's perspective, SMS, or texting, is the most important feature of the mobile. The growth in volume of text messages has been staggering. In the UK, at the beginning of 2003, 63 per cent of the population

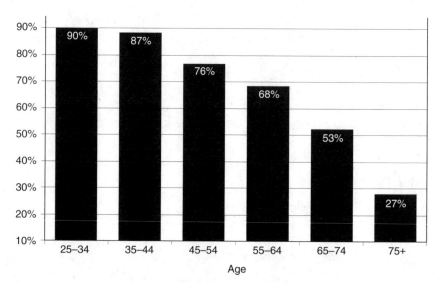

Figure 10.4 *Analysis of mobile phone use in the UK*
Source: OFTEL, August 2003 (now OFCOM)

used texting and generated over 52 million messages a day. A year later, this figure had grown to 64 million. MMS messaging is experiencing the usual pattern of growth for a new technology. During the first quarter of 2004 the number of MMS messages sent in the UK increased by 40 per cent.

Research conducted in mid-2002 indicated that the texting habit was dominated by the young, with a rapid fall in usage for people in their mid-50s. Anecdotal evidence suggests that while young people remain its primary users, the older age groups are catching up fast.

At long last, the obvious fact that older people have different needs from those of the young has been recognized by mobile phone handset manufacturers. The Japanese company Fujitsu has worked with the country's leading operator to develop the concept of the Raku Raku – the Easy Phone. This has been designed to satisfy the needs of the older age group, those with disabilities and people who still find using technology a threatening experience. The phone is designed to help with the most common problems older people encounter when using today's generation of mobile handsets. These problems, along with new design features, are set out in Table 10.3.

From the moment of the phone's launch it has been an instant success, selling over 3 million units.

A Swiss company, MobiClick, has gone much further and created a mobile phone with just three keys. The first button is on/off, the second is an alarm to call for assistance and the third connects to a pre-dialled friend

Table 10.3 *The facilities of the 'Easy Phone'*

The problem	Handset facility
Impaired vision	Large screen and font
	Voice guidance
	Distinctive key shapes
	Different tactile feedback for each function key
Hearing difficulties	Voice communication
	Easy access to the volume control
Difficulty using applications	Simple functionality for key tasks
	Quick-dial buttons
	Keyboard layout designed for easy recognition
Dexterity difficulties	Extra-large buttons
	Main buttons (dial and call end) made easy to identify

or family member. In 2005 Vodafone launched its 'Simply' mobile phone as a device that is 'an uncomplicated phone with built-in helpful tips' and 'easy-to-use for voice calls and texting'. For many people, not just the over-50s, it was great to read that the phone had been redesigned to put customer's needs not technology first!

It has taken far too long, but finally, slowly, the mobile phone industry is broadening its focus to satisfy the needs of more than just the youth audience.

Interactive digital TV (iDTV)

Interactive digital TV (iDTV) is the newest of the digital channels. It is still in an early phase of development and broadcasters and agencies have been slow to provide usage data. Part of this reticence is because the uptake has been slower than the industry pundits predicted. Its use is now increasing, most likely as a result of the demand for flat-screen TVs. It seems that consumers are taking the opportunity to convert to digital at the same time as they acquire their new wafer-thin TV sets.

According to Sky Broadcasting, in 2003, the UK had the highest penetration of digital TV at 44 per cent, closely followed by the US with 42 per cent. Japan was way behind, with 17 per cent, and mainland Europe in last position, with just 13 per cent.

Digital TV's emergence as an interactive channel seems to be following the growth profile of the web and SMS. For these, younger people were

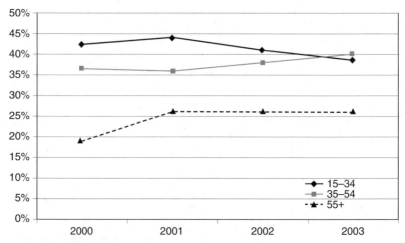

Figure 10.5 *The changing age profile for digital TV viewers in the UK*
Source: BMRB, 2003

the dominant early users of the technology, with the usage pattern gradually becoming age-neutral. Figure 10.5 shows the changing age profile for digital TV viewers in the UK between 2000 and 2003. As the popularity of the technology grows, its adoption by older people will undoubtedly increase.

The age profile for those using digital TV's more advanced features shows a similar skewed pattern, with younger people being the dominant users. Figure 10.6 illustrates this fact, showing the awareness and use of digital TV's interactive advertising facility.

The bar graph shows how the awareness of interactive advertising declines with age. Over 80 per cent of the 15–24-year-olds know about this feature, but the percentage falls to 40 per cent for viewers over the age of 65. Also shown in this figure by the line at the top is the percentage of each age group who both know about and have accessed interactive advertisements.

This profile shows that while the percentage of each age group who have accessed an interactive advertisement declines with age, it is less pronounced than the simple measure of awareness. In fact, the graph shows that in the 65+ age group, the percentage of viewers accessing advertisements is very similar to that of those aged 15–44. The message from this analysis is that older people who are aware of the channel, the early adopters, use it in a way that is not dissimilar to that of their younger counterparts.

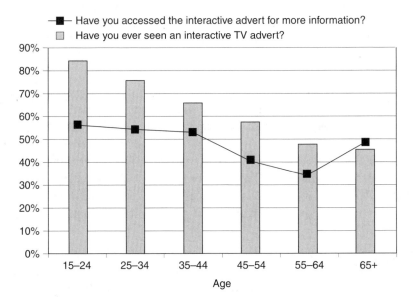

Figure 10.6 *Awareness and use of interactive advertising*
Source: BMRB, 2003

The BBC is one of the world's leading exponents of iDTV. Its inter-active service – BBCi – is accessed by large audiences and is becoming part of its mainstream television offering. BBCi's 'always on' text and video service was accessed by 10 million viewers in May 2004 and an estimated 13 million viewers accessed the interactive programmes during the 2004 Olympic games.

The BBC's own research shows that the audience for BBCi is skewed towards younger viewers, in the age range 25–44. The barriers that have discouraged people from using the digital text and video services have been:

▌ the speed of page loading on some of the digital platforms;
▌ the lack of page numbers;
▌ the audiences' familiarity and habit of using the existing analogue services (CEEFAX and Teletext).

To address these barriers, the BBC has introduced processes to improve the usability of the service, including page numbering to improve navigation and the relaunch of a faster service on Freeview – the UK's free digital service and cable platform. The changes are part of an ongoing plan to improve the usability of BBCi and should be available on all major digital platforms (Freeview, cable and satellite) in 2005.

It seems that all ages, both genders and every social class access inter-active programmes. The main factor determining the audience is the profile of people watching the programme. So, for example, two-thirds of the available audience for the Chelsea Flower Show in 2003 was aged 35+, but 80 per cent of the interactive audience was in this age category. The TV audience for the FA Cup is skewed towards males and this is reflected in the use of the interactive service.

The simple message that emerges from the BBC's experience is that when digital TV is simple to use and provides viewers with tangible benefits, then the take-up is only affected slightly by the age of the viewer. So, for instance, if people are watching Wimbledon and have the choice of six different matches at a simple click of a button, then they will use this facility. When there is a degree of effort and learning needed to use a channel, then older people tend not to bother. This is especially true if the digital service only provides marginal benefits over the existing analogue equivalent.

Instant messaging

It is arguable as to whether or not instant messaging can be categorized as an interactive channel, but, as it becomes more sophisticated, it is providing advertising opportunities and so deserves a mention.

Instant messaging (IM) began as a text-based tool that enabled somebody connected to the internet to exchange messages with a friend or colleague who was also online. It differs from e-mail by providing the ability to 'talk' to the other person, or people, in real time. Unlike e-mail, where there is a delay between the message's delivery and answer, IM is more akin to a conversation.

AOL was one of the first companies to provide IM services to its customers and has done much to promote the success of the service. AOL's most recent research, published in November 2004, showed that over 90 per cent of teens and young adults were IM users. The use of the service by the over-35s fell to a 50 per cent penetration level. These figures are a little higher than the results of research conducted by Pew Research, which showed all the age groups between 28 and 69 as having an uptake of around 30 per cent. The penetration levels differed by less than 8 per cent over this 40-year span of ages.

One simple, but profound, message emerges from these various pieces of research: older people are significant users of interactive channels. The recently introduced channels tend to be the most skewed to the younger user, but as the example of IM demonstrates, the differences in usage patterns can be very small.

Digital is the fastest-developing consumer marketing channel, in terms of its range of techniques, promotional expenditure and the time consumers spend using its various services. Marketers have no option but to ensure that this channel is effective across the whole age spectrum. The next chapter outlines the first steps towards achieving this goal.

OLDER WOMEN GET THE INTERNET HABIT

Historically, men have always been more interested in using PCs and the internet than women. The gender differences have now almost disappeared in the younger age groups, but older women have been slower to get the 'internet habit'. This imbalance is rapidly changing.

According to Nielsen/Netratings, in 2000, about 60 per cent of US adult internet users over the age of 65 were men. By 2004, the gender ratio had shifted to 50 per cent men and 50 per cent women – the same ratio as the total internet population.

The amount of time women spend using the internet is fast approaching the same levels as men. At the end of 2003, American men over the age of 65 were completing 63 sessions on the Web per month. Women of the same age were using the web 50 times a month. In a single year, women increased the average amount of time they spent online by 6 per cent, spending nearly 2 hours more online.

In Europe, the gender gap is more pronounced. In Germany, women make up only 20 per cent of the total of web users over 55 years old. Sweden is Europe's most gender-neutral country, with women representing 38 per cent of the users in this age group.

Younger women are becoming the primary users for some interactive channels. They are the main viewers of iDTV advertisements and play more interactive games on mobile handsets than men. No longer are technology geeks always men!

It is safe to say that older men and women will at least reach equality in their use of the internet. What we don't know is if older women will join their daughters and granddaughters and move beyond equality and become the prime users of certain channels.

THE OVER-65s MISSED THE DIGITAL REVOLUTION

Figures 10.2 and 10.3 above both showed how the over-65s are markedly less likely to use technology than the 50–60-year-olds just slightly their juniors. Only 21 per cent of UK adults over 65 are connected to the internet compared with 51 per cent of those aged 55–64. This difference is slightly less marked in the US, but even there the level of internet penetration for people aged over 69 years falls to 17 per cent. Equally, across all of the European Union countries, people over 70 are 6 times less likely to be using the internet than those in the 50–59 age group, according to a research study carried out by SeniorWatch.

The most obvious explanation for the poor uptake of the internet among the over-65s is their lack of experience of using PCs during their time at work. Once retired, people are deprived of the collaborative learning environment in which they could easily learn from their colleagues. After retirement, it requires a conscious effort to learn new skills like how to use the internet. The encouragement and assistance of children and grandchildren and the widespread availability of adult training courses makes this acquisition of skills relatively easy, but for many of the over-65s, it is easier not to bother.

Mediamark Research has been recording the growth in internet usage in the US since 1995 and has identified two types of people resistant to using internet technology. The first is the 'internet resisters' – people with no interest in or intention of going online. This group cannot see any advantage in using the internet and are adamant that that's how it will remain. The other group, 'the unconnected', consists of people who, owing to their financial position or where they live and work, have no access to the internet. Both these groups include a high proportion of older and less affluent people.

It seems likely that the cohort of people now aged 65+ will remain relatively low users of interactive technologies. The equivalent age cohort in a decade's time will have grown up surrounded by digital technologies so the figures are likely to be substantially different. Thus, today's 65+ will be the last age cohort to have grown up and worked in world without digital communications.

EDUCATIONAL BACKGROUND DETERMINES LEVELS OF INTERNET USE

The SeniorWatch project was the largest ever pan-European survey of the ways in which older people use computers and telecommunications. It was a financed by the European Community and concluded its three-year study at the beginning of 2003.

One of the key objectives of the research was to understand the factors affecting the over-50s' adoption of IT and recommend ways in which governments and companies could assist the process.

Users of PCs, mobiles and the internet were segmented according to their levels of skills. The most advanced group was labelled 'Frontrunners'. Figure 10.7 shows the profile for this group in terms of their age and educational attainment.

The level of educational attainment – as defined by the age they were when they left school – was found to be the most important factor in determining their capabilities in terms of using online technologies. For example, a person aged 80 who was 21+ when they left school is more likely to be in this group of leading internet users than somebody in their 50s who had little formal education. Indeed, educational attainment – a factor that is closely related to income – is the best predictor of who, in the 50-plus age group, uses technology. It's unlikely that this relationship will change in the foreseeable future.

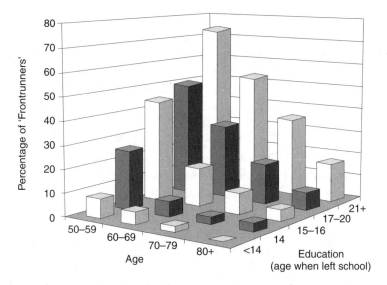

Figure 10.7 *The 'Frontrunners' show the relationship between age and level of education in determining internet use*
Source: SeniorWatch, 2002

AGEING AFFECTS HOW YOU USE TECHNOLOGY

It is a sad and unpalatable fact, but ageing is associated with a decline in our physical and mental abilities. This decline is hopefully balanced by an improvement in our knowledge, wisdom and mental attitude – but that is the subject of Chapter 13.

If interactive channels are to be effective for older audiences, their design and deployment must take account of these physiological changes. Sadly, there is huge gulf between the designers of interactive channels and researchers who understand the relationship between ageing and using technology. Most of the research is done in universities, particularly in the US, and, unfortunately, little of this knowledge is ever used by marketers in the corporate world. Fidelity Finance is one of the few companies with a research programme dedicated to understanding the special needs of older people and the Nielsen Norman Group – web usability consultants – has also researched the subject, but they remain in the minority.

Interactive channels are thus designed by the young, for the young. This has to change if they are to be effective with older audiences. A starting point for the marketer is understanding the implications of ageing for vision, dexterity and cognitive skills. The next chapter – 11, Interactive media for older eyes, hands and minds – explains how these problems translate into design requirements.

Vision

From about the age of 40 onwards, our eyes start to lose their ability to focus. Reading small text without the aid of glasses is difficult, as is staring at a computer screen for long periods of time.

Our eyes also begin to suffer from declining colour perception and contrast sensitivity. Our sensitivity to the colour blue reduces and it appears darker and harder to distinguish from green. Other colour combinations can become difficult to read, too, such as black on red and red on green.

Ageing results in our eyes needing higher levels of illumination. The eyes of a 60-year-old only receive a third of the amount of light as those of a 20-year-old. One decade later, the level of light received drops to 12 per cent and it continues to decrease with age.

As if these sight problems were not bad enough, ageing can also result in a degradation of peripheral vision. This results in problems reading a computer screen as the eye finds it difficult to locate the start of next line, differentiating it from adjoining lines of text, especially if there is insufficient contrast between each line.

These effects of ageing are in addition to the many natural vision problems that afflict all age groups. About 8 per cent of men and 0.5 per cent of women have some form of colour blindness, while another 2 per cent of the population suffer from other sight problems.

Motor movement

Older adults experience a reduction in their motor coordination. This creates difficulties when using a pointing device, such as a mouse, and small keypads. Dexterity problems make it difficult to control small cursor movements, resulting in an increase in the rate of errors and the time taken to complete tasks. Ageing also results in a loss of tactile sensation due to the degeneration of Meissner's corpuscles in the fingertips. This loss of sensation creates problems for many 70-year-olds using touch-sensitive controls for electronic devices.

In addition to these dexterity problems are those that occur because of age-related illnesses that damage joints and so on, restricting finger and wrist movements. Arthritis is probably the most common disease in this category. More than 7 million adults in the UK – 15 per cent of the population – suffer health problems due to arthritis and related conditions. The UK's incidence of this illness is similar to figures for other European countries and the US.

Cursor positioning difficulties are the most obvious manifestations of these problems. This skill does improve with experience, but older people and particularly those with arthritis are unlikely to achieve the same level of proficiency as younger people. Web designers rarely think of the difficulties that people who have problems moving a mouse experience when trying to position a mouse on small and closely spaced icons. When designers use complicated dynamic menus – the type that expand as the mouse moves over the menu graphic – they are oblivious of the frustration this causes older people. Similarly, mobile phone designers are besotted with loading more and more facilities into their devices that fewer and fewer people can and want to use. As phones become smaller, they demand ever-increasing levels of dexterity.

SeniorWatch concluded that a quarter of all Europeans aged over 50 seeking to improve their computer skills had some form of vision problems and 16 per cent had a serious impairment to their dexterity.

Cognitive skills

The effect of ageing on our cognitive skills is a complicated issue. There is no agreed model of how the cognitive processes work, but there is a general acceptance that ageing does lead to reduced performance when using interactive channels. This manifests itself in a reduction in capability in the following five cognitive processes:

▌ *working memory,* resulting in difficulty conducting multiple tasks and recalling the position reached in complicated processes;

▌ *spatial memory,* creating problems in visualizing and recalling where objects are located;

▌ *perceptual speed,* causing a slowing in the speed at which new information can be processed;

▌ *comprehension of text,* leading to a decline in the ability to understand certain aspects of text, such as inferences;

▌ *capacity to maintain attention,* resulting in difficulty concentrating when presented with multiple visual inputs. This becomes particularly difficult when the priority of the inputs is not obvious.

All of these different forms of cognitive ageing affect how older people use the web. Older users make more errors and take longer to complete tasks than their children and grandchildren. Nielsen Norman, web usability consultants, found that Web users over the age of 65 took significantly longer to complete tasks and made more errors than those aged 21–55. Fidelity, an American financial services company, also found a decrease in speed and accuracy levels among the over-55s. When these two findings were combined with the results of my own research, it was found that, on average, people 55 and over take 35 per cent longer to complete web tasks and make 20 per cent more errors than do their juniors. The over-65s took, on average, 60 per cent longer and made 50 per cent more errors than those under 55 did. These results are shown in Figure 10.8.

The obvious but false explanation for these results is the differing amount of online experience a young person, who has spent their life surrounded by screens, keyboards and the internet, has had compared to that of their late adopter grandparents. Surprisingly, this is not the reason. Researchers found that when they compared young and old people who had similar levels of internet experience, the older ones were still slower and less accurate when using the web than the younger ones.

Of all the age-related changes, it is the decline in cognitive powers that has the most impact on people's proficiency when using interactive channels. It has implications for the design of menu structures, levels of animation, presentation of information and provision of visual feedback.

It should be noted that vision, dexterity and cognitive problems are not limited to those who are older, but are also present in the population as a whole. In 2003, Microsoft published a study conducted by Forrester Research into the numbers of working-age adults in the US affected by different types of impairments. The results of this research are shown in Table 10.4.

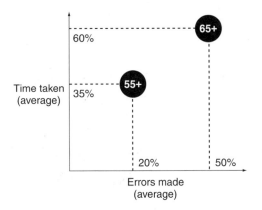

Figure 10.8 *The effects of ageing on performance when using the web*
Source: Nielsen Norman, 2000, Fidelity Finance, 2004, and 20plus30, 2004

Table 10.4 *Levels of visual and dexterity impairment in the US*

Degree and type of impairment	Incidence in US's working population (%)
Mild visual	16
Severe visual	11
Mild dexterity	19
Severe dexterity	7

Source: research commissioned by Microsoft, conducted by Forrester Research, 2003

This analysis shows that nearly a quarter of the US's population suffers from one or both of these impairments.

Another example of the physiological effects of ageing is provided by a UK government study (September 2003) showing that 2 million people are excluded from viewing the new digital services because of dexterity, sensory or cognitive problems. A further 700,000 people are excluded from using advanced features, such as digital text and interactive services, for these reasons.

Large numbers of people are excluded from using digital services, but even more require technical assistance to install the new television receivers. A staggering 15 per cent of viewers will require third-party assistance to make their equipment work.

The study also found that digital TV equipment is designed using the same menu-driven concepts found on PCs and mobile phones. People with dexterity, sensory and cognitive problems find this interface difficult to use. The report concluded that if the UK is to switch completely to the more complicated digital TV network, there will need to be a radical improvement in the design of the equipment if everyone is to be able to use it.

The results of ageing make it hard to use electronic devices. If these devices are designed assuming that their users have 20/20 vision, nimble fingers and perfect memories it compounds the problem. If it were not so serious it would be comical that we expect at least half of the population to cope with devices that are the key to interactive marketing channels which they find difficult and frustrating to use.

WE LEARN ABOUT USING TECHNOLOGY IN THE WORKPLACE

It is easy to forget that the widespread business use of the internet is less than ten years old. Amazon, Microsoft's Internet Explorer and Windows 95 have all appeared in the last decade. It was not until the new millennium that the internet really became welded into the day-to-day existence of the business world.

A great many older people retired with little or no first-hand experience of using the internet in their business life. For those aged over 70, it is very possible that they retired with no experience of using a PC.

This lack of experience with technology does not imply that these skills cannot be learnt – as witnessed by the many 80-year-olds who are extremely computer-literate. There does seem to be a direct connection, however, between the experience of using technology during one's working life and its use into retirement. Figure 10.9 shows the relationship between the number of years of internet experience prior to retirement and age. From the age of 60 onwards there is a rapid decline, closely matching the profile of internet use shown in Figure 10.3.

There are many pressures and incentives to persuade the over-70s to get online – the most powerful being the desire to maintain contact with family and friends. For a sizeable subset of this group – mainly the poorer and less well educated – the future will be one adrift from the internet and other interactive channels.

This will be the last ever non-digital age cohort. In the same way that we think it astonishing and quaint that our forefathers lived without experiencing electricity and running water, I suspect that the same thought will occur in the future about a life without digital communications.

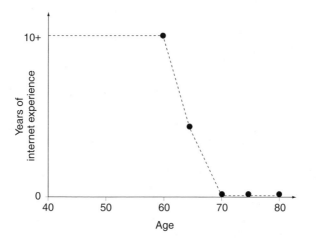

Figure 10.9 *Years of internet experience prior to retirement*
Source: 20plus30, 2004

MARKETERS ARE BAD AT CONTROLLING INTERACTIVE CHANNELS

Marketers must understand the fundamentals of the technologies that support interactive channels. A survey of UK marketers showed that the majority of the profession were baffled by much of the technology that they were responsible for managing. An astonishing 75 per cent of those working in the marketing, advertising and design industries said that they had difficulties using the technology required to do their job.

Managing interactive channels may be the responsibility of marketing, but, too often, the people making the day-to-day decisions reside in the company's IT department or its interactive agencies. These technologies are awash with their own jargon, which makes it difficult for the generalist marketer to question the specialist's decisions. Marketers are responsible for the success of these channels, but frequently lack the requisite knowledge and experience to make informed decisions.

This is a significant problem when the interactive channels are targeted at the marketer's own age group. It is doubly difficult when it concerns an audience twice or three times this age. As with so many issues related to age and marketing, the starting point is to take the issue seriously. Having done this, the secret is to use facts and experience rather than myths and prejudices.

As this chapter has shown, we know a lot about the relationship between age and how older people use the technology that enables interactive channels. These channels are increasing in importance, as is the number of older people using them. When formulating a marketing strategy, involving the internet, SMS, iDTV and IM, therefore, it is unforgivable if it does not take account of the needs of *all* audiences, including those aged 50 and above.

IMPLICATIONS FOR THE MARKETER

Interactive channels are multiplying in number, increasing in complexity and growing in importance.

! Marketing must understand how its audiences – of all ages – use and respond to an organization's interactive channels. In this respect, interactive channels are no different to traditional ones.

Older people are already significant users of interactive channels. There is little difference in the usage pattern from the ages of 30 to 55 years.

❗ Discard the myth that the young are 'good' with technology and the old are 'technophobic'. Older people are not a specialist niche group – they are part of the mainstream.

Because of the limited exposure of the over-65s to IT during their working lives they are significantly less likely to use interactive channels than those 5–10 years their junior. Their level of educational attainment is the most significant factor determining their adoption of digital technologies.

❗ Their lower level of technology usage is unlikely to change. This age cohort will remain a difficult and expensive group of people to reach.

Ageing results in a deterioration of vision, dexterity and the cognitive processes. These physiological changes have a significant effect on how older people use interactive channels.

❗ Marketing must ensure that designers understand the effects of ageing when setting up interactive channels. Unless there are specific reasons to target younger age groups, it is marketing's responsibility to provide channels that are age-neutral.

The newly emergent internet nations, such as China, are following the same usage patterns as Europe and the US. Initially, there is a preponderance of young users, followed by older people.

❗ Make use of the reliable data about usage statistics by country for the internet, iDTV and mobile phones. If you are planning international marketing campaigns, take account of differences in the numbers of older users in different countries.

Older women are reaching equality with men in their use of interactive channels. It is likely that they will become the primary users of certain types of channel, such as iDTV advertisements.

❗ Re-evaluate the extent of male bias in the content and targeting of your interactive channels.

Most marketers are under 35 years old. Soon this age group will represent a minority of users for most interactive channels. It is dangerous, and patently wrong, to believe that older people perceive using the web, SMS, instant messaging and iDTV as the province of the young.

! The item 'age-related considerations' must appear on the agenda
• whenever the subject of interactive channels is being discussed. Not understanding how older people use – and want to use – digital technology is a massive mistake that alienates a large group of customers.

SUMMARY

▌ Opinions about how older people use technology are littered with myths and stereotypes.

▌ As interactive channels are the fastest-growing method of customer communication, it would be wise for marketers to base their decisions on fact rather than unsupported assumptions. It is vital to understand the dynamics and motivations of older peoples' use of technologies such as the web, e-mail, mobile phone messaging and iDTV.

▌ The young are 'good' with technology and the old are reticent, late adopters and slow learners. This sentiment summarizes the commonly held view about the relationship between age and technology. It is a total distortion of the truth.

▌ The gap is reducing between the way in which technologies are adopted and used by young and older age groups. The over 65s, who retired before many of the channel technologies were widely adopted, are an exception. The pattern of technology usage for people from their early 30s to middle 50s is similar and becoming more so.

▌ Ageing affects a person's sight, dexterity and cognitive powers. These problems result in differing degrees of difficulty when using all of the interactive channels. Better-educated people – and especially those with a longer history of using the technologies in the workplace – are able to compensate for some of these physiological problems. For many older people, using a mouse, typing on a keyboard, viewing a screen and navigating a website can be a nightmare.

▌ Older people are not alone in encountering such problems. People with visual, dexterity and cognitive disabilities that occur at all ages represent a sizeable proportion of the population.

▌ Interactive channel designers should take account of these physiological difficulties, but rarely do. The plight of older people and those with disabilities are regularly ignored by channel designers – not out of malice but rather a lack of knowledge and appreciation of the number of potential customers affected.

▍ It is difficult for marketers to manage the ever-increasing number of interactive channels and have a real understanding of the enabling technologies. Marketers often find themselves instructing the technologists implementing these channels without having a thorough understanding of what the channels can and cannot do. It is not surprising that the issue of the age of the user is often missed out during the channel's design phase. It is vital, however, that this issue is included in the design specification as older age groups represent an extremely large group of important potential customers who are being badly served by the current generation of interactive channels.

11

Interactive media for older eyes, hands and minds

The previous chapter described the reasons for marketers needing to understand the effects of ageing. This chapter explains how to transform this knowledge into making interactive channels effective for older audiences. It details the practicalities of using interactive technology to fulfil, rather than frustrate, the older user.

An 80-year-old can have the same attitudes, interests and zest for life as his or her grandchildren – even great-great-grandchildren – but will not possess the same quality of eyesight, dexterity and cognitive ability. Our lifestyle and genetic history influences the form and pace of our ageing, but a decline in sensory and cognitive abilities is inevitable. Sorry if this sounds somewhat melodramatic, but that is how it is! The wonders of genetic engineering might change this rule sometime in the future, but not soon enough to be useful to you as you use this book!

As the web and e-mail are the most widely used forms of interactive media, this chapter focuses on ways in which to improve their effectiveness. The same principles and techniques are equally applicable to multimedia messaging and interactive TV channels.

There is a wide variation in the depth of involvement that marketers have in the technical implementation of their websites and e-mail marketing. For some marketers, the technical aspects of the web and e-mail are a 'black art' that they delegate to their technical experts. For others, often in smaller organizations, understanding the technical issues is part of their job. With this in mind, I have written this chapter so that you can select the level of detail appropriate to your needs.

Marketers make a disastrous mistake when they believe that their in-house website developers or their external web design agency understand the science of designing for older people. Producing age-friendly websites is not something that many web designers understand and very few of them possess more than a rudimentary knowledge of the subject. So, if you decide that your interactive channels should be as effective for the over-50s as the under-30s, your web designers must be instructed about this requirement. This chapter helps you to formulate your instructions and gives you the tools you need to make sure that they have been followed.

WHAT'S THE PROBLEM?

Very few websites, web advertisements or e-mail marketing campaigns take any account of the older audience's needs. Even websites specifically targeting older people often contain examples of the most rudimentary mistakes. After a decade of the web's existence, far too many sites are constructed to look pretty but with little consideration given to how they will be used. Younger people have the experience, patience and resilience to cope with poorly designed sites, but older people are less able and less willing to endure such frustrations.

The following example illustrates the nature of this problem. In 2004, my company tested the websites of eight major companies in the cruise industry. This industry was selected as its customer base is more likely to be older than younger. A panel of people between the ages of 50 and 60 years visited each of the chosen websites to search for a particular type of cruise, find information to help them to decide if a cruising holiday was something that they would enjoy, and tried to book the cruise. These seemed very basic tasks and ones that we expected it would be possible to carry out on all cruising websites. We were surprised at what we found.

The websites appeared to be dominated by the companies' marketing messages and with conveying the glitz of the cruising experience. Most of the sites failed to satisfy the basic requirement of being easy to search and providing comprehensive information about cruise itineraries.

The following comments are typical of the panel's responses:

'a mixture of company promotion and customer information without doing either well'

'frustrating to use'

'irritating flash bang graphics'

'too controlling – they have forgotten that I am the customer'

'busy and muddled'

'hard work finding the simplest information'

The panel scored each website against three criteria.

▌ Would you refer this site to a friend? (Only one of the websites was considered good enough to be referred.)
▌ When using the website, how frustrated were you? (The average score was 'significantly frustrated'.)
▌ Before leaving the website, how successful were you in achieving your goals? (On average, the panel members would have abandoned the websites having only achieved 40 per cent of their requirements.)

The problems encountered when using these cruise industry websites are not untypical. Wichita State University – a centre of expertise on website usability – evaluated 36 websites that were designed for older people. They found that the websites varied greatly in quality and all of them had design faults that caused significant problems for the older person.

Marketers spend a lot of time talking about their organizations' brand values and their 'passion' for being 'customercentric'. Every time somebody abandons a visit to their websites in frustration, those brands' reputations are diminished. Companies sometimes spend an inordinate amount of time and money on perfecting the visual design of their website, but give only cursory consideration to the question of how it will be used.

Websites that are simple and satisfying to use make for happy and loyal customers. The same applies equally well to e-mail marketing and mobile messaging.

So, where to begin to achieve this state of marketing nirvana?

THE FIRST STEP IS TO TAKE IT SERIOUSLY

Why do so few companies try to make their interactive channels 'friendly' to older people? As this chapter demonstrates, it is not a lack of knowledge about what needs to be done. It is not because there are any inherent technical reasons for it being impossible to achieve. It is all to do with taking the issue seriously and having the commitment to do something about it.

Sometimes designers rationalize the situation by saying that it is impossible to design a site for both a young and an old audience. I have met designers who believe that satisfying the requirements of older people inhibits their creativity or freedom to use the latest technical innovations. I have even heard the argument that designing for older people means breaking the sacrosanct corporate style rules. Satisfy customers at the expense of breaking style rules – what a suggestion!

If these lame excuses were the only reasons for so little having been done, it would be simple to rectify the situation. Unfortunately, there is a much harder problem to solve. The reason so few marketers and designers attempt to make their interactive channels friendly to older users is very simple: they are unaware that they have a problem.

Even when the issue and its solution are explained to people, it is difficult to generate in them the resolve to take it seriously. One catalyst for change is to focus attention on the age of the audience expected to visit the website. Figure 11.1 shows two types of profile for people visiting websites. The category 'For young eyes only' could be a tween music or fashion website. The 'Older the better' web audience profile could be for a site where the products and services are targeted exclusively at older people.

Of course, just because the products and services are aimed at an older age range doesn't mean that all the people visiting the website will be old. The children and grandchildren may well be the people who buy or advise on purchases for their older relations. Thus, the majority of websites will not be at one or the other end of the age spectrum, but more like the profile shown in Figure 11.2.

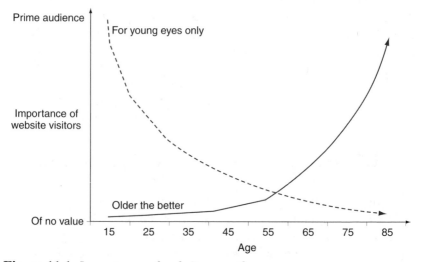

Figure 11.1 *Importance of website users by age*

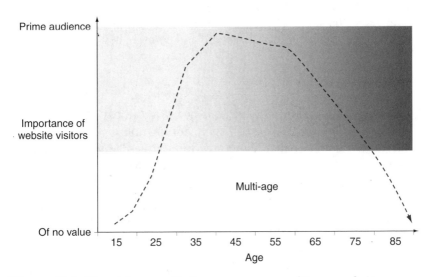

Figure 11.2 *The visitor profile for an average, multi-age website*

The sole reason for conducting this exercise is to ensure that the age of an interactive channel's users is considered. If the analysis shows that a substantial – even possibly the majority of the audience – is aged over 50, it is extremely difficult to ignore the fact.

Apart from the downright foolishness of ignoring the requirements of an important audience, all the evidence shows that making channels work well for older people also improves their effectiveness for younger age groups.

Once the decision has been made to take the issue seriously and make interactive channels friendly to the older age group, the implementation of the necessary changes is relatively straightforward.

OLDER EYES, HANDS AND MINDS

Chapter 5 discussed the effects of ageing on vision, dexterity and cognitive skills. If a website attracts visitors of widely different ages, which, as we have seen, is likely, then the objective is to apply this knowledge to ensure that the site is age-neutral – that is, the site delivers a constant level of satisfaction, irrespective of the person's age.

The following section provides a basic set of guidelines for deciding the most appropriate design and technology options. All marketers should have a basic understanding of these factors (if you want a more detailed version of these guidelines, see Appendix 1). These guidelines are intended to be used for websites and e-mail, but the same principles apply to all channels using a screen, keyboard and pointing device.

Older eyes

As eyesight deteriorates with age, it is necessary to pay attention to the fonts, colours and format used to display information.

The most common belief about how to improve the visual quality of websites is 'make the font bigger'. When measured under research conditions, the size of the font appears to have little or no effect on the speed or accuracy of use. Older people have a preference for larger fonts, but using them doesn't necessarily change the speed or number of errors made. Websites using very small fonts are both difficult and unpleasant to use – a view shared by the over-50s *and* teenagers.

In addition to using a sensible font size, what else can be done to make things easier for people as the quality of their eyesight declines? The following are the main factors that will improve performance and ease of use when reading text on a website:

- whenever possible, use sans serif fonts, such as Arial, rather than fonts with serifs, such as Times Roman;
- try to use fonts no smaller than 12-point and certainly no smaller than 10-point;
- the fonts and colours must provide a clear visual contrast between the navigation and content areas of the screen;
- there are certain colour combinations to avoid – black on red and using red and green together;
- the length of a line of text on the screen should be around 40–50 letters – this helps to reduce eyestrain;
- backgrounds and watermarks should be avoided – if it is necessary to use a background, then it should be as light as possible;
- older people have difficulty distinguishing between design elements that are used to improve the screen layout – bullets, icons and headings, for example – and text and images associated with hyperlinks, so make a clear distinction between design and navigation and use a consistent treatment of links and layout throughout the site.

Older hands

Older people can have difficulty in accurately positioning a PC mouse. Using the pointing device on a notebook or PDA is even harder. Watching older people use a mouse for the first time is a painful experience as they edge the cursor across the screen. Practice and regular use improves their ability, but for people who infrequently use computers, it remains an ongoing difficulty.

The following design features assist people who find taming an errant mouse a problem:

■ An addressable graphic – that is, a small picture, or button, that can be clicked on – needs to be sufficiently large. It is suggested that no graphic should be smaller than 18–22 pixels.

■ There must be sufficient space between active links to avoid difficulty in positioning the mouse cursor.

■ Avoid dynamic menu systems with nested dropdown menus. These are menus that expand as you roll the cursor over the menu graphic with the mouse. They are a very elegant and visual way of displaying the menu options, but their weakness is the precision of mouse movement they demand to make them work properly. They are also very 'search engine unfriendly', so on all counts their use should be avoided.

■ Wherever possible, ensure that you can navigate a web page using the directional keys on the keyboard.

Remember that many older people have no keyboard skills – something that is not uncommon with teenagers, too – and have to resort to one-finger typing. Minimize the amount of text that needs to be keyed.

Older minds

Ageing brings with it difficulty in maintaining concentration and it takes longer to learn and remember new information. These problems are exacerbated when combined with having little experience of using a PC and the web.

There are two things that can be done to alleviate these problems:

■ make the content of the website relevant and easy to understand;
■ ensure that the navigation is simple to use.

The following design suggestions will improve both navigating the website and making sense of its content.

■ Whenever possible, use 'goal-centred' navigation. By anticipating the questions people have in their minds when they visit the website, you can structure and phrase the navigation elements in the same terms.

▌ Make the search facility easy to locate and use. Too often, on-site search engines rely on a level of knowledge about web terminology and its mechanics that older people don't possess.

▌ Provide as much visual feedback as possible to tell the user where they are on the site.

▌ Older users are less able to recover when they make an error and find themselves stranded in the wrong part of the site than more experienced users. To avoid this, provide as much 'recovery' navigation as possible.

▌ The website text should be clear and precise. Paragraph and sentence structure should be short and simple and devoid of technical jargon.

▌ Only use animation if it is really necessary. Let me say that again: *only use animation if it is really necessary.*

▌ The effects of animated advertising on a website are just the same – maybe even worse – than the site's own animation.

▌ Make the text concise. Use single-subject sentences and reduce the word count as much as possible. Writing for the web should use half the word count (or less) of conventional writing.

You will probably have noticed that these recommendations are directly linked to sight, dexterity and cognitive performance. There is also a set of technical guidelines about a website's construction that will improve its suitability for older audiences.

▌ Once the design of the site is stable, minimize the changes to the navigation structure to avoid the user having to relearn how the site works. Designers are often temped to change things for the sake of change. Unless there are sound marketing or customer service reasons, don't.

▌ Avoid using multiple browser windows – that is, when a link is clicked, it opens another browser window rather than showing the results in the same window. It is possible that the opening of a second window might be blocked by the software settings and it may well confuse the user.

▌ Do not use plug-ins that the visitor needs to download before being able to use the website. This is especially common on travel companies' websites where they feel impelled to use 360-degree animation and rich media.

▌ Site load times should be as short as possible. A lot of older people will not migrate to using Broadband, so websites should not be constructed assuming that all audiences have a fast connection.

▌ Older, and younger, people often want a hard copy of a web page. Anticipate this need and provide a 'print this page' facility where it is appropriate.

Web designers often quote the fact that older people spend longer on websites, are willing to wait longer for websites to load and switch between sites less often. It would be totally wrong to interpret this as an excuse for not making a website as friendly as possible for the older age group. Older people may be willing to spend more time trying to use a website than younger users, but that doesn't mean badly constructed sites have no adverse effects. It is just as easy to construct sites that are friendly to older age groups as not. All it requires is that the decision is made to do so and then ensure that the designers follow some very simple rules. The trouble is, designers don't like following rules!

WHAT CAN GO WRONG?

When I interview older people about their experiences of using the web, I keep hearing the same complaints. These gripes are not limited to one age group and the same comments are just as common coming from somebody in their 40s as in their 50s or 60s.

Like most things in marketing, problems that beset websites obey the Pareto principle – a few faults cause a disproportionate number of problems. If marketers would focus on the most common gripes users mention, they would be 80 per cent towards resolving them. The following are the top five gripes of older website users:

▋ *Gripe 1: 'I cannot find what I am looking for.'* In the early days of website design, there was a technique called 'scenario planning'. This is a complicated-sounding name for the very simple process of documenting the most common activities that visitors to the website undertake. From studying numerous company and government websites, it is obvious that many organizations have stopped using this technique. During our research of cruise company websites, we tested how well they allowed the visitor to answer the simple question 'Does the cruise visit a particular country?' To our astonishment, we found that, in most cases, we couldn't locate the information needed to answer this most basic of questions. To resolve the situation, start by ensuring that your website does the basics very well and most of the visitors will get most of the information they require most of the time.
▋ *Gripe 2: 'I find it difficult to read the text.'* The most common reason for this is a lack of contrast between the text and the background. Sometimes it is because the colours used for the links, before and after they are clicked, have insufficient contrast. Sometimes it is because

companies insist on following their design style rules even if they create problems for the site user.

Whatever the reason, if it is difficult to read a website's text, there is little likelihood of it providing the visitor with a rewarding experience.

▌ Gripe 3: *'I don't understand what they are talking about.'* Company terminology, technical gobbledygook, marketing-speak and verbose copy – all contribute to the emotion that makes you want to throw the mouse through the PC's screen! Writing plain, simple and easily understandable English for websites is a skill. Too often, it is left to untrained marketers to create it or modify text that was intended for other media. Even worse than the marketer with poor writing skills, however, is the member of the IT department who is designated to write website copy.

▌ Gripe 4: *'I keep forgetting where I am on the site.'* Google's home page contains 32 items of text and 12 navigational links. At its most bloated, Yahoo! contained well over 20 times the words and the number of links it has now. Google is simple to use and structured so that it is impossible to get lost. Yahoo! can be great fun to navigate for the expert user, but may be a potential maze for the older person. Designers need to understand that ageing – especially when combined with little experience of using the web – increases the chances of getting lost on a site. It is their responsibility to construct websites in such a way that they minimize the chance of this happening. Aim to be a Google, not a Yahoo!

▌ Gripe 5: *'It keeps stopping me doing what I want to do.'* This problem occurs when websites are designed with the marketing and commercial objectives of the company in mind rather than those of the customer. The cruise industry, as we saw earlier, provides a perfect example of how this can lead to annoyance and frustration. It is not unreasonable to think that, having selected a cruise, it would be a simple operation to proceed and book it. One would think that this would be the ultimate aim of having a website.

Our researchers found this to be far from the case. We subsequently learnt that few cruise companies take orders directly, but, instead, direct people to travel agents. Instead of clearly stating this fact, it is left to the hapless customers (most of whom will be aged over 55) to discover it by trial and error.

This last is an extreme example of what happens when companies don't consider adequately how their websites will be used. This problem affects all ages, but disproportionately older people.

BE SYSTEMATIC

Most marketers already have their interactive marketing channels in place and don't have the luxury of discarding them and starting again. The challenge is to evaluate what already exists and decide what needs to be changed.

Once you have decided that your website must appeal to all ages, where do you begin the evaluation and planning process? The starting point is to define two key characteristics of the website. First, the audiences who will use the site – what is known about them, their experience of using the web and their age?

Second, what do visitors want to achieve when they visit the website? This requires an understanding of what the website must provide in order to ensure that visitors leave feeling totally satisfied.

This simple analysis is such an obvious thing to do, but is too often omitted. It applies equally well to any interactive channel used by any age group.

The next requirement is that the website be evaluated in a systematic way, using our knowledge base of how ageing affects the use of this technology. Figure 11.3 shows how this knowledge can be structured into a pyramid of factors. The foundation is the website's navigation structure. When that is poorly constructed, it is immaterial how the rest of the site works.

The other factors are:

▮ *functionality* – this includes all of the website's processing features, such as orders, enquiries, searches, forms and so on;
▮ *design elements* – how the site uses colour to present text and imagery and the way it incorporates animation;
▮ *language and imagery* – the appropriateness of the site's language and imagery.

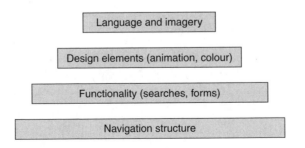

Figure 11.3 *The pyramid of factors affecting a website's age-friendliness*

Websites' audit methodologies normally focus on either the site's technical or design and aesthetic features. When evaluating a website for its age-friendliness, it is necessary to check both these sets of factors with equal rigour.

The questions in Appendix 2 form an audit document for evaluating a website's age-friendliness using the same structure as the pyramid of factors. The audit document also contains a set of questions to help define the types of people who are expected to visit the website and how they are expected (predicted) to behave.

The breadth and number of the questions makes this the most comprehensive age-friendly audit document available. It does not require any specialist technical knowledge, but it is necessary to evaluate each facet of the website in a systematic way. On completing the audit, you will have a thorough understanding of how good, or bad, your website is at meeting the requirements of the older user. Equally, website designers will find that the audit process is a valuable way to guarantee that they deliver to their clients' websites that work equally well for the whole age spectrum.

As well as conducting a detailed appraisal of the website, the audit is also a useful and revealing way to review the level of commitment your organization has to making all the various components of your interactive strategy age-friendly. Reaching a final picture of this situation is not the most important outcome. By going through the process of answering the questions, some difficult organizational issues have to be confronted.

The matrix shown in Figure 11.4 is a simple model that represents pictorially the state of an organization's preparedness in each of the key areas. The horizontal axis is divided into six elements, four of which were explained earlier in relation to Figure 11.3:

▋ navigation structure;
▋ functionality;
▋ design elements;
▋ language and imagery.

There are two additional factors:

▋ *promotion* – this includes the techniques used to generate Web traffic, such as Web advertising, paid-for search, comparison sites and affiliates;
▋ *e-mail marketing* – this includes standard person-to-person e-mail, e-zines, alerts and newsletters.

The vertical axis of the matrix represents the level of commitment the organization has to becoming age-friendly. Starting with 'not considered', the level of commitment increases by four increments:

- *aware of the issues factor* – knowing the age-friendliness could be improved;
- *made ad hoc changes* – have made changes to improve age-friendliness, but not as part of an overall strategy;
- *programme in place* – there is a funded programme to improve the element's age-friendliness;
- *continually reviewing* – changes have been made and there is a programme in place to repeatedly review their effectiveness.

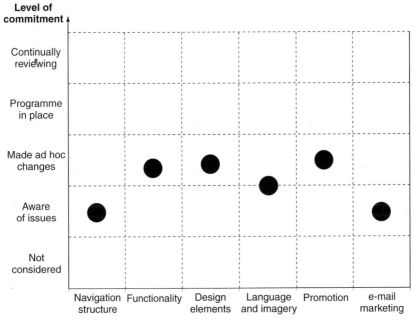

Figure 11.4 *Matrix showing the organization's level of commitment to age-friendliness*

The profile shown in the matrix is typical of the level of commitment I have found in my experience of working with companies.

Most organizations have some awareness that their websites have to be able to satisfy the needs of older people. Where this awareness translates into actions, it invariably results in a series of ad hoc changes to different parts of the web channel. It is very unusual to find companies that organize their age-related changes into a formal programme and exceptionally rare to encounter this happening on an ongoing basis.

When older people form a significant number of a website's users, the objective is for all of the components of age-friendliness to score in the 'continually reviewing' category.

THE NEED FOR RESEARCH

How do you know what functionality your audiences want from your interactive channels? Without research, it is close to impossible to know, in detail, what people of different age groups want from a website. A 60-year-old would readily admit to having little idea about the website needs of somebody in their 20s. If you asked 20-year-old about the site requirements of their grandparents, they would not be reticent about giving an opinion. The reality is that most websites are designed by young people for young people. Very few companies make any attempt to find out about and understand the motivations and needs of the people visiting their websites. If they did, they would be in for some shocks and surprises.

One company that takes audience research very seriously is Fidelity Investments, an American finance company. It is one of the very few companies with a human interface design laboratory where the requirements of different web users and their online behaviour are studied.

To illustrate the ways in which people's requirements of websites change with age and gender, Fidelity asked a group of potential customers to define their requirements of a financial services home page. Here are some of the findings:

▌ men wanted more news content and secondary navigational items, such as site maps, international sites, company information, additional news and FAQs;
▌ women wanted more special deals and promotions and liked having photographs of the company's management;
▌ older people showed a significant preference – 40 per cent of people over the age of 65 years – for navigation that included large, button-like bullets located next to each link, but none of the sample under the age of 40 years wanted this type of navigation;
▌ older people wanted the website to incorporate a 'Help' feature – it was the choice of 30 per cent of the over-65s, but only 5 per cent of the under-65s requested this feature.

Another example of how a person's age determines their preferences for website functionality is the desire for personalization of the content. Research conducted by ChoiceStream (May 2004) showed that 80 per cent of older consumers were interested in receiving personalized content. Nearly 90 per cent of younger people (18–24) expressed an interest in this feature. The level of interest fell to 76 per cent for those aged 35 and older.

Understanding the needs of different website audiences also includes factors as fundamental as their literacy levels. According to the National Adult Literacy Study, 92 million adults in the US – almost 48 per cent of the population – have low or very low reading skills. This report makes very depressing reading. It concluded that 'many adults lack the basic reading, writing and computational tasks necessary to understand health, personal finance, travel and governmental services information'.

A person's age is relevant to their likely literacy level. Two out of five older Americans (those who are 65+) read at or below the 5th grade reading level, while the average younger adult reads between the 8th and 9th grade levels. The stark message from this research is that just because a person uses an interactive channel doesn't mean that they will have a high or even medium level of reading attainment.

The purpose behind quoting these different examples is to emphasize a simple truth. How can a 25-year-old with a university degree have any idea what a 65-year-old who left school at 14 wants from a website? Research is not an option, it is a necessity.

THE IMPORTANCE OF TESTING THE CHANNEL

The latest generation of mobile phones are technological wonders. Voice is but one of the features of these phones, alongside them being camera, games console, text message sender and receiver, internet browser and music centre. For the gadget geek, they are a treasure trove of functionality, providing hours of amusement. For somebody with poor eyesight, clumsy fingers and a low frustration threshold, though, they are a nightmare.

I would be astonished if the new generation of phones were ever tested with an older audience during their development. If they were, then the feedback received must have been ignored!

At the other end of the complexity spectrum is the interface for viewing enhanced programme services on digital TV. The BBC tests its digital channel interface with all ages and has achieved a wonderfully simple way of accessing its services. Audience research shows that the service is used by all ages and sectors of society.

The Web is somewhere between these two extremes. Mostly, website testing is limited to ensuring that the site's functionality works. That does not necessarily mean the website is usable, let alone a marketing asset. In those cases where usability testing is undertaken, it is rare to find that the research group includes older people.

Compared with the thrill of the creative phase of site design, testing is perceived as a laborious and expensive exercise. Steve Krug, who is one of the leading writers about usability testing, lists five plausible, but incorrect, excuses for not testing websites. These are shown in Table 11.1.

Irrespective of the age of a website's audience, usability testing should be an integral part of the site's lifecycle. It should be conducted when a site is first created and whenever it undergoes significant change. As the age of the site's audience increases, so does the need for testing.

Some usability experts, including Steve Krug, argue that the profile of the people used for testing is unimportant. I disagree with this view. My experience is that the best testing results for sites being used by older audiences come when testers are of an equivalent age.

The option not to test a website's usability might soon become a thing of the past. Disabilities legislation is being invoked throughout Europe and in the US for its federal government websites. A website that is difficult to

Table 11.1 *Plausible, but incorrect, excuses for not undertaking website usability testing*

We don't have the time	It is wrong to assume that testing is a long and complicated exercise. It can be done quickly and ends up saving time as it highlights problems when it is relatively simple to correct them.
We don't have the money	You can spend a lot of money on testing, but it can also be done on a limited budget. The testing does not have to be comprehensive. It is better to test and correct a website's top five problems than not test it at all.
We don't have the expertise	The basics of usability testing are easy to understand. Read Steve Krug's book, *Don't Make Me Think* (Que, 2000); it's a good place to start.
We don't have a usability lab	You don't need one. All you need is a quiet area with a PC. It is best if the environment is as much like real life as possible. With the advent of inexpensive testing software, such as Camtasia, any company has the ability to undertake its own usability testing.
We don't know how to interpret the results	This is the hardest part of usability testing. Either hire a usability consultant or, if budgets are very limited, refer to one of the many excellent usability guides.

use will not just result in disgruntled users – it could also lead to legal action being taken.

The connection between disability issues and ageing is the topic of the next section.

ACCESSIBILITY IS PART OF THE SAME SPECTRUM

As people age, they begin to share some of the problems – or, more accurately, they exhibit some of the same symptoms – as people with disabilities. These, as we have seen, include eyesight, hearing, dexterity and cognition-related difficulties. It is very wrong, though, to lump the issues of ageing and disability together as an amorphous set of 'problems'. The UK's regulator for the communications industries, with responsibilities across television, radio, telecommunications and wireless communications services, OFCOM, has done just this. It has established a single committee to advise on the interests of old *and* disabled people. The rationale for this decision was one of saving costs, not because of a natural affinity between the two groups. It is equally wrong, however, to ignore the multiple technical overlaps between making interactive channels effective for the old and those with disabilities.

There is very little legislation related to ageing but an increasing amount is concerned with disabilities. In the UK, Part 3 of the Disability Discrimination Act 1995 (DDA) requires:

> Providers of goods, facilities and services to avoid the less favourable treatment of disabled people and to make reasonable adjustments, including the provision of auxiliary aids and services, to any practices, policies or procedures which make it unreasonably difficult for disabled people to make use of the services they provide.

A website is deemed to be a service and so is covered by the Act.

In the US, the 1998 amendment to Section 508 of the Rehabilitation Act requires:

> All federal agencies must ensure that their electronic and information technology is accessible to disabled people whenever those agencies develop, procure, maintain or use such technology.

In most parts of the world there are moves to legislate that people with disabilities share the same access to the web and, in the future, other interactive channels as other members of society.

The difficulty comes in defining exactly how this law translates into technical requirements. In 2004 in the UK, there is no case law on the application of the law's provisions to websites. In November 2004, the Disability Rights Commission released the results of research into the accessibility of UK websites. It showed that most websites – 81 per cent – fail to satisfy the most basic Web accessibility tests. The same research showed that website designers are woefully ignorant of the needs of disabled users and how to create websites that they can use. Only 9 per cent of web designers claimed any sort of expertise in creating accessible websites and although 70 per cent had conducted user testing, only 9 per cent had ever included disabled users in such tests. If the same analysis were to be conducted to discover web designers' skills in building sites for older people, I expect the results would be even worse.

The message for marketers is clear: the 'big stick' of legislation is already forcing the accessibility of interactive channels to be taken as a serious issue. As age discrimination legislation starts to be enacted, the same might also apply to the age-friendliness of interactive channels.

Figure 11.5 shows how age, accessibility and the usability of a channel are bound together. Unfortunately, these factors are not popular with web designers taken singly, so the combination of all three must be their worst nightmare. The challenge marketers must take on is that of ensuring their designers take these issues seriously, as their importance, both legally and functionally, is destined only to increase.

It cannot be stated enough times that if you ensure that your website works well for older people, this improves its performance for all ages. Web designers need to be told this message repeatedly!

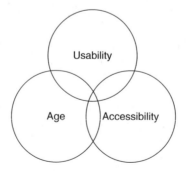

Figure 11.5 *The relationship between usability, age and accessibility*

DON'T FORGET THE TELEPHONE

The telephone is a vital one-to-one marketing and service channel for doing business with older consumers. Telephones are all pervasive and simple to use, although, with the mushrooming number of function keys that keep on being added to handsets, that statement might not be true for much longer.

Mike Bingham is the UK's leading expert on techniques for improving telephone contact with the over-50s consumer. He is the founder of Senior Response, a call centre company catering to this age group. I asked Mike to detail the most important issues for the effectiveness of telephone contact with older people.

His starting point is to remember how the telephone was perceived and used by older people and how this still impacts their attitude to telephones today. In the early 1950s, the UK was coming to terms with the economic effects of almost a decade of World and Cold Wars. Televisions, washing machines and refrigerators were still the props of American TV sitcoms rather than essentials of everyday life. For most people, the nearest telephone was located with a wealthy neighbour or relative. Most often, using the telephone was an uncomfortable experience in a cold telephone box, some distance from your home.

The over-50s remember:

▌ telegrams, which were pieces of paper delivered by young men on motorcycles and normally bore bad news;
▌ demand for telephones exceeding supply – even for those who could afford a telephone, it was not uncommon to have to wait for year to be connected;
▌ large differences between the costs of calls made at peak and standard rates;
▌ hurrying telephone conversations because of their high cost.

All of this is so different from today's world where young people spend an extraordinary amount of their lives talking or keying into their mobile phones.

Research by the University of Copenhagen investigated how older people react to the telephone. The research showed that sales-related calls were unwelcome – they were instinctively seen as being intrusive. However, they were seen as less intimidating and easier to control than face-to-face contact. On the other hand, regular calls from relatives and friends form a vital support mechanism for older peoples' health and well-being. Thus, when the telephone rings, it engenders in older people a degree of apprehension, yet welcome calls are beneficial and an important way of keeping in contact with the world. Understanding this love–hate relationship between older people and the telephone is important for marketers using it as communications channel.

Mike believes that there are seven cardinal rules for making the telephone channel effective for the older age group:

I   schedule calls to fit with the older person's day, which will be very different from that of somebody 20 years younger;

I   speak slowly and distinctly – by the age of 70, most people will be suffering from a deterioration in their hearing;

I   don't overwhelm the person with too much information – in the same way that the designers of websites must recognize the effects of ageing on people's cognitive abilities, so must people in call centres who specify the operators' calling scripts;

I   avoid using modern or technical language that may not be part of the older person's vocabulary, so, for example, don't use words such as 'equity' when you could say 'the value of your house less what you owe';

I   quickly establish a rapport with the person – the caller must be able to empathize and sympathize with mature customers and instantly gain their trust;

I   use direct questions – for example, instead of talking about a questionnaire or survey, say 'I would like to ask a few questions', or instead of talking about food intake or consumption, talk about what they had to eat yesterday;

I   convey to the person a sense of caring and interest in what they have to say rather than trying to end the call as soon as possible.

If the caller is of the same generation as the person being called, this makes it easier to satisfy a number of these rules. Table 11.2 shows the results for research by Senior Response UK in 2004 into how effective callers of different ages were in making appointments as part of a marketing campaign for a hearing aid supplier.

This analysis shows that the older call centre operator achieved a better conversion rate than all the younger ones. Obviously, a poorly trained older person with little aptitude for the job is not automatically going to be better than an enthusiastic and talented young person. Assuming the same level of ability, however, the older person has distinct advantages over the younger person because of their ability to understand the general culture, language and mindset of the person being called. Young people can be

Table 11.2 *Success rates of call centre staff of different ages*

Age of operator	People contacted	Appointments made	Conversion rate (%)
54	70	25	36
51	55	11	22
28	63	10	16
25	86	14	16

Source: Senior Response UK, 2004

taught these things, but their knowledge will always have gaps because they did not live through those times.

Many companies use interactive call technology (that is, 'for ..., press 1 on your keypad, for ... press 2' and so on) and have outsourced their call centres, often to overseas locations. When doing this, it is vital to consider the impact this will have on their older customers.

The telephone will continue to be an ·important marketing and support channel. By obeying a few simple rules, its effectiveness when used with older people can be greatly improved. The techniques discussed in this chapter are not complicated or difficult to apply. The really difficult thing is for marketers to get their organizations to see the value in taking them seriously.

IMPLICATIONS FOR THE MARKETER

It is a disastrous mistake to believe that in-house web developers or external designers will automatically create websites that are suitable for older people.

! If your interactive channels are to be age-neutral, then this must be clearly specified in the design brief. It is unwise to assume that all web designers have the necessary skills to ensure this happens, let alone automatically.

The primary reason for marketers and designers failing to make their interactive channels friendly to older users is that they are unaware they need to do so. Even when this is recognized, there is often too little priority given to solving the problem.

! Determine the age profile of people using your interactive channels. If your audience contains a significant number of older people, then understand that by not adapting the channel to their needs you are intentionally damaging your competitiveness.

There is a sound body of research proving the design and technical rules that improve the usability of websites for older people. All marketers should have a basic knowledge of these rules and how they should be applied.

❗ Understand how the problems caused by eyesight, dexterity and cognitive deterioration can be minimized. Ensure that the people responsible for building your interactive channels also understand these rules.

Badly designed websites affect all people, but they affect the old disproportionally. Most problems are easy to remedy and only arise in the first place because of a few basic mistakes.

❗ Focus your attention on solving the top five problems that older people encounter.

Understand the characteristics of the types of people visiting your website and what they want to achieve by visiting the site.

❗ Lesson 101 of marketing is about understanding your market and its needs. This is equally valid for interactive channels. To validate whether or not you have a sufficient depth of understanding of your older audiences, answer the questions in Appendix 2.

Understanding your organization's existing level of commitment to providing age-neutral interactive channels is the first step towards changing it for the better.

❗ Create a profile of your organization's commitment to age-neutral channels using the matrix in Figure 11.4.

You need to understand the functionality that older people want from your website or any other interactive channel.

❗ There is no substitute for face-to-face research of people's requirements.

There are many overlaps between the techniques used for designing interactive channels that are accessible to people with disabilities, satisfying the needs of older people and following best practice for usability.

❗ Accessibility, age-friendliness and usability should be dealt with together and must be on the agenda of all marketers with responsibility for interactive channels.

The telephone is, and will remain, an important marketing and support channel for contacting older people.

❗ You should optimize the way your call centres operate to cater for the needs of older people and evaluate whether or not your operators have the necessary 'soft skills' to deal with this audience.

SUMMARY

▌ This chapter explains how the special needs of older people can be incorporated into the design of all interactive marketing channels, but especially the web.

▌ Unfortunately, web designers do not instinctively consider the problems caused by age-related deterioration of eyesight, dexterity and cognitive abilities. Websites continue to be built by the young for the young. Older peoples' needs are rarely considered. Not surprisingly, many websites are difficult for older people to use, leading to frustration and annoyance.

▌ It doesn't need to be this way as there is a large body of knowledge detailing how to build age-neutral websites – that is, sites that are equally easy to use whatever the age of the user. This chapter contains a comprehensive list of guidelines for building such websites.

▌ Most marketers have the technical knowledge to apply these guidelines. The reason for their not doing so is because the companies don't perceive it as a serious and high-priority issue. This chapter contains a simple set of tests that reveal the priority your organization gives to this topic.

▌ Understanding customers' wants and needs is part of the bedrock of marketing. For some reason it is ignored when dealing with older people and their use of the interactive marketing channel. This includes not asking questions as basic as 'What does the audience want from the channel?' and seeking opinions on how well they work. In most instances, companies rely on instinct rather than research to provide this knowledge. This chapter explains the basics of how to research this area and ways in which to use the information it elicits.

▮ With so much focus on the web and other data channels, the importance of the telephone is often forgotten. Like all other channels, there are some important 'dos and don'ts' for how to use it with an older audience.

▮ Digital interactive channels are used by all sectors of society. This chapter focuses on the needs of older people, but these channels also need to take account of people with disabilities. Fortunately, there is a significant overlap between building channels that are accessible for the disabled and meet the needs of older people. Marketers should be aware of the linkages between age, disabilities and the science of usability.

12

Communicating with the over-50s

This chapter argues that it's time for advertisers, agencies and media owners to revisit the over-50s and develop a more contemporary approach to communicating with them in the 21st century. It draws on the findings of the research study that OMD conducted in 2004 that challenged the industry's beliefs about those over 50 and is our guide for communicating with today's older consumers. The research study, which we named UFO (Understanding Fifties and Over), is also described in Chapter 6. My thanks to Jo Rigby, Head of OMD Insight, for contributing this chapter.

THE FORGOTTEN AUDIENCE

Most communications agencies when asked to produce case studies of how they have communicated with an audience aged 50 and over, would struggle to find more than a handful in the past 10 years. A couple of times a year we may work on a communication brief that specifies the target audience should be over 50 and it will almost certainly be for financial services, holidays or products specifically aimed at older people, such as denture cream or stairlifts. It is also a rarity to work on a communication brief where the age profile is wide enough to include consumers aged 50 and above. The majority of briefs an agency receives or collaborates on with their clients will specify a much younger audience – the profile '18–34 ABC1' appears with such regularity that it has become a cliché.

It is almost unheard of for a media owner to present their title or role to an agency and proudly say that they enjoy a significant readership or viewing audience of those aged over 50. Media owners actually go to great lengths to avoid any mention of older viewers or listeners, preferring to reflect solely on their younger audiences. One example of this is *Metro* – a UK daily newspaper that is freely distributed in urban areas, which packages its readers as 'urbanites' – consumers aged 18–44 ABC1. *Metro* invites readers to join its 'Urban Life' online research project, which is an online panel of 3,000 urbanites, including representatives from all of Britain's major cities. However, on reaching their 45th birthday, they are removed from this panel. Of *Metro*'s readers, 26 per cent are aged over 45, yet they are not considered to be valuable enough to canvass opinions from.

There are many more examples of media owners glossing over their older audiences. The question is, why do they feel the need to do this? They are simply responding to the pressures of advertisers and their agencies to deliver a youth audience.

The over-50s currently represent 40 per cent of the UK adult population, own 70 per cent of the UK's wealth and control 60 per cent of its disposable income. On paper, they are a pretty attractive audience whose wallets more advertisers should be battling for. So, what are the reasons for ignoring this them? Here are some of the reasons that I have encountered.

'The product is aimed at a younger audience'

This is often a 'default' approach to media planning, based on a presumption that it is only the youth who will be attracted to the brand, particularly if it is stylish or modern. Advertisers should ensure that they haven't reached this decision by gut feel or only researching their product among a younger audience. There are instances where it is more appropriate to launch a brand at a younger audience – for example, some fashion or beauty brands aimed specifically at a youth audience. Often brands launch to a cutting-edge youth market, but should consider broadening this in subsequent years.

'Older consumers are loyal to the brands they consume'

The UFO findings identified a number of brands that over-50s have abandoned. The poor performance of Marks & Spencer, the one-time premier UK high street retailer, is testament to older consumers turning their backs on the 'most loved' high street brand and choosing more fashion-forward brands on the high street. UFO also identified that 42 per cent of respondents had switched the company providing their gas or electricity supply.

These examples show how dangerous it is to assume that the over-50s have unquestioning brand allegiance. The success of new entrants to the airline market, such as easyJet, have been helped by the huge customer base of over-50s who have rushed to take up this no-frills proposition, even if they had previously chosen to fly with British Airways.

That said, of course we found some clusters of consumers who are fiercely loyal to their brand of choice rather than all the brands they use. As with consumers of any age, there will always be those who are easy to convert and those stalwarts who rarely switch.

Based on our research, we would urge advertisers to move away from the myth that all consumers become more loyal as they age. Brands cannot afford to be complacent about brand loyalty among any consumer group and fickleness is not age-specific.

'Older consumers will not experiment with new brands'

This belief leads marketers to the conclusion, invariably reached without market research, that they would be 'wasting' time and money trying to convert the older audience.

Our findings from UFO reveal that consumers switch brands for better value, as a result of a bad experience with their existing brand choice or as a result of pure and simple brand appeal. Counter-evidence to the belief that older consumers prefer traditional brands is that newer brands, such as amazon.co.uk, Ikea and easyJet, received very positive brand affinity scores among a significant proportion of our respondents.

It is often true that the speed at which older consumers adopt new products can be slower than among younger people. This is often the case with the take-up of newer technologies, such as the internet. There are examples where this isn't so, however, such as the early uptake of digital radio among older consumers. However, as the rate of technological change gets ever faster, the time lag between generational take-up is decreasing.

The conclusion from analysis of commonly held beliefs

These reasons – and other even more outdated ones – used to exclude older people from advertisers' plans are not substantiated by research. The consumer we see emerging from UFO is one who is informed, demanding and unlikely to spend time or money with brands that consistently fail to communicate with them.

LACK OF DIVERSITY

We have all been young and can easily relate to the concept of youth and what it represents. We have never been old and it's almost impossible to comprehend what it is like to be older. So, it's no surprise that the majority of stereotypes about the over-50s come from the incredibly young media and advertising industry. Over 80 per cent of people who work within the UK's advertising and communication industry are aged under 40 and, of these, 50 per cent are aged under 30 (IPA Agency Census, 1999).

My own experience within media backs up these statistics. I've always been intrigued as to where media people go to work when they reach their 50th birthday. The industry's lack of diversity – in age as well as other areas – is problematic as it results in us being incredibly removed from the world we need to communicate with. One could argue that it makes us look quite old-fashioned, living in a micro-bubble, rather like politicians!

Perhaps the UK's Age Discrimination Act (October 2006) and the proposed changes to the retirement age will help encourage people of a more representative age profile to enter or stay in the industry!

CREATIVE STRATEGY V MEDIA STRATEGY

The target audience selected for a media brief often mirrors that of the creative brief. Brands wanting to exude a youthful and contemporary image will often borrow imagery relating to consumers much younger than those who actually purchase the products. This can lead to the assumption that the communications planning must follow suit and be based on communicating with a youth audience. This approach can result in consumers simply not seeing or hearing a brand message as it has been placed in environments that do not touch their lives. An example of this could be a healthier option snack brand that uses certain magazines to communicate to women. If the title selection is skewed towards those titles that reach an 18–34 audience, the message will be lost to women over 50 who read magazines with an older profile.

This approach is also misleading. UFO respondents mentioned many brands with youthful positioning that they were buying into. Positioning a brand in this youthfully aspirational way can be successful in attracting older consumers who identify more with this positive image than more staid approaches aimed at their age group.

The issue of advertising and the over-50s is hotly debated, with the majority view being that this audience can't relate to the brand messages generally put out and so, instead, seek out more product information than other audiences. UFO research identified respondents' favourite current TV advertising. Among the top campaigns were Peugeot 206, Stella Artois and the John Smith's bitter campaign featuring Peter Kay. These campaigns were very brand-led and also weren't specifically 'aimed' at older people.

When prompted to explain why they liked these campaigns, the respondents cited the cleverness, sexiness or just pure production values of the advertising. The Stella Artois campaign was enjoyed for its cinematic production qualities and beautifully scripted stories. John Smith's campaign featuring Peter Kay was found to be witty and a brilliant use of a popular comedian.

Debates about how to advertise to the over-50s invariably include the notion that ads need to be made that overtly target this age group. However, there is no evidence that older consumers need to see themselves represented in adverts in order to identify with a brand. As an aside, one element of the research involved asking male respondents who their favourite female celebrity was and, far from being older female celebrities, at the top of the list were Kylie Minogue and Jordan.

The attitude change needed is for advertisers and agencies to recognize that youthful branding does not necessarily equate to the youth being targeted. The best option would be a shift towards integrated communications planning rather than building communications around a prebriefed creative.

RECOGNIZING THE DIFFERENCES

UFO identified seven cluster types, outlined in Chapter 6. The research also showed us the media consumption of each cluster and the relationship they had with their media choices.

To try to draw up a media plan for the over-50s would be as pointless as attempting to devise one for the entire population of Australia. There isn't a bespoke channel mix that can be used to communicate with the over-50s, just as there isn't one for 15–24-year-olds.

To illustrate the diversity of this audience, we can look at two of our cluster groups – Live Wires and Living Day-to-Day – and explore just some of the channels that might be appropriate when considering communicating with them. The Live Wires group has a female skew, is financially comfortable and has an age range that includes those who are working and those who are retired. Living Day-to-Day has a broad age profile, but the shared demographic factor is a low household income. It's important to bear in mind that, while the Live Wires have more disposable income, Living Day-to-Days are still important consumers for packaged consumer goods, holidays, consumer durables and so on.

The range of channels we might consider in order to reach Live Wires is dictated by their extremely active lifestyle. Those in this group have many interests and hobbies that take them out of the house throughout the week. This leaves little time for watching TV – a fact that was backed up by the media diaries we asked members of this group to keep for a week. Their TV viewing was extremely selective, focusing on programmes such as Channel 4's *Sex and the City* and the plethora of property programmes. This group also enjoyed reading upmarket glossy magazines that fed their interests in fashion, travel and well-being. Some favourite titles that might surprise are upmarket fashion monthly magazines such as *Vogue*, *Marie Claire* and *Glamour*.

The time that Live Wires now have to invest in their interests opens up opportunities for brands to access this group by associating themselves with their passion centres. This could be sporting events, outdoor concerts or fashion tie-ins. Cinema visits are more frequent among this group than the other clusters, with films such as *Calendar Girls* (starring Helen Mirren and Julie Walters as middle-aged women who appear in a nude calendar to raise money for charity) sparking off a renewed interest in the big screen.

Live Wires are big fans of internet shopping, finding it more convenient and offering more choice than the high street. Of those with internet access, 75 per cent of our Live Wires have bought something online. They also use the internet to research issues such as holidays, health and finance. On average, they spend an hour a day on the internet.

A media plan designed to reach Live Wires could include the following elements:

- sponsorship of a high-quality drama or property show;
- internet campaign on health or beauty sites;
- tie-in with an upmarket magazine to create a supplement;
- brand association with a relevant film release.

On the other hand, if a brand needed to speak to the less affluent Living Day-to-Day consumers, marketers would have to look at using more home-based channels. TV viewing is significantly higher in this group, with less of an 'appointment to view' approach. This group particularly enjoys the trend for reality TV, with programmes such as *Pop Idol* and *The X-Factor* (talent shows where viewers vote to decide the winners) being popular. Those in this group are also more likely to have access to multichannel TV, broadening the range of stations to choose from to reach them.

The Living Day-to-Day cluster read tabloid newspapers such as *The Sun* and *The Mirror*. The women in this group expressed a strong interest in celebrity culture, enjoying reading newspaper and magazine features about their favourite celebrities.

A media plan designed to reach the Living Day-to-Days could include the following elements:

▌ token collection campaign with a tabloid newspaper;
▌ sponsorship of TV reality show;
▌ press advertising in TV listings magazines;
▌ advertorial in a celebrity-focused magazine.

While the Live Wires spend, on average, two hours per day listening to the radio, this tends to be to the non-commercial stations, such as Radio 2. The Living-Day-to-Days, in contrast, are heavier consumers of commercial radio.

This very brief overview of media channels in relation to just two groups within the older audience illustrates the pointlessness of approaching it as purely one group of people defined solely by the fact that they are over 50 years old. The very different media habits of these people are lost in the aggregate media consumption data shown in Figure 12.1. As with all

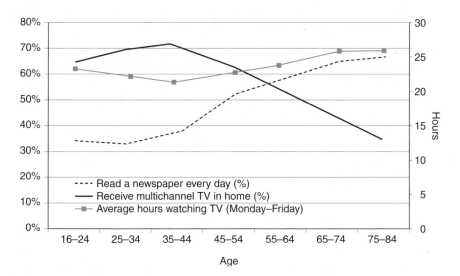

Figure 12.1 *Readership of newspapers, access to multichannel TV and hours spent watching TV (October 2003–September 2004)*
Source: TGI, 2004

consumers, there is so much more to consider, which should not be overlooked at any age. It is important to note, too, that while this segmentation was necessary to break down the older audience taking part in our research, there are many similarities between the attitudes and behaviour of our clusters and consumers of all ages.

WORD OF MOUTH

The power of word of mouth (WOM) is widely recognized by media planners, and specific activities that will generate a high, positive level of WOM often appear in media plans. WOM is often associated purely with youth targets, however, overlooking the role older people play in amplifying brand messages.

UFO explored the communities that the older market interacts with, which included the workplace, immediate and extended family groups, friends and the local community. Each cluster group had different levels of contact with each of these communities – some stronger than others. For example, those in our Anchored in the Past group were predominately home-based, with little contact with extended family or friends. Conversely, our Live Wires had large friendship circles, often built up again once their children had reached an independent state. Over 25 per cent of our Live Wires had contacted old school friends using the website Friends Reunited and told stories of frequent reunions. Of this group, 23 per cent agreed that they often talk about advertising they've seen with friends. While this figure can be higher among 15–24-year-olds, it demonstrates that consumers such as the Live Wires can be valuable messengers of relevant brand messages. Sharing news of the latest fashion find at Topshop (a hugely successful high street fashion brand that has successfully positioned itself as young yet attracts all ages) or a new music release that they had heard on the radio were typical of the snippets of information passed around their friendship groups.

INTERGENERATIONAL COMMUNICATIONS

The value of the older audience as guides and validators of their children's brand decisions should also be considered, particularly for high-ticket items and those where parents are financially contributing. With today's generation of twentysomethings living at home for longer, it has become increasingly important to consider that parents in their 50s and 60s will be having an input in their decision-making process. UFO revealed that the financial services sector is one example of advice being sought on which mortgages or savings plans to choose. Media plans should therefore consider speaking to a secondary audience, using the relevant title and station selections.

The role of grandparents should also be considered. UFO research revealed that 44 per cent of grandparents claimed to be 'heavily involved in the care of my grandchildren'. With more women returning to work after having children, it is increasingly falling to grandparents to provide primary care. This introduces new dynamics in the decision-making process. Who is really responsible for buying snacks, treating the kids to a McDonald's Happy Meal or a cinema visit? Once we could assume it was the child's mum, but now there is every chance that it is its grandma.

We also now recognize that over-50s seeking to pursue a youthful and active lifestyle are seeking out clues for brand choices from younger consumers. There are lots of clever ways in which brands can talk to both audiences without alienating one or the other and communicate an aspirational and contemporary message. One example would be Apple's use of U2 in its recent advertising campaign and for a special edition of the iPod – a band recognized by both 25- and 50-year-olds.

MEASURING SUCCESS

All communications activity should have an element of measurement included. This can range from the ultimate evaluation of econometrics, through to a pre- and post-campaign evaluation. Equally valid are more qualitative techniques to capture perception shifts. However, even in the area of evaluation, the over-50s can find themselves overlooked.

Advertisers invest huge sums of money in advertising and brand-tracking studies, yet it is surprising how many of these only speak to consumers aged 16–34. How many omnibus surveys set their upper age band for respondents at 55+ and do not break this group down further? This either misses out on large numbers of consumers or buries aspects of consumer behaviour within too wide an age group.

Finally, respondents invited to take part in qualitative work are usually from the younger end of the scale, with either budget or oversight excluding older participants.

As the focus on the over-50s becomes greater, it will be paramount that the topic of measurement is reassessed to ensure that the information needed to judge whether or not an activity has been successful is available. We need to be careful to avoid research that, as the result of an oversight or poor design, fails to capture the views of the older consumer and, thus, results in reinforcing some of the old ideas about this demographic.

EXCITING TIMES AHEAD

The 1980s and 1990s proved to be such an exciting time for youth marketing, with numerous groundbreaking youth research and communication campaigns being launched. As advertisers begin to re-evaluate their priorities to embrace the over-50s, I predict that the next 10 years will see innovative and creative approaches to communicating with older consumers that will be exciting, too. Brands will begin to break out of their well-worn tracks and seek out strategies and plans that communicate to the over-50s in a contemporary, fresh way. The web, iDTV and in-store advertising all provide opportunities for brands to target the older person. Communicating with this audience by connecting with their self-perceptions and imagery will be far more successful than playing back a stereotype that no one over the age of 50 relates to anyway.

We are wedded to age in a deeply unhealthy way – it blinkers us and prevents us from breaking out of our well-worn media approaches. Today, we have the research resources and techniques to learn so much more about our consumers than just their age. So, why don't we release ourselves from our shackles?

For too long now, age has played a dominant role in media planning and prevented us from keeping pace with how consumers have changed. An interesting exercise would be to remove the age field from your next media brief – pretend that there isn't a measure for age. Imagine all consumers as ageless and, instead, focus on what else you could find out about your potential customers. Think about their need states, what they enjoy doing in their leisure time, why they might enjoy your brand. Constantly deferring to age is a hard habit to break, but if it can be achieved, the solutions that you can explore are infinitely more creative and exciting.

If this is too radical, then simply ensure that you haven't defaulted to an age profile based on your perception of the brand or audience. The lack of diversity within the media industry results in an extremely one-sided view of the world, so it's even more important to carry out research that starts from an age-neutral point of view. Our image of the over-50s is totally out of sync with reality and is showing the industry up as being out of touch with consumers.

I'm constantly surprised at the laissez-faire attitude towards this audience of many advertisers. There is a huge gulf between the potential riches to be gained from capturing certain clusters of this market versus the insignificant amount of strategic thinking that goes into marketing to them. Any forward-thinking advertiser should be devoting resources to exploring the scope of this audience, whether this be as a discreet group or an integrated audience.

Could we ever move towards age-neutral media planning? The deeply entrenched attitudes towards this age group need to start to be eroded more generally. It seems unlikely that this will happen overnight.

IMPLICATIONS FOR THE MARKETER

Creating a media plan for the over-50s is as pointless as attempting to devise one for the population of Australia.

! Before attempting to create a media plan, it is vital to divide the over-50s market into non-age-related segments.

There is no difference between the processes for creating a media plan for the over-50s and one for teenagers.

! The same principles of marketing apply to the over-50s as to any other age group. The same rigour of media planning that is applied to the teen market should be used with the over-50s.

Word of mouth is an important technique for amplifying brand messages generally. It doesn't just apply to young people.

! Review how word of mouth can be used with the older age groups.

The over-50s will guide and validate their children's brand decisions. In many cases they will be financially contributing to the purchase.

! Just as tweens influence what car their parents purchase, so parents and grandparents influence their children's purchasing decisions. Evaluate the effects of intergenerational influences on purchases of your company's products.

Many of the omnibus market research surveys and bespoke research studies have an age limit on their respondents of 55 years old.

! Ensure that the market research used to make decisions provides adequate insight into the full age range of older people. It should at least cover the range 50–70+.

SUMMARY

▌ The majority of briefs an agency receives or collaborates on with its clients target a young and affluent audience. The terminology '18–34 ABC1' appears with such regularity that it has become a cliché. Similarly, media owners go to great lengths to avoid any mention of older viewers or listeners, preferring to reflect solely on their younger audiences.

▌ The over-50s is a forgotten audience for the agencies, clients and media.

▌ To better understand the consumer habits of the older age group, OMD conducted a research study in 2004 called UFO – Understanding Fifties and Over. This study showed that the different segments of the over-50s market have widely differing behaviour patterns and this includes their media habits.

▌ To consider drawing up a media plan for the over-50s is pointless. There isn't a bespoke channel mix with which to communicate to them specifically, just as there isn't one for 15–24-year-olds.

▌ The UFO study identified other media-related areas where the over-50s are ignored. The power of word of mouth (WOM) to amplify brand messages is widely recognized by media planners, but only associated with the young. Older people have an important role in guiding and validating their children's brand decisions, but this is mostly ignored. Finally, advertisers invest huge sums of money in advertising and brand-tracking studies, yet it is surprising how many of these only speak to consumers aged 16–34 and how many omnibus surveys only offer the views of respondents up to the age of 55+.

▌ For too long now, age has played a dominant role in media planning and this has prevented us from keeping pace with how consumers are changing. Our image of the over-50s is totally out of sync with reality and this is showing the industry up as being out of touch with consumers.

13

Thoughts about the creative

It is impossible to define the dos and don'ts of *the* creative for TV, print, packaging and point-of-sale that works best with older people. The instant you start writing guidelines, you are forced into making assumptions and gross generalizations. Prescribing the rules of the creative for the over-50s might be a futile quest, but it does not stop a lot of people from trying!

Although no rules exist, there are some guidelines as to what might work and what will probably not.

WHY IT'S SO DIFFICULT

A person's age is one of the many factors influencing the response to the combination of imagery, sound and copy that we call the 'creative'. We know by now, if we didn't before, that age alone is a poor determinant of consumer behaviour. The same applies to predicting the response to the creative.

The following are two totally different UK advertisements that gained accolades from the media industry and consumers of all ages.

One of the UK's five most popular advertisements of all time is of a man, probably in his 40s, sitting in an automated photo booth. He has a few long, whispy pieces of hair meticulously arranged to cover his bald head. As he waits for the camera to flash, he desperately tries to maintain a natural smile. The camera refuses to flash. As he bends forward to investigate, he disturbs his carefully arranged strands of hair and the camera flashes.

He sits upright and grimaces and the camera flashes again, at which point his seat collapses. You can still see the top of his bald head and you hear a match being struck. He reappears, bathed in smiles and smoking. The music starts (Bach's 'Air on G-string'), followed by the spoken words, 'Happiness is a cigar called Hamlet'.

Over a quarter of century later and another advertisement received widespread acclaim, especially from the over-50s. It features Peter Kay, a UK comedian. He comes home and greets his mother, who is vacuuming the floor, with the statement, 'Come on, Mum, time to go'. She answers, 'Go where?' He then says, 'To an old people's home – they will look after you now.' With an astonished look on her face, she says, 'Are you mad? I am 55 – why should I go and live in an old people's home?' He concludes, 'Because I want to put a snooker table in your bedroom and the kids are frightened of your moustache.' The advertisement finishes with a picture of a pint of beer sitting beside her photograph. His hand removes the photograph and replaces it with one of a well-known British snooker player.

The reason for recounting these advertisements is to illustrate why it is impossible to be prescriptive about the creative. In both advertisements, an older person is the target of the humour, but it doesn't seem to matter. The advertisements could be accused of being ageist, sexist and even baldist, but it's not important. The subtlety of the portrayal is what makes them both succeed and this is something that cannot be distilled into a few simple rules.

SOMETHING IS WRONG

Whenever older people are asked about advertising, they give the same responses. Either they don't understand or relate to much of the advertising or, even worse, they believe that it is condescending.

Millennium, a UK agency, surveyed 22,000 people aged over 50 in 2003 and found that 86 per cent of them claimed they did not relate to most of the advertising they watch. Sweeney Research, an Australian research company, found that 67 per cent of 45–54-year-olds said that advertising was not in tune with their needs or entertaining to watch. The UK charity Help the Aged (2002) found even higher levels of disengagement.

One explanation for these reactions is that older people have seen and heard a lot more advertisements than the young. The over-50s have been exposed to more advertising than 99 per cent of the creative directors working in the advertising industry. They have seen some great advertisements and a lot that range from the mediocre to the diabolical.

Another explanation for these negative views is that this outcome is intentional and welcomed. If you subscribe to the '18–35s rule the world' philosophy, then it doesn't matter what older people think. In fact, if your creative idea is one of youthful non-conformity, then the greater the negative reaction from the oldies the better.

The most likely reason for clients and agencies tolerating these negative reactions from such a large part of the population is because they don't care, or don't care enough, to do anything about it.

Assuming that there is a desire to produce a creative that works for older people, then what are the issues that need to be considered? Are there any lessons that can be learned from a creative that appeals to this audience?

OPTIONS FOR THE CREATIVE AND MEDIA

The diagram in Figure 13.1 is an extremely simple representation of the combinations of media and creative focus a company might pursue. The ages associated with 'young' and 'old' will vary from company to company. For most organizations, though, the 18–35 group represents 'young' and anything older is 'old'. The combinations are as follows:

- ▐ *Option 1: young creative, young media* – This represents how much of today's advertising expenditure is focused. Advertising designed for the young, using a media biased towards youth.
- ▐ *Option 2: old creative, old media* – When the subject of an age-friendly creative is discussed, it mainly refers to this combination. This is the 'age ghetto' combination aimed at appealing directly to old people. A good example of this is the Heinz soup advert aimed at older men (see Chapter 4, Figure 4.1).
- ▐ *Option 3: young creative, varied media* – This represents a large part of the advertising industry's output. The creative is produced for the young, but the media profile includes older people. This approach assumes that, even though the advertising was created for a young audience, it will somehow be effective when viewed through older eyes.
- ▐ *Option 4: neutral creative, varied media* – This is a much rarer combination. The creative is age-neutral, while the media profile is the tool used to achieve the targeted exposure by age or other segmentation criteria. Good examples of an age-neutral creative are the Guinness

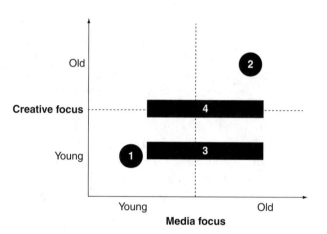

Figure 13.1 *The focus of the creative and media spend*

Olympic swimmer and Honda's car advertisements (see Chapter 1, Figures 1.2, 1.3 and 1.4).

In reality, few campaigns will have such a clearly defined creative and media focus, but it is useful to separate them for the purpose of this discussion.

Any discussions about options 1 and 3 are best left to somebody who understands the mind of the young, which excludes me. The remainder of this chapter concentrates on the issues affecting the creative for options 2 and 4.

THINGS TO CONSIDER

In Chapter 4, A global snapshot, Reg Starkey wrote:

> Older consumers know that advertising which ignores us, excludes us, patronizes us, offends us, insults our intelligence, treats us like stereotypes, provides inadequate information or rewards, or fails to engage us for any reason whatsoever will fail.

You have been warned!

Previously, I stated that when producing a creative for the over-50s, you cannot use a set of universal rules. There is not a simple cookbook of recipes that says, 'This works for 50-year-olds but not somebody 20 years older.' However, there is something that is not a rule but a statement of the obvious: the older person must be able to understand the combination of images and sounds'. If, when viewing an advertisement, it is impossible to determine if the product being promoted is a car, soft drink or bank account, then the chance of the brand retaining the over-50's attention or creating recall is zilch. If the choice words, images and music are impossible to understand, the creative doesn't get to first base. If the objective of the creative is to satisfy Option 1, then that is fine, but if it is intended for Option 3, then it fails. No understanding = no impact = wasted use of media.

The following are the main techniques and 'rules' that are often applied to the older market, together with a discussion of why they should be approached with care.

Associate vigour and excitement

The covers of most books about marketing and older people feel compelled to use the imagery of youthful 70-year-olds jogging, skiing, leaping, swimming and other variants on physical exercise. The same happens with newspaper and web articles about older people. Clearly, the imagery is attempting to demonstrate that old does not mean being frail, unhealthy and reliant on a Zimmer frame.

This approach might work for those older people who are serious about having, or aspiring to, an active lifestyle. The risk is that the imagery looks unreal, contrived and faintly comical.

There might be circumstances when it is necessary to emphasize the youthful aspects of life older people still enjoy. It can create real problems when a company's image becomes associated with a concept of ageing that is unadventurous, lacking excitement and predictable. Wallace Arnold is a UK holiday company renowned for providing good-value coach holidays for older people. As its Sales Director commented, 'Older people are more active and adventurous – now retirement is not about closing down, but going to all the places you have wanted to visit.' In response to this, the company embarked on a repositioning exercise to stress the active and adventurous aspects of their holidays. To a lesser extent, SAGA, a major over-50s holiday provider, found itself in the same position and has been trying to reposition its image for the active and energetic old.

Token oldies

One of the most often produced pieces of proof of the advertising industry's lack of interest in older people is its reluctance to use models in their 50s and 60s, let alone their 70s. This is a horribly simplistic argument.

It is illogical and unsubstantiated by research to say that older people expect to see older people in adverts or respond better if they are there. In some types of creative this might be true; in others it is not. Indeed, one of the UK's biggest mail-order companies says that it receives complaints from its female customers when it uses older models. It would be a sad day if age legislation ever reached the point of forcing agencies to always include a 'token oldie'.

National differences

OMD's research (see Chapter 5) showed that there are significant national differences in the ways older people view brands, accept change, respond to new experiences and perceive the future. It is not unreasonable to believe that the same differences exist in their reactions to a creative.

De Beers, the diamond company, experienced these national differences when it tried to use the same campaign to market its 'three stone jewellery' in Japan as it had in the US. It found a significant difference between the two countries. In the US, a man buys a ring for a woman, but in Japan, a ring is mainly purchased by a woman for herself. Research conducted by JWT, the advertising agency for De Beers in Japan, showed that older women, after years of self-sacrifice, were thinking of themselves and willing to spend on large-ticket items such as jewellery.

Being sensitive to such variations between consumers in different countries is not exactly a new concept. However, the idea needs to be refined to also take account of the specific differences in the behaviour of older people and between men and women.

Perceived age

One of the reasons marketers give for using younger people in advertising is that a person's perceived and chronological ages are different. They argue that if 60-year-olds think of themselves as being 40, then appealing to a 40-year-old might be best achieved by using somebody aged 25. A great theory, based on the simple assumption that we retain a younger mental picture of ourselves than is the reality physically. Some small element of proof of this idea is the horrible shock I get when unexpectedly seeing myself in the mirror!

Undoubtedly there is truth in the dual age argument, but the relationship between the ages is a complicated thing. What does this mean for how a 60-year-old woman feels?

▌ Does she feel as she did when she was 45, but her body is 15 years older?

▌ As she would like to have felt, aged 45, but her body is 15 years older?

▌ Like somebody aged 45 today?

▌ As if she is 15 years younger one minute and 15 years older the next?

The answer is that, at different times, all of the above might apply. The relationship is thus far more complicated than is normally portrayed.

Associated with this argument is the trap of confusing 'youth' and 'youthfulness'. One is a state of mind, the other is how people look and behave when they are young. 'Youthful' branding does not necessarily equate to 'youth' targeting. A 65-year old's idea of youthfulness is far more complicated than wanting to look and behave like a youth in 2005 or one in the 1960s.

Pigeon-holing

Thomsons is a large UK holiday company and in 2004 it decided, after 23 years, to abandon its 'Young at Heart' brochure, which was aimed at the over-55s. The company's spokesman said, 'These people do not think of themselves as old and are just as likely to go on the same holidays as couples in their 20s and 30s.' Perhaps not surprisingly the company found that today's over-55s did not identify with the label 'young at heart'. Does this prove that overtly labelling and pigeon-holing people as old doesn't work?

On Best Western's website, the list on the left-hand side, which is the navigations for the site, has a label '55+ Travellers' alongside one for AARP. The hotel company has mounted direct mail campaigns with over 2 million items aimed solely at the over-50s.

When asked about the overt use of age labels, a representative for the company said, 'This was never a marketing issue. We want to appeal to our customers throughout their life stages and have no problems in mixing campaigns for different age groups.' Perhaps the explanation for Best Western's success with the overt use of age labelling is that being 55+ means that you can receive a discount.

A popular UK travel company called Inntravel generates 75 per cent of its business from people aged 45 to 70, but the company's promotional materials give no indication that its prime market is older people. Alternatively, Elderhostel, an American travel company, claims to be 'the world's largest educational and travel organization for older adults'. It would be difficult to label your market more clearly than by using the name 'Elderhostel'.

It is safe to assume that using a mix of advertising proclaiming that a product or service is for old people is a high-risk strategy, but, as these examples demonstrate, it is not an immutable rule – it can be broken.

The importance of music

A great many of the over-50s enjoyed the music of their youth and still do. The flocks of older people attending the Rolling Stones concerts and those of lesser bands of the 1970s show how important music is to many of that generation.

As Dustin Hoffman's youthful face appears in the opening sequence of *The Graduate*, accompanied by Simon and Garfunkel singing the 'Sound of Silence', it is as if the intervening 38 years had never happened. Music has the power to associate feelings with specific times in our lives. It is something that cuts across social backgrounds and lifestyles and directly affects our emotions.

Research by the University of Leicester that involved showing advertisements with music that 'fits' the brands found that they are 63 per cent more likely to be recalled than those with 'non-fit' music. These results make it all the more surprising that music is often something that is added as an adjunct after the visual creative has been produced.

Some companies, though, do understand the power of music. In the US, music by Janis Joplin and Led Zeppelin was used in Mercedes and Cadillac advertisements. Pepsi used Britney Spears, with a retro-makeover, to promote its product.

It would be wrong to conclude from this that simply putting a 1950s or 1960s song in an advertisement is the key to success with older consumers. The UK's Capital Radio and NOP researched how people's age affected their ability to identify the brand by just hearing the advert's musical accompaniment. They tested eight major brands with well-known musical themes and discovered that the over-35s had the lowest level of recall, even with long-established brands.

Few would dispute that music is an important factor in the creative mix, but the evidence suggests that older people's love of music may not translate into the ability to associate music with specific brands.

Nostalgia

Recapturing memories of the past – real or imagined – has become a popular theme for new product development. In the past couple of years, many products from the past have been relaunched with a 21st-century makeover. Retro candy – or, as it is known by the confectionery trade, nostalgic candy – has soared in popularity. DaimlerChrysler revamped its old Thunderbird car as the PT Cruiser and Volkswagen, after it restyled the Beetle, decided to bring back the Microbus Campervan. In the UK, the Chopper bike was relaunched and hugely popular after being out of production for a quarter of a century. Even Nike, which seemed destined to always focus on the teen segment, purchased the company Converse, famous for its canvas and rubber basketball shoes in the 1970s.

Clearly nostalgia engenders powerful human emotions – among them the desire to buy products from the past. In addition, there is the small matter of the fact that promoting a brand consumers are already aware of – even loved and missed – is likely to be a lot easier than starting from scratch.

Music from the 1950s, 1960s and 1970s has been the most popular technique for evoking nostalgia and memories of happier times. Visually, the most common ploy has been to electronically manipulate old film and TV imagery into a modern context. Volkswagen's TV advertising for the Golf, for example, used Gene Kelly's famous dance sequence to 'Singing in the Rain' but transformed it electronically into modern dance and music.

What is surprising is how few older celebrities are used in advertisements. Various members of the *Star Trek* crew appear from time to time and Dennis Hopper, of *Easy Rider* fame, has been used in advertisements for the Ford Cougar and Gap clothes. There are not many high-profile brands that have adopted this approach.

Celebrities are used for other reasons. For example, the famous 1960s' model Twiggy is central to the UK charity Age Concern's marketing campaign. It is about changing attitudes to age and beauty, not nostalgia. Very often, healthcare, finance and mobility assistance products use celebrities, but this is about endorsement, not nostalgia.

The marketing importance of nostalgia looks like it is here to stay. Music and imagery, not people, seem to be the best way to capture the emotion.

Other guidelines

There are many other guidelines that may help in the creative process. These are listed in Table 13.1, along with a view of their value.

Table 13.1 *Techniques that are thought to assist in making a creative that is appealing to older people*

Guideline	How valuable?
Use humour.	Humour is a powerful tool, but it is difficult to get right and potentially destructive when it goes wrong. It is particularly difficult to use humour that spans multiple generations.
Be positive – don't focus on the problems of being old.	In most cases, this is sound advice – as it would be for most generations.
Older consumers are much more wary of advertisers' arguments than the young.	This depends entirely on the types of consumers in each age group who are being compared, but if the argument does have validity, it is difficult to know how it can be applied.
Keep messages honest and literate.	Probably good advice for all ages.
Combine with people of other generations.	This is a widely used technique. Confectionery, cosmetics, home entertainment, healthcare and sanitary products all used a creative that included images of grandparents, parents and children. It is a simple approach that appears to work.
Reduce the 'marketing-speak' and concentrate on the facts.	This argument is too simplistic. When researching products with the intention to purchase, older people want the facts, not just imagery and marketing copy. For instance, a common complaint about websites is that they are 'marketing heavy' and 'information light'. This is because they are created as a promotion – rather than a customer service – vehicle. In addition, brand advertising is also effective with this age group, especially when it has a high production quality.
Target attitudes, not age groups.	This is not an absolute rule, but is true in most circumstances.

THE AGE-NEUTRAL CREATIVE

The age-neutral creative is Option 4 in Figure 13.1. This is a creative that is effective with a wide spectrum of ages. It is difficult to achieve, but when it does work it can result in outstanding advertisements. You will recall that earlier we looked at the adverts for Honda, Guinness and John Smith. These are all examples of this type of creative. To take two more examples, Nike and Unilever's ads appeal, and are relevant to, multiple generations. As will be seen, they use radically different concepts and techniques to connect with their audience.

Nike is often quoted as a brand with its focus firmly on the youth market. One of the UK's marketing pundits joked that if the company's tagline 'Just do it' was adapted for older people, it should be 'Just watch it', on the basis that older people are not likely to be involved in active sport. It is ironic, then, that one of Nike's most talked about advertisements is an excellent example of an age-neutral creative. It is also, by any measure, an example of a brilliant creative.

For those who are not baseball fans, it is useful to have a little background to the advertisement. In 1918, the Boston Red Sox beat the Chicago Cubs in the baseball World Series. They have not won the series since – until 2004.

The advertisement is staged in the stands of Fenway Park, with two young boys and their parents watching the game. A clock shows the passing years and, as it races along, the characters and their costumes age. The two boys become teenagers, their girlfriends replace their parents and then their own children join them, watching the game. As the fashions and styles change, there is the constant swell of a violin, punctuated by outbursts of disappointment as the Red Sox fail to win. The advertisement goes through the anticipation, excitement, letdown and glory, then the clock reaches 2004. In the last frame of the ad, you hear the crack of ball on bat, the members of the family rise to their feet in anticipation and the screen goes black. As the music stops, the 'Just do it' words appear, followed by the Nike logo.

In 60 seconds, the ad shows the passing of 84 years – children becoming old men, sitting with their own grandchildren and all sharing a passionate desire for the same thing – for the Red Sox to win again, as they did when they beat the St Louis Cardinals. The ad uses nostalgia, multiple generations, shared passions and the human values that transcend age. At the end of the ad, Nike is associated with perseverance, excitement and, above all, winning.

The second example is a campaign launched in January 2005 by Dove – a subsidiary of Unilever that sells a range of toiletries. Called the

'Campaign for real beauty', it is a mix of advertising and PR that challenges society's conventional and narrow view of what constitutes female beauty.

The creative for the advertisements is a series of photographs of women, each accompanied by a question about a facet of beauty. To support the campaign, Dove commissioned a global research study, conducted by two respected academics, to explore women's relationship with beauty and self-image. A website was created to support the campaign, provide additional material and the mechanism for women to share their views on the questions raised by the campaign.

Three of the campaign's photographs targeted society's stereotypes about the effects of ageing and beauty with text that asked the following questions.

▌ 'Wrinkled? Wonderful?' Will society ever accept that old can be beautiful?
▌ 'Grey? Gorgeous?' Why can't more women feel glad to be grey?
▌ '44 and hot? 44 and not?' Can women be hotter at 40 than 20?

These photographs are shown in Figure 13.2.

In its PR campaign, Dove emphasized that none of the women appearing in the campaign were professional models. All were 'real' women, who represent a broader spectrum of female beauty. The lady with the wrinkles was 96-year-old Irene, Merlin was the 45-year-old woman with grey hair and Alison was the 44-year-old 'hot' lady.

The other three photos were of women with ages ranging from 22 to 35. They, too, challenged the traditional views about what constitutes a beautiful woman's body shape and complexion.

The campaign uses imagery from multiple ages (22–96), challenges stereotypes and involves the consumer. Dove's brand is positioned as being on the side of 'real' women of all ages, shapes, sizes and complexions.

Not a different breed

When a person celebrates his or her 50th or 70th birthday, this does not mean that they suddenly adopt a different set of responses to a creative. The challenge for the creative industry is that of understanding this simple fact and then identifying the emotions and behaviour that are as close as possible to being ageless. Not an easy task.

Martin Smith, the Sales Director of SAGA Publishing, said, 'When I talk with clients and agencies they often think it is necessary to customize their

Figure 13.2 *Photographs from Dove's 'Campaign for real beauty' that challenge the stereotypes of female beauty*

advertising for the over-50s. I tell them that our readers are mainstream consumers and to use their existing campaigns. Getting marketers to understand this message poses a challenge.' If a campaign is devised to appeal only to a twentysomething, then this approach won't work. The previous examples show that producing an age-neutral creative is possible, but not necessarily easy.

The final words on this subject I will leave to Jeremy Bullmore, a past chairman of both J. Walter Thompson and the UK's Advertising Association and a non-executive director of WPP. When he was asked, 'How should communicators approach the 50-plus market?', he gave a disarmingly simple and brief response. He believes that there are four things to get right: select the right media, see the world through their eyes, treat them as people and don't be surprised if they don't differ too much from other members of the human race.

IMPLICATIONS FOR THE MARKETER

Whenever older people are asked about advertising, they give the same responses. Either they don't understand or relate to much of it or, even worse, they believe that it is condescending.

! Do you know, or care, if this applies to your advertising? Understanding the response of the over-50s to your advertising is the starting point for making changes.

Age alone is a poor determinant of consumer behaviour. The same applies to predicting the response to a creative.

! If in your marketing you make assumptions about the relationship between age and the creative, they need to be substantiated.

The creative can be used either for campaigns to be targeted at older people or for those appealing to a wide range of ages, including the over-50s.

! Ensure that you have considered both options and are not confusing the two types of creative.

There are various creative techniques that have been used to appeal to the over-50s. They are not guaranteed to work, but they are a starting point.

! Does your creative use any of these techniques? Evaluate them to see if they are appropriate for your product and market.

Using the same creative to appeal to a wide range of ages is not easy, but has resulted in some outstanding advertisements.

! All companies should decide the extent to which their creative is to be age-neutral.

Unless you are testing the reaction that older people have to your creative, you will never know what their response is.

! If your customers are of all ages, ensure that your market research is adequately sampling the views of the over-50s.

SUMMARY

■ A person's age is just one of the many factors influencing the response to the combination of imagery, sound and copy that we call a 'creative'. We know that age alone is a poor determinant of consumer behaviour and the same applies to predicting the response to creative.

■ It is impossible to distil the dos and don'ts of producing creatives for older people into a simple set of rules. Creative that is offensive to older eyes can, with a few subtle changes, be converted into brilliant and effective advertisements. It is just not that simple to do well.

■ Older people's opinion of much of the creative offerings they see is low. Research consistently shows that either they don't understand them or they cannot be bothered to try. Perhaps this is not surprising when the creative were not produced with them in mind.

■ Producing creative that appeals to older audiences is done for one of two reasons. The most common is when targeting them to promote products only they need. The rarer and more difficult type is when the creative has to appeal to a wide range of ages. This is an age-neutral creative.

■ A number of creative techniques are used to appeal to the older audience. These range from portraying older people in a youthful and energetic way to using children, parents and grandparents to accentuate a product's age appeal. Sometimes these work, but not in all circumstances.

■ A person's 50th or 70th birthday does not mean that they suddenly adopt a different set of responses to creative. The challenge for the advertising industry is to understand this simple fact and then identify the emotions and behaviour that are as close as possible to being ageless.

What of the future?

Throughout this book I have avoided attempting to predict the future or discussing the wider business and economic implications of the world's changing age profile. In this final chapter, though, I am relaxing this constraint a little. That the population is ageing has far broader implications than those we see in marketing and these other effects need highlighting.

This chapter starts by discussing the circumstances that must exist if business is to broaden its focus out from its hitherto favoured 18–35-year-olds. Specifically, what insights can be gained from using the 'tipping point' theory?

Marketing is only one part of business and society that is being affected by the changing age demographics. Very soon, large numbers of people will reach retirement age. Companies have to contend with managing this haemorrhaging of skills and knowledge, and society has to cope with the economic implications. These issues, along with the division of the world into young and old regions, are discussed in this chapter.

THE TIPPING POINT

Can the 'tipping point' theory help answer the question 'What circumstances will make marketers understand the business value of older consumers?' What must occur for marketers to instinctively devote as much attention to the growing hoards of the wealthy over-50 consumers as they do to the shrinking numbers of young adults?

Malcolm Gladwell's book *The Tipping Point* (Little, Brown & Co., 2000) was a bestseller and firmly cemented the phrase into the general vocabulary, so most people have a sense of what the phrase means. It is that point when attitudes towards a product, fashion, theory or an opinion suddenly change. It is why something is banal and boring one day and the next it is extraordinary and exciting.

Underlying the concept of the tipping point is a simple model that defines what conditions are necessary for the phenomenon to occur. There are three basic elements to the theory. Let us look at these in turn.

A few people can make a big difference

The reason a radical change occurs is not because the majority of people suddenly start behaving differently, but, rather, is due to the actions of a few very special people. If this select group of people start to act differently, they will influence the majority to change their behaviour. There are three groups of people who have this extraordinary influence:

▌ *Connectors* – the people who bring the world together. They have a natural and instinctive gift for making social connections across different groups, subcultures and niches.
▌ *Mavens* – obsessive watchers of the marketplace who have the knowledge and social skills to rapidly spread new ideas. The word 'maven' is Yiddish and means 'one who accumulates knowledge'.
▌ *Salesmen* – life's natural communicators and persuaders. They can take a dull message and sell it to any audience.

The stickiness factor

Being 'sticky' is being memorable. It is that 'bit of magic' that converts the bland into something you cannot get out of your head. A product, idea or behaviour must have stickiness if the connectors, mavens and salesmen are to create a tipping point. It is why 'Save the Earth' has more impact than 'Keep the environment clean'.

The power of context

Malcolm Gladwell's explanation of the power of context is that 'Epidemics are sensitive to the conditions and circumstances of the times and places in which they occur.' The tipping point, like an epidemic, requires the presence of the right conditions in the environment in order to support the change.

This is a very simple explanation of the theory, but provides enough information for us to analyse what must occur if the concept 'older consumers are important' is to reach a tipping point.

Who are the connectors, mavens and salesmen?

Who are these three types of people in the context of marketing and the over-50s?

I *Connectors* – It is difficult to identify these individuals, groups and organizations. Issues related to older consumers have low visibility and importance with marketing networks. The whole area still ranks as a niche subject that occasionally gains visibility and then disappears.
I *Mavens* – There are a few individuals who collect and distribute information on the subject – me included. The role of the maven is most obviously being filled by a few, powerful organizations. In the US, AARP is highly visible. To a lesser extent, CARP fulfils this role in Canada. Age Concern in the UK is beginning to behave like a maven. Because of the wider social effects of an ageing population, national governmental organizations are also becoming mavens – especially in Australia and the US.
I *Salesmen* – There are few high-profile businessmen, such as Sir Martin Sorrell, Chief Executive of WPP Group, and Jeremy Bullmore, a non-executive director of the Guardian Media Group, who speak about the subject. They are a rarity. As more well-respected businesspeople enter their 50s, they may become salesmen. So far, they have been slow in arriving.

Do we have 'stickiness'?

This is the weakest of the three factors. At the moment, the message about marketing and older consumers is either a barrage of statistics to prove their marketing importance or a plea for fairness, that they should be just as valued as their children and grandchildren. There is very little that is magic or memorable in either of these arguments, even though they are both correct.

Marketing concepts such as branding, return on investment (ROI) and customer relationship management (CRM) reached a tipping point and then became something marketers became excited about and had to understand. Imagine the MD of Unilever asking a senior marketer what the branding strategy is and receiving the answer that there isn't one! It wouldn't happen, yet how many companies can honestly say that they have an AMS (ageing market strategy)? The truth is that the words 'ageing', 'old people', even the annoying term 'baby boomers', are a huge turn-off.

Is there the right 'context'?

Yes. This is the most powerful and visible of the three factors. Every day the population ages a little more, the spending power of the over-50s becomes more visible and examples of the power of the older consumer increase.

Governments are beginning to take the matter seriously as they confront the huge social implications for healthcare and pensions. The economic, social and commercial environmental conditions are all aligned to support the occurrence of a tipping point. The downside is that much of the context is associated with negative factors, such as 'pensioner poverty' and an 'age crisis'.

Without doubt, the main thing stopping marketers from taking the subject seriously is the lack of 'stickiness'. So far, the massive commercial upside of exploiting the economic power of the over-50s has not been translated into ideas and images that have that 'bit of magic'. Hopefully, the concepts in this book will help make the subject a fraction 'stickier'.

The context is right, and once the subject achieves stickiness, there is a core of connectors, mavens and salesmen who can promote the idea. The difficult thing is saying when this will happen!

IT'S A YOUNG AND OLD WORLD

'Demographics are the single most important issue facing the Arab world', said Usamah M. Al-Kurdi, Secretary-General, Council of the Saudi Chambers of Commerce and Industry. His concern about demographics is not about an ageing and shrinking population, but the diametric opposite – a population with large numbers of young people that is rapidly growing. A world that divides into rich and poor also splits into old and young.

The proportions of the total populations of the world's largest countries aged over 50 are shown in Figure 14.1. The 'old' world consists of Japan and Europe, with over 35 per cent of the populations in this category. In

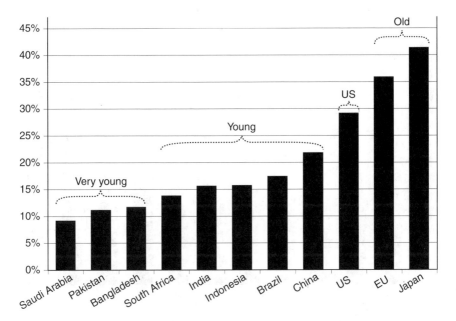

Figure 14.1 *Percentages of the populations of the world's largest countries aged over 50 in 2005*
Source: World Bank Group, 2005

the 'very young' countries of the Middle East and parts of Asia this figure falls to a tenth of the population.

In South Africa, large parts of South America and Asia, the proportions of older people are slightly larger. The US's population is somewhere between being 'young' and 'old'.

How is the population profile of the world expected to look in 2020? On first glance at Figure 14.2, it would appear that other than all of the countries becoming older, little else has changed since 2005. Closer inspection of the chart reveals, however, that China has aged more than any other country. In another five years, by 2025, the US and China are predicted to have very similar proportions of their population in the over-50 age category.

In Japan, the proportion of over-50s has grown by less than it has in Europe and the US, but the composition of the older age group is very different. Table 14.1 shows the proportions of the populations in the US and Japan in the 50–59 and over 75 age categories.

Japan has moved from being 'old' to being 'very old'. The consequences for business and society when 21 per cent of a country's population is aged over 75 are impossible to imagine, at least for me. In 2020, just 2 per cent of Saudi Arabia's population will have reached this age. The

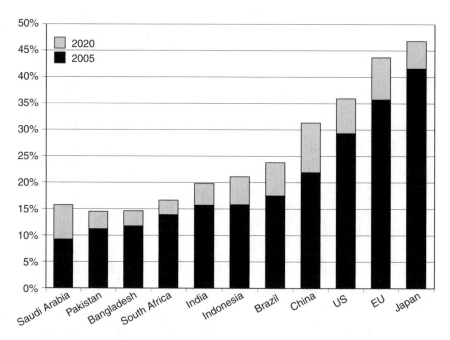

Figure 14.2 *Percentages of the populations of the world's largest countries aged over 50 in 2005 and 2020*
Source: World Bank Group, 2005

caveat with using these predictions is that they are only as good as the population models used by the World Bank. Disturbingly, in the past, errors in forecasts of population ages have mostly been those of underestimating both the rate and extent of ageing.

In Chapter 2, data from the United Nations showed how the ratio of the over-50s to under-50s is changing. Irrespective of the sources of data and how it is analysed, the conclusion remains the same – the divisions between 'old' and 'young' countries are increasing at a frightening rate.

Table 14.1 *The percentages of 50–59 and over-75-year-olds in Japan and the US in 2005 and 2020*

Japan	2005	2020
50–59	15%	13%
75+	14%	21%
US		
50–59	13%	13%
75+	9%	11%

Source: World Bank Group, 2005

For the marketer, this raises a simple question. Will the global companies' mantra of 'act global, think local' still apply in a world that is so differentiated by age? How will you manage a brand where in one country 25 per cent of the population is 75+ (Japan) and in another 2 per cent (Saudi Arabia)?

SCHIZOPHRENIC ABOUT OLDER WORKERS

There is a strange schizophrenia-like condition that afflicts companies when they think about older workers. One minute they are loath to employ them, the next they are frightened of losing skills and knowledge when they retire and moments later they talk of them as being the solution to filling the gap caused by the falling numbers of young people. To confuse matters further, companies are happier employing older women than they are their male counterparts.

Table 14.2 shows the participation rate of men and women aged 55–64 in the labour force. In every country, there has been a reduction in the percentage of men aged over 55 years and an increase in the number of similarly aged women. The expansion of part-time employment explains much of the increase in female employment, but the constant decline in the numbers of older men in the workforce results from a number of factors.

Some older men accumulate enough wealth to retire and leave the workforce, voluntarily. For a good many, however 'early retirement' is not

Table 14.2 *The labour force participation rates for men and women aged 55–64, 1979–2000*

Country	Men (percentages of populations aged 55–64 working)			Women (percentages of populations aged 55–64 working)		
	1979	1990	2000	1979	1990	2000
Australia	69	63	61	20	25	36
Finland	56	47	48	41	41	45
Germany	67	58	55	28	28	34
Japan	85	83	84	45	47	50
Netherlands	65	46	51	14	17	26
UK	–	68	63	–	39	43
US	73	68	67	42	45	52

Source: OECD, 2002

something of their own choosing. The simple fact is that getting a new job when you are the wrong side of 50 – some would say 45 – is difficult. In exactly the same way that companies have an irrational preference for young consumers, they also have a predilection for recruiting younger employees. I suspect that many of the reasons for the youthcentric marketing bias are equally applicable to recruitment.

There are some economic reasons that explain why older men have been forced to re-enter the job market. Declining heavy industries have been large employers of men in the past, but with the drop in demand have had to make them redundant and they have skills that are inappropriate for the newer industries. Generally, too, when companies make staff redundant, it often has a disproportionate impact on older workers. Bizarrely, employment initiatives by governments have contributed to the problem as they are invariably aimed at encouraging companies to employ young people.

At the very same time as this is happening, companies and governments are wrestling with the problem of losing large swathes of their older employees who are about to reach the age of retirement anyway. According to consultants Deloittes, one-third of companies in the US expect to lose 11 per cent or more of their workforce to retirement by 2008. By 2010, the Bureau of Labour Statistics in the US has calculated that the country will have a shortfall of 10 million workers. In Western Europe, the staffing shortfall will occur sooner and be more severe. The fact that a half of America's federal government workers will be eligible to retire in 2005 illustrates that this is a 'today' not a 'tomorrow' problem.

As large numbers of people leave the workforce, this causes two distinct problems. The most obvious and the easiest to solve is how to substitute for their headcount with other people or ways of doing business. Perhaps their jobs could be outsourced overseas, replaced with new business processes, operational efficiency could be improved, immigrant labour could be brought in or a combination of all approaches. The solution and how simple it is to apply depends totally on the type of job concerned.

The second problem is how to replace the accumulated knowledge, experience, contacts, and customer and client relationships that disappear when this cohort of employees retires. Ironically, this problem is not so acute at the most senior levels of companies, where formal succession planning techniques are commonly used. It is the middle ranks of the corporate hierarchy that are most exposed as large numbers of employees bid their farewells and leave.

Because few marketers are in the ranks of the 'about to retire', this problem will have little direct effect on the marketing function. Like all departments, though, marketing is reliant on company-wide support services and these are bound to be affected.

Question – what do all of these older people intend to do when the 'retire'? Answer – keep working.

Ken Dychtwald consults companies about the impact of ageing on their workforce. In an article published in the *Harvard Business Review* he writes, 'In short most baby boomers want to continue working – and they need to for financial reasons – but they may not want to work for you.' His views are echoed in a report from AARP that shows nearly 80 per cent of boomers plan to continue in paid labour during their 60s and 70s. Research in the UK, Canada and Australia came to similar conclusions.

Companies must resolve their conflicting views about older employees and do it fast. If they do nothing, they will lose large numbers of valuable employees who are motivated to continue working. It is a crazy situation.

IT IS NOT LOOKING GOOD

In the short-term, the new generation of older consumers provides marketers with a fantastic business opportunity. However, when today's generation of 20- and 30-year-olds reaches their 50s and 60s, the predictions are not so good.

Knowing exactly how the ageing population will affect the world 20 to 30 years from now is impossible. A lot of things will occur in the intervening years – new technologies will be developed, natural disasters will occur, the world's economic and actual climate will change, wars will be fought... All we can say for certain now is that things are not looking good.

Let us look at why we need to be concerned.

Tomorrow's problem

National governments are exactly like companies – they have an ostrich-like approach to their ageing populations. In 2004, AARP collected together 158 opinion leaders to discuss how global ageing will impact the economics of the G7 countries. Their conclusions were not encouraging.

Figure 14.3 shows their responses to the question 'To what extent do you think your country will be affected by an ageing population?' Over half think that they will be greatly affected. This certainty is not matched with much confidence about how they should react. AARP's report of the meeting contains the following quote, which perfectly illustrates how

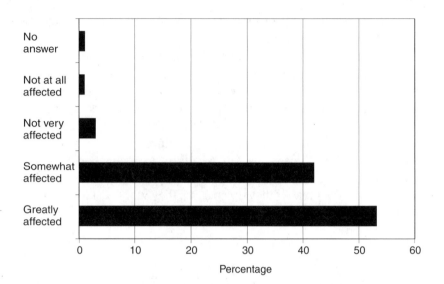

Figure 14.3 *Responses from the G7 opinion leaders to the question
'To what extent do you think your country will be affected by an ageing
population?'*
Source: AARP, 2004

governments react to the issue: 'Leaders are optimistic that their countries
will be able to handle the challenges and opportunities of populations
ageing, but admit that there are few concrete plans in place.'

Each year brings a major new global catastrophe. The tsunami in the
Indian Ocean, 9/11, flu outbreaks, Middle Eastern conflict, plus assorted
civil wars – all claiming more global attention than a 0.25 per cent
increase in the number of over-50s. The following comment from Allan
Meltzer, a professor at Carnegie Mellon University, goes to the root of the
problem: 'Governments are elected for 4–5 years and are asked to solve a
problem over 20 years or more.'

There is no mystery to what is happening to the world's population. The
UN, OECD, World Bank, IMF and national governments have collec-
tively written millions of words on the subject. Knowing what the issues
are is one thing; doing something about them is a different matter.

Economic woes

Laurence Kotlikoff, Chairman of the economics department at Boston
University, paints one, extremely depressing, view of the future:

Close your eyes and imagine it's 2030. What do you see?

A country that's older than present-day Florida, a country with only 15 per cent more workers to pay benefits to 100 per cent more retirees, and a country with high and rising poverty rates among the elderly.

You see a government in desperate trouble – raising taxes to unprecedented levels, making drastic benefit cuts, cutting domestic government spending to the bone, borrowing far beyond its capacity to repay. You also see major tax evasion, high and rising rates of inflation, a growing informal sector, a rapidly depreciating currency, large capital outflows, and more people leaving than entering the country. In short, you see an America in 2030 that looks a lot like Russia circa today.

He is writing about the US, but his views of the future are just as applicable, in some cases more so, to the situations in Europe, Japan, Canada and the other 'old' countries.

Others have less pessimistic views of the future, but all are agreed that the central, unresolved issue is that there will be fewer younger people supporting a lot of older ones. The economic implications of this are many and profound.

▍ *Pensions* – How much of their pensions does the existing generation fund and how much is paid by the next? What happens when the recipients of State pensions increase much faster than the numbers of taxpayers to fund them? (These and other predicaments relating to pensions were discussed in Chapter 2.)

▍ *Household savings* – During the lifecycles of households there are times when savings levels are high and times when they decline and then go into reverse (people spend their savings). McKinsey, a strategy consultancy, has calculated the effects of the changing age profile on household savings. An increasing number of older people results in fewer 'high' and more 'low' savings households. McKinsey forecasts that by 2024 this change in household composition will result in $30 trillion less in global net savings than would have been the case had higher historical growth rates persisted. A reduction in household savings means that there is less capital for businesses and government, which means less economic growth. How a $30 trillion decline translates into business realities is beyond me. Clearly, it doesn't sound good.

▍ *Immigration* – Politicians often proffer the solution to an ageing population as being immigration. There is a disarming simplicity to the concept of moving the surplus youth from the 'young' to the 'old' countries. It sounds like a perfect win–win solution. In fairness, the arguments are a little more sophisticated than this, but they all rely on it as an underlying principle. Undoubtedly, the infusion of young people from overseas will form part of the solution, but it is not without its negative consequences. The UK's attempt to solve its healthcare skills shortage by using scarce resources from the emerging nations, for example, is already happening. It raises significant moral questions as countries with few skilled professionals, such as teachers, doctors, nurses and engineers, lose them to 'old' counties. There is a counter-argument, too, which is that as immigrants send much of their earnings back to their families, it is similar to providing the countries with financial aid. Immigration does have a part to play, but it is only a small piece of the solution. The net benefits it provides and the realities of making the process work are far more complicated than politicians suggest.

▌ *Pay now or later* – Who should pay for the effects of an ageing population: this generation, the next or the one after that? It is estimated that in the UK there is a 'gap' of £690 billion, which is required to fund the pensions of workers employed by the government. The people who will have to provide the funds to fill this 'gap' are current and future generations of UK taxpayers. To give some measure of the enormity of the gap, it is equal to 20 times the UK's annual defence expenditure. Professor Kotlikoff thinks that there is an imbalance in how the problem is likely to be shared between the generations. In the US, he believes, 'higher net taxes, levied on current generations, means that future generations will face lifetime net tax rates almost twice as high as those we face.' The BBC TV programme 'If the generations fall out' described a future in which the intergenerational resentment about funding pensions and healthcare becomes violent. Who can tell if this will ever occur, but there is no doubt that somebody – more accurately, some generation – will have to pick up the bill for demographic change. The longer it is postponed, the more there will be to pay.

IMPLICATIONS FOR THE MARKETER

As this chapter has been a broad discussion about the business and economic affects of ageing, it did not result in a long list of implications and actions for marketers. Just three issues concern marketers – either directly or as part of their broader business responsibilities.

The countries of the world are dividing into those where the populations are expanding and young and those where they are declining and old.

! Companies that trade in both the 'young' and the 'old' parts of the world will need to adapt their marketing strategies to account for the increasing age divergence. In particular, the implications for the branding of products need to be understood.

Large numbers of people are reaching retirement age and leaving their employers. This presents companies with a resourcing problem and, more worryingly, a loss of knowledge and experience.

! Because marketing departments are staffed by young people, they are partly insulated from this problem. However, marketing departments do rely on other parts of their companies that will be affected. Marketers have a responsibility to ensure that their companies confront the manpower implications of the ageing population.

The economic effects are many and difficult to define. They range from the increased demands placed on pensions and healthcare to the resulting reduction in the level of households' savings. Few, if any, countries are implementing policies to deal with these issues. Most appear to be adopting a 'muddling through' approach or clinging to simplistic solutions based on immigration.

! These issues are as much to do with politics as economics. We all have a responsibility to ensure that our politicians take them seriously – if not for altruistic reasons, then because we will all suffer from the effects if nothing is done.

SUMMARY

▌ This final chapter has covered a range of subjects to do with the economic and business implications of the population ageing. The starting point was using 'tipping point' theory to understand the circumstances that must exist before companies start valuing older consumers.

▌ The main conclusion was that the lack of an understandable, attractive and easy-to-communicate message about the economic power of the over-50s was the main reason for the tipping point not having yet been reached. The logic and facts that justify this subject deserving attention are not disputed. As yet, however, they have not been wrapped in words and images that capture this attention.

▌ While one part of the planet faces an era of living with more older people, another has the opposite challenge. The world's countries are dividing into 'young' or 'old'. In the next 20 years, 21 per cent of Japan's population will be aged over 75. At the same time, in Saudi Arabia, just 2 per cent of its population will be in this age group. International marketers will be faced with the problem of operating in two very different worlds.

▌ There is a strange schizophrenia-like condition that afflicts companies when they think about older workers. One minute they are loath to employ them, the next they are frightened of losing skills and knowledge when they retire and moments later they talk of them as being the solution to filling the gap caused by the falling numbers of young people. Because the marketing profession is predominately young, it is protected from the problem to a degree. Other parts of companies and government, however, could suffer a crisis as so much knowledge and experience suddenly disappears.

▌ The two other topics are the economic implications of the demographic changes and the lack of resolute political action. There is a mountain of research and analysis about ageing and its implications. Missing are the plans and policies that will enable something to be done about its findings. Central to any policies will be how the impact and costs of the population ageing are shared between the different generations. As most countries are adopting a 'wait and see' approach, it seems that it is today's younger generation that will face paying the bill.

Appendix 1

Older eyes, hands and minds

The following is a detailed listing of the things that improve the effectiveness of websites and e-mail marketing for older people. The same principles apply to all interactive channels that use a screen, keyboard and pointing device.

DESIGN FACTORS THAT HELP OLDER EYES

Dos and don'ts about displaying information

Fonts

Avoid using serif fonts, such as Times Roman. If you have to use them, make the font size larger than 12 point. It is better to use sans serif fonts, such as Arial, Verdana and Helvetica.

Do not use condensed type – that is, type where the width has been reduced without changing the height. It is an effective way of squeezing more copy on to a page, but it can make the text blurry and cluttered and is harder to read.

Font size and colour should be combined to make it easier to understand how the navigation works – that is, the navigation hierarchy should be reinforced by the size, boldness and colour of different parts of the text.

The combination of fonts and colours must make a clear visual contrast between the navigation and content areas of the screen. It must be obvious to users which bits they can click on to navigate and which bits are for reading only.

It is better to justify the text to the left-hand side of the page and leave the right-hand side ragged as the gaps between words are even, which makes the text neater and easier to read.

Colour

For some older and partially sighted people, light (white or light yellow) letters on a dark (black) background can be easier to read than dark letters on a light background. However, the traditional dark text on a light background is often preferred for aesthetic reasons.

Colours should not be mentioned by name – do not say 'click on the red', for example – as they do not always display as intended and some people are colour blind.

There are certain colour combinations to avoid – black on red and using red and green together, for example.

Don't use the colour blue for text or small objects.

Use dark colours – choosing those from the bottom half of the 'hue circle' – against light colours – from the top half – and avoid contrasting hues from adjacent parts of the circle.

Where possible, use a high level of colour brightness.

Format

The line length for the text on the screen should be around 40–50 letters maximum. If the line length is too short, it will cause eyestrain, as the user's eyes need to travel back and forth from line to line.

Headings should be 4–6 points larger than the text in the body of the page so that it is easy to differentiate one from the other.

Text and graphics should still read well even if the browser is set to display the page in black and white.

People with poor sight – particularly those with poor peripheral vision – have difficulty finding the beginning of the next line while reading. It is important that text has a sufficient gap between each line as this makes finding each new line much easier than when they are too close together. These gaps are called the 'leading' and are specified in points. The spacing between lines should be 25–30 per cent of the text size. If bold type is used, then more space should be added to improve the ease and speed of reading. As text gets smaller, the leading should be increased to help readers cope better with the small letters.

Backgrounds and watermarks should be avoided. If it is necessary to use a background, then it should be as light as possible.

The meaning of the text should be capable of standing alone without the need for graphic images as people browse the Web without displaying the images.

Explain what happens when you click on a link. Increase the redundancy of links by making both the text and image active. A simple rule when deciding the text and image combination is 'What you click is what you get'.

Make a clear visual distinction between the website's content and its navigation. Older people are more likely to attempt to click on non-links, such as bullets, icons and headings. Employ a consistent treatment of links throughout the website.

DESIGN FACTORS THAT HELP OLDER HANDS

Dos and don'ts about designing for using the mouse

Mouse movement

Older people can have difficulty positioning the mouse and so the addressable graphics need to be sufficiently large to make this as easy as possible. It is suggested that no graphic – that is, graphic buttons – should be smaller than 18–22 pixels. The purpose of the icon must be obvious to all ages. Do not use symbols that will only be understood by certain age groups.

Avoid using objects that cannot be resized – especially navigation bars, graphics and other critical elements.

Ensure that there is sufficient space between active links to avoid the need for a high level of accuracy when positioning the mouse cursor.

Avoid dynamic menu systems with nested drop-down menus. These are menus that appear or expand as the mouse is rolled over the menu graphic. Normally, there is only one level of expansion, but some websites use three and even four levels of menu hierarchy. They are a very elegant and highly visual way of displaying the menu options, but their weakness is the precision of mouse movement they require to operate correctly. As a rule, people with reduced mobility have problems using this kind of navigation. It is also very search engine-unfriendly, so should be used with great care.

Wherever you can, make it possible to navigate a web page using the tab or directional keys on the keyboard to assist people who find it difficult to control a mouse precisely.

Many older people have no typing skills and so can find it difficult or slow to use a keyboard. The amount of text keying required should therefore be kept to a minimum.

DESIGN FACTORS THAT HELP OLDER MINDS

Dos and don'ts about structuring websites

Navigation

Goal-centred navigation works by anticipating the reasons for people visiting a website. For instance, instead of using a link called 'Ordering process', you would put 'Do you want to place an order?' The intention is to phrase the sentences describing the navigation in language that is easy for a person visiting the website to understand. This form of navigation can reduce the time taken to find information by over 20 per cent, while also improving the user's experience of the site.

It is very important to make using the search facility as easy and obvious as possible. Ensure that the language describing how to use the on-site search engine is simple and free from jargon.

Try to keep pages short by organizing the text into readable elements. If pages have to be long, then include page navigation.

Older people often use the browser's 'back' button. This should be taken into account when designing the website.

One of the biggest complaints is that of getting lost when navigating a website. Provide as much visual feedback as possible to tell the person where they are on the site.

Older users are less able than younger ones to recover when they make an error and find themselves in the wrong part of the website. Provide as much 'recovery' navigation as possible.

Avoid the amount of learning required to understand how the website works. Keep the page design, symbols and icons consistent throughout the site. Wherever possible, use standard Web conventions and styles of navigation.

Content

The website's text should be clear and precise. Paragraph and sentence structure should be short and simple to understand.

Do not use technical jargon, industry- or company-specific words or language that will only be understood by a limited number of people. Terms such as URL, 'resolution', 'web address', 'plug-in', 'skip intro' are part of the everyday vocabulary for the under-55s. They are terms that many people in their 70s will not understand.

Flashing graphics are distracting for users, especially those with diminished peripheral vision or bifocal glasses. Only use if it is absolutely necessary.

Use objective and direct language. State facts and draw conclusions rather than using sales and marketing language.

Make the text concise by using single-subject sentences. Writing for the web should use half the word count (or less) than conventional writing. Remember, website visitors scan rather than read the text.

It is better to use factual language rather than directives, so do not use phrases such as 'you must' or 'you should'. Older – and, hence, more experienced – people prefer to come to their own conclusions, and not necessarily accept those presented to them.

Avoid extravagant and exaggerated claims. There is a risk that words such as 'fantastic' and 'the best' will be discounted or ignored.

Where possible, use the active voice – that is, 'the dog bit the boy' rather than 'the boy was bitten by the dog'.

TECHNICAL REQUIREMENTS

Dos and don'ts about selecting the technology

Technology

Ensure that the website is easy to view, with screens set to an 800–600 resolution.

Once the design of the website is stable, avoid making changes to the navigation structure to minimize the amount of relearning required by older users.

Avoid using multiple browser windows – that is, those of the kind that when a link is clicked on, it opens another browser window rather than showing the results in the same window. If it is necessary to use multiple windows, then tell users that the results of the operation are in a new screen.

Use style sheets to ensure a consistent layout of the site. Style sheets are an extension to standard HTML that allow designers to control multiple web page styles from a single file. They are used to predefine page elements such as font size, colour and style.

Unless there are special reasons, do not use a 'splash screen'. This is the first screen that a person sees when visiting a site, but it provides very little of value other than a link by means of which users enter the main website. Splash screens are very search engine-unfriendly, too – another good reason to avoid their use.

Do not use plug-ins that have to be downloaded before the site can be viewed. Because of the constant fear of viruses, many older (and younger) people refuse to download and install software just to view information on a website.

The load time for a site should be as short as possible, even though older people are less likely to abandon a slow-loading site than the young. While older people may not abandon the website it does lead to considerable frustration, which will condition how they perceive the site's content afterwards.

Anticipate the likelihood that the website visitor will want to print pages that contain a lot of text. Provide 'print this page' facilities for these types of pages.

If the website attracts a high proportion of older users, provide a facility to increase the size of the text displayed. Explain what this means rather than use abbreviated terms such as 'larger font' or 'magnify text'.

Appendix 2

A website audit for age-friendliness

PURPOSE OF THIS DOCUMENT AND HOW TO USE IT

This document contains a summary of the best practice guidelines for reviewing websites and e-mail marketing materials to evaluate their suitability for older audiences.

To provide a context for the evaluation, the starting point is to define the type of audience using the website and the user scenarios – that is, how the site will be used. Section 2 of this document details the questions that need to be answered.

Many of the guidelines will also improve the usability of a website for all age groups. They appear in this document, however, because they have a huge effect on improving sites for older people.

Multiple resources have been used to produce this checklist. Particular use has been made of research from the following organizations: AARP, Fidelity Finance, the Psychology Department at Wichita State University, the Nielsen Norman Group and National Institute of Ageing.

DEFINITIONS OF AUDIENCES AND USER SCENARIOS

Best practice guidelines help to identify the most obvious ways in which to improve the effectiveness of a website. A deeper and more valuable analysis comes from understanding the characteristics of the website's audiences and the types of transactions that they want to conduct. The following questions assist in defining these two sets of factors.

Website audiences

What are the assumed levels of experience of the older people using the website? What percentages of older visitors belong in each of these categories? Defining the levels of competence of the site's visitors assists in evaluating whether or not the language and functionality are appropriate for the audience's levels of skills.

Level of internet experience	Percentages of older people expected to visit the website
Experienced user – familiar with commonly used PC/Web terminology, likely to purchase and have an online bank account.	
Regular user – familiar with commonly used PC/Web words. Possibly experienced with online commercial transactions, but this cannot be assumed.	
Beginner – little knowledge of PC/Web terminology. Very unlikely to buy products or services online or use an online bank account.	

What types of people are using the website? Identify the top five groups of users. The reason for ranking the importance of site visitors is that it helps in evaluating the appropriateness of the content and navigation.

❏ Prospects
  ▪ Consumer
  ▪ Purchaser
  ▪ Intermediary
	❏ Customers
	  ▪ Consumer
	  ▪ Purchaser
	  ▪ Intermediary

❏ Shareholders/City	❏ The media
❏ Staff	❏ Suppliers
❏ Salesforce	❏ Potential employees
❏	❏ ....

Which audiences will contain a significant number of people aged over 50? This forces the question 'Which types of older people will be visiting our website?' to be answered.

Prospects/Customers

	Age ( )	Age ( )	Age ( )
Consumer			
Purchaser			
Intermediary			

Other significant audiences

	Age ( )	Age ( )	Age ( )
....			
....			
....			

WHAT USER SCENARIOS ARE THE MOST IMPORTANT FOR OLDER AUDIENCES?

To answer this question, it is necessary to think, in detail, about exactly what older people will do when they visit the website. An example of such a scenario could be that they do so to find out if they are entitled to purchase a particular type of insurance. An example of an audience could be people using their home internet connections, aged over 50, with little experience of purchasing financial services online.

Scenario	------------------	**Audience**		---------------------------
	Description of the action	The functionality required to satisfy the action
Action 1		
Action 2		
Action 3		
Action 4		
Action 5		

This procedure would be repeated for the five most important user scenarios.

NAVIGATION

The questions in this section evaluate the effectiveness of the website's navigation structure and how it is implemented. Older people experience more problems navigating sites than younger users. They perform more top-down search strategies (80 per cent more) than their younger counterparts. For these reasons the usability of the site's prime navigation processes is extremely important.

Structure

The questions in this section relate to the website's navigation architecture.

	Navigation options
	Goal-orientated – related to what the user wants to achieve.
What is the primary form of navigation from the home page	Business function-orientated – sales, support, products, 'Who we are' and so on.
	Type of user – existing customer, media, investor and so on.
	Not clear.

Implementation

The questions below relate to how the navigation architecture is implemented on the website.

What is the primary form of menu presentation?	Non-expandable – where a new page is used to show the next level of navigation. Beware!
	Expandable – where the higher level of navigation is left visible and supplemented by the next level. OK.
	Drop-down menus. Beware!
	Index menus. OK.
	Cascading menus with nested drop-down menus. These can be difficult to navigate for individuals with poor mouse control. Beware!

Does the navigation provide clear visual feedback as to the user's position within the site?	Y	N
Does the site have an easy-to-understand visual hierarchy?	Y	N
Is it obvious which parts of the home page are clickable?	Y	N
If it is necessary to scroll a page, does the navigation remain visible?	Y	N
Is the navigation non-standard? Might the older user find it confusing? Remember, older people find standard navigation formats easier to use.	Y	N
If an icon is adjacent to a text link, is it part of the link?	Y	N
Is there sufficient space between links? (There should be approximately a 5-pixel margin surrounding a link or button.)	Y	N
Do links go directly to the content rather than the site's home page? This applies to off-site links and e-mail marketing.	Y	N
Is the site navigation reliant on opening additional windows?	Y	N
Is the default size of pop-up windows large enough to accommodate all the information without needing to scroll?	Y	N
Is it obvious how to access the home page from all parts of the site?	Y	N
If the organization's name or logo appears, does this link to the home page – except on the home page itself, of course?	Y	N
If the term 'home page' is used in the navigation, does it remain inactive when the home page is displaying?	Y	N
Do the font size, colour and shading combine to reinforce the navigation's hierarchical level?	Y	N
Can both the text and graphics be understood if the browser is set to black and white?	Y	N
Can the navigation operate with the image download turned off?	Y	N
Are colours mentioned by name (such as 'click on the red link')? This should be avoided.	Y	N
What is the size of the smallest addressable graphic used for navigation? (They should not be smaller than 18–22.)	Y	N
Can the 'back' button be used to navigate the site? An important feature for older people as they use it more than the young.	Y	N
Does the site have a consistent page design and use of symbols and icons (the amount of navigation learning to use the site should be kept to a minimum)?	Y	N
If the pages are greater than two screens, do they include on-page navigation?	Y	N

FUNCTIONALITY

Search

Do the complexity and volume of information on the website suggest that it should have an on-site search feature?	Y	N
How useful and easy is it to use the site's search feature? (The quality of the on-site search is extremely important as younger people are 25 per cent more likely to find the correct answer when using search than older users.) Is the feature: ▋ difficult and confusing ▋ providing some assistance but could be improved ▋ easy to use and gives good results?	Y	N
Was it easy to locate the site's search functionality? Is there any possibility for confusion as to whether or not it was the main search feature?	Y	N
Were the search results visible without needing to scroll the page?	Y	N
Is it obvious what is being searched – the web, the site, the first set of search results?	Y	N
Does the site provide any assistance with possibly misspelled words?	Y	N
Is it clear what the exact syntax is of the phrase being used in the search?	Y	N
Does the search feature provide any help options?	Y	N
Is the help feature written in terms that can be easily understood?	Y	N
Does the search feature detect common keying errors, such as a dash for a hyphen, and either correct the problem or tell the user to remove it and search again?	Y	N

Forms

Does the site use common keyboard shortcuts?	Y	N
Is the need for typing kept to a minimum and are common typing mistakes automatically corrected? It is likely that older people will have less advanced keyboard skills and much less experience than younger users.	Y	N
If there is an error in a form, is the problem highlighted with all of the correct text repeated?	Y	N
Is the explanation of errors easy to understand?	Y	N
If it is necessary to enter the details of 'occupation' is the choice 'Retired' an option?	Y	N
When completing fixed-format fields, such as dates, sort codes, credit card numbers, phone numbers and so on, is the task simplified by using multiple fields and drop-down menus?	Y	N
Are common keying errors in fixed-format fields automatically corrected? An example might be accepting dashes *and* hyphens as part of the credit card number.	Y	N

Transaction mechanism

Is it necessary for users to register or sign in before starting a transaction? Whenever possible, allow as much of the transaction to be completed as you can before demanding personal details?	Y	N
If the transaction mechanism involves purchasing a product, does the product details page provide the following information: ▪ item's name ▪ short description ▪ link to long description ▪ price ▪ picture?	Y	N
Is information about the company written using terminology that is easy for older people to understand?	Y	N
Is the quality of the product pictures sufficient to make an informed purchasing decision?	Y	N
Is the categorization of the product accurate and helpful? Too often, companies categorize products using their own terminology and practices.	Y	N
After purchasing a product, is it obvious that is has been added to the shopping cart and what action to take next?	Y	N
Is the shopping cart easy to navigate?	Y	N
Is there any visual representation of the purchasing process and which stage the person has reached?	Y	N

Assistance tools

Does the site offer any facilities to increase the size of the text?	Y	N
Does the site contain recovery navigation – that is, assistance for users who get lost navigating the site?	Y	N
Does the site provide a 'print page' facility for pages containing a lot of information?	Y	N

Comparison tools

Does the site make it easy for users to compare different products and services? A facility to sort by price, popularity, type of functionality and so on is useful.	Y	N
When there are multiple products that might satisfy the person's requirements, does the site present the product information in a simple way to help the user make the decision?	Y	N

DESIGN ELEMENTS

Text

	Dense and exhausting to read?	Y	N
How would you describe the way the text is presented?	Similar to the written format?	Y	N
	Blocked in easy-to-read segments?	Y	N

When viewed on the default browser, is the font size less than 12-point?	Y	N
When viewed on the default browser, is the font size of the links less than 12-point?	Y	N
Are headings and links presented consistently throughout the site?	Y	N
Is the default font used a sans serif one? (Note that, due to the effects of anti-aliasing, it is best to avoid using serif fonts.)	Y	N
Is condensed type used on the site? This should be avoided.	Y	N
Is the on-screen line length greater than 50 letters? It should be less than this to reduce eyestrain caused by having to frequently scan back and forth across the text.	Y	N
Is the line spacing (leading) less than 25 per cent of the point size?	Y	N
Are there adjacent lines of bold type? If yes, then additional space should be inserted.	Y	N
Is the size difference between headings and the main body of the text less than 4–6 points? It should be greater than this so the two can be easily differentiated.	Y	N

Colour

Is the default representation of links used (bold, coloured blue or underlined)? If not, is there an obvious reason for choosing something else?	Y	N
Does the link's colour change after it has been clicked?	Y	N
Does the link's colour contrast well with the background, both before and after it has been visited?	Y	N
Do the colours (and their combination) cause problems when viewing the site?	Y	N
Are any of these colours and their combinations used? ■ Blue – this might appear darker and is hard to distinguish from green. ■ Black on red. ■ Red and green. People with poor eyesight can experience problems with these last two combinations.	Y	N
Does the site use a background and/or watermark? This should be avoided.	Y	N

Animation

Moving images – Flash animations, marquees (scrolling lines of text) and animated GIFs – can both confuse and annoy older people, and younger ones, come to that. They should only be used if it is absolutely necessary.

Does the site include any moving elements as a standard part of the page design? Animation might be used during the site's opening sequence, but it might be inappropriate in other parts of the site.	Y	N
Does the animation element require a plug-in to be downloaded? This should be avoided at all costs.	Y	N
Is the user provided with the options not to view and to view the animated part of the site and given sufficient explanation about its content, implications on download speeds and the need for a plug-in, if required?	Y	N

THE USE OF LANGUAGE AND IMAGERY

The following questions evaluate the style and content of the website's text.

Computer jargon and icons

It cannot be assumed that all website users have a similar level of web and PC literacy. Remember, many people in the 1960s and 1970s will not have experienced using a PC during their time at work and their knowledge will only have been acquired since retiring.

The questions listed below are intended to check the potential of the website to confuse and alienate the user.

What level of internet/PC knowledge does the site assume? (See Appendix B.)	*Experienced user* – familiar with all commonly used technical terminology.
	Regular user – familiar with commonly used PC and Web words.
	Beginner – no knowledge of PC or Web terminology.

Is the iconology likely to confuse the user? For example, printer or e-mail symbols that do not have any associated explanation?	Y	N
Is jargon supported by a non-technical explanation?	Y	N
Does the site assume prior knowledge of using a browser? An example would be the presence of a 'back' button with no text.	Y	N

Generation-specific text and imagery

Will the over-50 age group be familiar with all the words used in the site copy?	Y	N
Is the site imagery orientated towards a younger age group? There are many legitimate reasons for selecting such imagery, of course.	Y	N
Could the site's text be interpreted as condescending to or stereotyping the user? This can happen if assumptions are made about the users' requirements, views and attitudes.	Y	N
Does the site convey a value system that is associated with younger people?	Y	N

Clarity and relevance of language (navigation and site copy)

What is the Flesch score (measure of readability) for a 1000-word sample of the website's text?	Y	N
Is the text in an inverted pyramid style – that is, starting with the conclusion, followed by text in decreasing levels of importance?	Y	N
Are any of the words and phrases difficult to understand or ambiguous? A low predictability level for the language used can reduce the efficiency of reading, particularly for older adults.	Y	N
Does the text contain jargon, either industry- or company-specific, that might confuse the reader?	Y	N
Does the navigation include jargon, either industry- or company-specific, that might confuse the user? Was it necessary to click on any of the navigation links to understand their purpose, for example.	Y	N
Does the text achieve the correct balance between: ■ factual and descriptive information ■ sales messages ■ humour and entertainment?	Y	N
Is the layout of the text easy to scan due to: ■ highlighted keywords ■ meaningful subheadings ■ bulleted lists?	Y	N
Can the text be comprehended without reference to the supporting graphics?	Y	N
Is there a hierarchical structure to the text blocks, such as scanable headlines, an intermediate précis, then the main text?	Y	N

Site configuration

With a monitor setting of 800–600 resolution, is it necessary to scroll the home and first-level web pages to view their content?	Y	N
Are there any anomalies if the site is viewed using AOL or with an Apple computer?	Y	N
Are their any parts of the site that cannot be resized, such as navigation bars or graphics?	Y	N
Does the site require multiple browser windows? This can be confusing for older users. Provide the user with an explanation if it is necessary to use more than one window.	Y	N
Does the site use style sheets? They assist in ensuring a consistency of layout.	Y	N
Does the site use a splash screen? This should be avoided, especially if older people use the website.	Y	N
Is it assumed that the site's visitors use a broadband connection? The home page should take no longer than 25 seconds to load on a standard dial-up connection.	Y	N
Are misspelled variations on the site's URL registered to capture traffic that would otherwise be lost?	Y	N

Appendix 3

Questions that test a company's age-neutrality

The ten questions below test whether or not a company has an age-neutral approach to its marketing.

	Age-neutral tests	
1	With regard to the consumer's age, is the marketing strategy and its implementation unbiased, dispassionate and based on facts only, not assumptions?	Yes?
2	Is the *application* of the marketing strategy regularly reviewed to ensure that it remains age-neutral?	Yes?
	Consumer behaviour	
3	We assume that the consumers' behaviour is age-neutral unless there is convincing evidence to the contrary.	Yes?
4	We make no decisions based on assumptions about the effects of ageing on consumers' reactions to new brands, technology, change and new experiences.	Yes?
5	We have plans to exploit the changes to consumer markets created by changes in population age and economic structure.	Yes?
6	We account for the differences in the behaviour of older people on the basis of their nationality and ethnic origin.	Yes?
	Scope	
7	We apply an age-neutral approach to all areas of marketing, not just communications.	Yes?
8	We are aware of the physiological effects of ageing and incorporate them into all aspects of our marketing.	Yes?
9	Our intention is to make age-neutrality part of our marketing strategy.	Yes?
	Segmentation	
10	Unless we have convincing research evidence, we do not use the chronological age of consumers to segment our market.	Yes?

Details of OMD's market research programme

RESEARCH TECHNIQUE

The research was conducted using OMD's internet panels, with the exception of the Czech Republic, where telephone interviewing was used. The research was undertaken during the period from September to October, 2004.

THE QUESTIONNAIRE

Each respondent was asked to score their agreement with the following pairs of statements.

Brands

▌ I am willing to try new brands.
▌ I tend to stick to well-known brands.

Change

▌ Change is something that benefits us in our lives.
▌ I don't understand why people want to keep changing things.

Technology

▌ Technology is moving so fast I don't even try to keep up.
▌ I really enjoy the challenge of keeping up with technology.

Financial security

▌ I'm anxious about the future, especially my financial security.
▌ I view the future with confidence knowing I will be financially secure.

New experiences

▌ Life still holds new experiences for me to enjoy.
▌ I prefer enjoying things that I am familiar with rather than seeking new experiences.

SIZE OF THE SAMPLE

The size of the research sample in each country was as shown below.

The Czech Republic	Australia	France
Sample: All respondents (980)	Sample: All respondents (608)	Sample: All respondents (1,117)
15–29 (268) 30–44 (250) 45–59 (262) 60–79 (200)	18–24 (62) 25–34 (108) 35–44 (112) 45–54 (132) 55–64 (126) 65–74 (68)	15–24 (162) 25–34 (202) 35–44 (207) 45–54 (170) 55–64 (176) 65+ (200)
US	**UK**	
Sample: All respondents (998)	Sample: All respondents (1,147)	
16–24 (180) 25–34 (180) 35–44 (200) 45–54 (200) 55–64 (138) 65+ (100)	Under 24 (106) 25–34 (194) 35–44 (296) 45–54 (273) 55–64 (206) 65–74 (72)	

Index

Further reading from Kogan Page

Commonsense Direct Marketing, 4th edition, Drayton Bird, 2000

How to Advertise: What Works, What Doesn't and Why, 3rd edition, Kenneth Roman and Jane Maas, 2003

Market Intelligence: How and Why Organizations Use Market Research, Martin Callingham, 2004

Market Research in Practice: A Guide to the Basics, Paul Hague, Nick Hague and Carol-Ann Morgan, 2004

Marketing Communications: An Integrated Approach, P.R. Smith and Jonathan Taylor, 2004

The Marketing Plan Workbook, John Westwood, 2005